# TRANSNATIONAL BUSINESS CULTURES

# Cross Cultural Management Series

*Series Editor:*

Kwok Leung, *Professor of Management at City University, Hong Kong, China*

This series provides high quality research monographs and edited volumes that examine key issues in cross-cultural management such as workplace diversity, varieties of capitalism, comparative national performance, international joint ventures, and transnational negotiations. The series encompasses multidisciplinary perspectives and is aimed at an academic readership. The purpose of the series is to provide a global academic forum for the study of cross-cultural management.

*Other titles in the series:*

*Cross-Cultural Management: Foundations and Future*
Dean Tjosvold and Kwok Leung
ISBN 0 7546 1881 1

*Management and Organization in Germany*
Thomas Armbrüster
ISBN 0 7546 3880 4

# Transnational Business Cultures
## Life and Work in a Multinational Corporation

FIONA MOORE
*Kingston University, UK*

ASHGATE

Published by
Ashgate Publishing Limited
Gower House
Croft Road
Aldershot
Hants GU11 3HR
England

Ashgate Publishing Company
Suite 420
101 Cherry Street
Burlington, VT 05401-4405
USA

Ashgate website: http://www.ashgate.com

**British Library Cataloguing in Publication Data**
Moore, Fiona
   Transnational business cultures : life and work in a
   multinational corporation. - (Cross-cultural management)
   1.International business enterprises - Management
   2.International business enterprises - Cross-cultural
   studies 3.Germans - England - London - Cultural
   assimilation 4.Management - Cross-cultural studies
   5.Business anthropology 6.Corporate culture
   I.Title
   658'.049

**Library of Congress Cataloging-in-Publication Data**
Moore, Fiona.
   Transnational business cultures : life and work in a multinational corporation / by
Fiona Moore.
        p. cm. -- (Cross-cultural management)
   Includes bibliographical references and index.
   ISBN 0-7546-4265-8
  1. International business enterprises--Management. 2. International business
enterprises--Cross-cultural studies. 3. Management--Cross-cultural studies. 4.
Business anthropology. I. Title. II. Series: Cross-cultural management series.

   HD62.4.M656 2005
   306.3--dc22

2004024199

ISBN 0 7546 4265 8

Printed and bound in Great Britain by MPG Books Ltd, Bodmin, Cornwall

# Contents

# List of Figures and Tables

# Acknowledgements

Grateful acknowledgement is due first of all to Professor Steven Vertovec and everyone in the Transnational Communities Programme at Oxford University. Thanks is also due, in no particular order, to Professor Mari Sako, Dr Alisdair Rogers, Dr Maria Jaschok, Shirley Ardener, Dr Marcus Banks, Dr Roger Goodman, Dr Jonathan Beaverstock, Dr Malcolm Chapman, Professor Jonathan Zeitlin, Professor Ray Loveridge, Professor Hilary Harris and Dr William Kelly for invaluable academic advice, assistance and comments. I would also like to thank Dr Steven Collins, Professor Willi Patterson and Herr Doktor Professor Norbert Walter for assisting with issues of access and of finding a suitable fieldsite. The staff of the Deutsche Bank Archive also deserve thanks for taking the time to locate specialised material and provide research resources for me. Amy Scott and Sylvester von Hermann assisted with the provision of comparative material; April DeLaurier and Robert Atwood provided accommodation and advice in London and the family of Mrs Gisele W. were of similar help in Frankfurt; the late Peter Humble was an invaluable presence in a number of areas. I would also like to thank Alan Stevens for physical and emotional support, patience and for reading and commenting on the text.

Lastly, I wish to thank the employees of "ZwoBank," as well as the many other people who took the time to speak with me over the course of my research, without whom this project would never have taken place.

This project was funded by an SSHRC Doctoral Fellowship, an ORS Award, and grants from both the Peter Lienhardt Memorial Foundation and the Nuffield Foundation. The *Alex* cartoon on page 145 is reproduced here with the kind permission of Alex Cartoon Inc.

All translations from German to English, both of written texts and of interviews, are my own except where otherwise specified. All errors and/or missed nuances are therefore my responsibility.

*For Alan*

# Chapter 1

# Introduction

## Introduction

Although culture and transnational business is currently a subject of great interest in all disciplines of the social sciences, researchers in business studies have tended to treat businesspeople as a single unit, without the complex explorations of culture necessary to understand human behaviour under globalisation. Anthropologists, by contrast, have focused for the most part on non-elite groups, ignoring the possibility that the employees of multinational corporations might have equally complex social engagements. Through an examination of German transnational businesspeople in London and Frankfurt, I argue that "culture" is in fact a complex, shifting concept which is used and reinterpreted according to the strategies of individual managers and groups, and that this fact is leading to the development of a new "transnational capitalist society" incorporating both local and global cultures in a complex, ever-changing system of interconnected relationships.

In this introductory chapter, I will discuss the study's background as well as briefly describing the issues which affected my research. This will include a critical overview of the way in which "culture" has been treated in the literature on business, particularly that regarding MNCs, and of how my work relates to these earlier studies. I will consider the literature on the role of national and organizational culture, and the recent studies on the development of "third cultures," incorporating national and organizational elements, in the branches of MNCs. I will then summarise the approach of this book, derived from Erving Goffman's theories on strategic self-presentation. I will then outline the methodology used in conducting the study and describe the structure of the book: an overview of earlier research done in this area and the formulation of a hypothesis based on this work, followed by an ethnographic case study, and concluding by reconsidering the earlier research in light of my new findings. I conclude with a brief restatement of my hypothesis: that the nature of global finance means that one cannot simply isolate "global" from "national" culture, but must think in terms of "culture" as a concept which is under constant negotiation in a loose social structure focused on transnational business activity.

## Two Ships Passing: Anthropology and Business Studies

In order to combine the most useful aspects of anthropology and business studies in this context, I will consider the ways in which the concept of culture, both "national" and "global," is used by the employees of the London Branch of a German financial MNC. Initially, however, we must consider the theoretical context of this study in terms of the way in which anthropology and business studies have dealt with the concept of culture in such situations.

German businesspeople in Britain are a particularly interesting group in terms of culture and business. For one thing, they have a long history as a labour diaspora which maintains active connections with its home country, and yet is not "visible" in the same way that, for instance, the Italian labour diaspora is (compare Panayi 1995 and Grass 1990 with Banks 1996: 72). Furthermore, the simultaneous admiration and jealousy expressed by the British media for the economic success of German firms in Britain suggests a problematic relationship between a "global" elite and "local" workers (Roth 1979: 115-119; *The Economist* 1998c). German transnational businesspeople in the UK are thus a group with an interesting relationship to both organisational and national cultures, and which can be isolated for study purposes on the basis of its members' shared nationality.

Anthropology and business studies have historically worked very much at cross-purposes when it comes to the study of transnational business. Anthropologists, for instance, despite occasional calls to "study-up" (Nader 1974) tend to eschew studies of elite groups (in particular white, male and European ones) in favour of small-scale and third-world societies. Although ethnographies of large corporations do exist (see Baba 1998, Schwartzman 1994, Nash 1979, Kasimir 2001, Graham 1995), they still tend to focus on the lowest level of the workforce and ignore the transnational aspects. Consequently, although it is not true to say that anthropologists do not study transnational business, their research tends to focus very much on small businesses and migrant labour, with transnational businesspeople featuring mainly as two-dimensional oppressors. Portes, for instance, in his study of Dominican peasants in New York City, dismisses their involvement with state bureaucracy and global capital, portraying them instead as resisting First World domination through transnational practices, when it could be argued that by acting as cheap labour to First World organisations, they are in fact supporting it (1998). Also, as Guarnizo and Smith cuttingly point out with reference to such studies, that simply because a group is "oppressed," it does not mean that they do not share exactly the same hegemonic outlook as their oppressors (1998: 24). Nancy Lindisfarne's otherwise-excellent overview of globalisation and imperialism nonetheless writes off transnational capitalists in a single line as the main cause of imperialist practices, tarring expatriate managers and two-person Internet startups with the same brush as Rupert Murdoch (2002). This volume thus endeavours to redress this balance and place a human face upon the elite: to make a reasoned examination of their place as part of the transnational economic system and, perhaps, to shed some light on how they truly relate to other groups within it.

Business studies, by contrast, has no lack of monographs on transnational businesses, with the bulk dating from the 1970s onwards (e.g. Bergsten et al. 1978). However, there are very few which actually deal with the lived experience of culture: while the work of Carroll and Fennema and Carroll and Carson (2002,

2003) on the formation of global elite networks and Harzing (2001a, b) on expatriate businesspeople are valuable and interesting, their quantitative focus leaves little room for considering the lived experience of culture in a transnational organisation. Studies of organisational culture in general tend to consider it very much in the abstract, rather than as something which is experienced daily by ordinary people (e.g. Garth Morgan 1997, Trompenaars 1993). Consequently, I intend to build on the qualitative approach taken by such researchers as Czarniawska (1997) to look at the people within the corporation under study as individuals, acting within the organisation according to their personal strategies for success rather than as simply individuals following prescribed roles.

This study thus aims to contribute to both anthropology and business studies by combining the ethnographic, qualitative approach of the former with the traditional area of study of the latter, to cast some light on how individuals behave in transnational economic organisations.

## Background to This Volume: "Culture" in Studies of Corporations

While much has been written on transnational businesspeople in business studies, these works tend to dismiss the significance of culture in their daily lives. By contrast, although anthropologists have recently developed some thought-provoking insights into the nature of transnational cultures, they have contributed little to the study of business. An ethnographic study of a particular group of transnational businesspeople thus might allow us to combine the best of both approaches, and to explore the lived experience of culture in transnational organisations.

### "Culture" in Business Studies

In applying anthropological methods to a setting normally the domain of business studies, the chief difficulty which must be addressed is the fact that anthropologists and business studies researchers have quite different definitions of "culture." The main points of the debate have been effectively summarised by Wright (1994); however, I shall briefly outline the situation here. While both disciplines seem more or less to agree on what a company or nation's "culture" consists of—its values, myths and rituals, collective symbols and so forth (Mead 1994: 155-156; Turner 1971: 21)—they disagree on how it is formed. Business studies views culture as a solidary, unified property belonging to a group—a property which is manufactured, and changed at will, by the group collectively or by powerful individuals within it. Hofstede, for instance, refers to culture as "the collective programming of the mind which distinguishes the members of one human group from another" (1980: 21), thus likening it to a computer programme which can be installed and edited at will. Although this approach is useful for developing theoretical models, it tends to afford too much agency to powerful people within the group, ignoring the fact that secretaries, for instance, may have as much influence in the definition of a corporation's culture as its general managers

(Anthony 1994: 2). Furthermore, this approach tends to gloss over the complexity of culture. In studies of German businesses, for instance, most tend to treat them as a unified whole, speaking, like Randlesome, of "German" traits which have an existence in and of themselves, rather than considering these as symbols which can be redefined according to the context (1993: 1; this approach is criticised in Millar 1979: 43). Furthermore, such studies often avoid explorations of the role of national culture in transnational business in favour of simply setting up German companies as the antitheses of Anglo-American ones, in a manner disturbingly reminiscent of the way in which Japanese companies were treated by the "learn from Japan" movement (compare, for instance, Sorge and Warner [1996] with Chapter 6 of Vogel [1979]). The view of culture in business studies is thus as a unitary property of groups, whether corporate or ethnic, which is more or less the same throughout the group and is bounded off from other groups.

This approach also leads researchers in business studies to differentiate more or less firmly between "national" and "organisational" cultures. This results in, for instance, Hofstede's *Culture's Consequences* (1980) focusing solely on the difference which the host country culture made to each branch of IBM included in the study, and Garth Morgan's *Images of Organisation* describing the development of the cultures of individual corporations without reference to the countries hosting them (1997), with neither researcher considering (as an anthropologist might) the branches as organic and dynamic syntheses of the corporation's history and practices and those of the host country. More recent studies have begun to critique this approach, considering the cultures of branches not simply in terms of corporate culture or home versus host country effect, but as "third cultures" made up of a synthesis of elements from both inside and outside the organisation (e.g. Ghoshal and Nohria 1989; Andersson et al. 2000; Mueller 1994). In business studies, therefore, we are beginning to see a recognition that culture may be subject to more in the way of negotiation and change than was formerly believed.

The "third-culture" literature does go some way towards acknowledging the complexity of culture in organisations. Ghoshal and Nohria, for instance, come up with a complex typology of ways in which home, host and organizational cultures can interact to form a variety of different patterns (1989). Kristensen and Zeitlin's ongoing studies of dairy-product multinationals go even further than that, considering that a variety of factors other than home, host and organizational culture—including history, mode of acquisition and market sector—go into forming the culture of the branch (2004). During a 1998 conference at the Goethe Institut, Stephen Hagen observed that much of the emphasis on MNCs developing a distinctive, global "corporate culture" comes from American MNCs who, rather than hiring local managers for their branches, hire American-educated people originating from that area; in such a situation, one might well question whether these individuals are part of "local," American or corporate culture, if indeed any of the three are separable from the others. Kogat suggests that MNCs are conduits of national culture, not simply from the home to the host country, but also from the host to the home, through their employees' social networks (1993). Ohmae questions whether IBM, which has a Japanese workforce but American origins and management, can be said to be Japanese, American, both or neither (Ohmae 1990:

10). It is thus not so much that MNCs are "nationalityless," as Ohmae argues, as that they are, by virtue of their involvement with the processes of globalisation, engaged in complex "trialectics," to coin a phrase, between two local cultures and at least one transnationally operating global culture (1990: 195; see Vertovec 1999: 449). However, these accounts generally do not take into account the influence of global cultures, or the possibility that these cultures change over time in response to different social pressures. In order to analyse its effects on MNCs, then, business studies thus need to consider culture not in terms of particular unitary entities, but as changing concepts subject to diverse pressures; more than this, however, the dynamic character of culture in organisations must be acknowledged.

## *"Culture" in Anthropology*

Anthropologists, in contrast to business researchers, tend to consider culture as a common repertoire of ideas which is reworked in ways which are systematic, but not predictable (Wright 1994: 4). Culture is seen, not as a bounded, unified entity, containing distinct national and organisational forms, but as subject to continuous negotiation as different groups overlap, come together and move apart. Wallman's study of two London neighbourhoods, for instance, considered how, while the groups might appear to have solid, definite boundaries, these "boundaries" were in fact composed of a variety of different ways of considering different groups (ethnic affiliation, class, occupation, etc.) which intersected in some ways, and acted in opposition in others (1986). The key aspect of the anthropological view of culture is thus its shared, dynamic and negotiable quality, constantly changing in response to inside and outside pressures; however, this view is generally applied to small-scale and, especially, third-world groups, without considering the applications for business.

   With the advent of globalisation studies, with its interdisciplinary approach, the tendency is to regard culture as even more complex and multifaceted. Globalisation studies focuses, more or less directly, on the complex relationship between global and local cultures, activities and groups. Tomlinson, for instance, in his seminal book *Globalization and Culture*, argues that the relationship between global and local reflects a "complex connectivity" (1999a: 2, 71). He argues that while people engage in activities which take place in "global spaces"; flying on airplanes, using the Internet, and other practices which cannot be said to take place in one locality or another; they are at the same time embodied and physically located (149, 141-3). As he puts it, this process of deterritorialisation does not mean "the end of locality, but its transformation into a more complex cultural space" (149). Globalisation studies thus builds upon the anthropological view to create a picture of culture which, due to the complex nature of the relationship between the global and the local, is necessarily fluid, with diverse groups blending into each other. It thus seems that the nature of global finance means that one cannot simply isolate "global" culture from "national" culture, or indeed either from "organisational" culture, but that we must think in terms of "culture" as a concept which is under constant negotiation in a loose social structure focused on transnational business activity.

In this book, I propose to develop this view of culture to argue that transnational businesses and the people associated with them do not in fact form solidary cultures, but a kind of global "Transnational Capitalist Society," in which various groups of different degrees of global integration coexist, interact and develop their cultures in response to each other and to outside pressures. Effectively, this involves viewing transnational businesses not as individual entities, influenced by national and organisational cultures, but as existing in the sort of "complex connectivity" described above, linked to other groups and internally divided, and with their cultures being ongoing, dynamic processes in constant development through interaction with other groups and through internal debate. As this theory will be outlined in greater detail in the final chapters of the book, I will simply state here that the transnational capitalist society hypothesis argues for a more dynamic, less bounded view of culture and social interaction in the global business world.

This volume thus takes as its starting-point the idea of culture as a fluid, dynamic property of particular groups, subject to constant negotiation, which does not define single cultures, but contributes to the development of a globe-spanning social construct incorporating many different groups. As such, we shall consider how one group which operates in transnational business circles makes use of culture and its fluid properties, and in turn influences the way in which different local and global cultures connect with each other, through the way in which its members present themselves.

## Theoretical Approach of This Volume: Strategic Self-presentation in Transnational Business

The main theoretical position in this work stems from Erving Goffman's theory that the driving force behind this dynamic system of culture, or transnational capitalist society, has to do with the self-presentation of individuals and groups. Goffman's argument, that the way in which people and organisations act to present themselves in the most positive light possible according to their own strategies for success, goes some way towards explaining the dynamic nature of culture in transnational business settings.

### Understanding Strategic Self-Presentation

Many of Goffman's works focus on exploring the ways in which people define themselves and their allegiances, most famously in his monograph *The Presentation of Self in Everyday Life* (1956), but also in many of his other articles and books (e.g. 1961, 1963, 1970, 1979). Goffman describes individual and corporate actors strategically combining and selecting between expressions of allegiance in order to maximise their benefits in particular situations (1961: 101; 1963: 243). Actors, he says, may define themselves predominantly according to a connection with one group (as "a Jew," for instance, or "medical doctors" or "employees of IBM"), but within that there is a constant interplay of allegiances to many groups and institutions, with different ones prioritised in different situations according to which the actor feels best suits their aims (1961: 143). While Goffman has been rightly accused of verging too much on rational action theory, people do use symbolic self-presentation strategically at least to some extent; one might also argue that to act strategically is not necessarily to act rationally, or even, as Bourdieu's theory of social practice suggests, to act entirely consciously (Burns 1992: 119; R. Jenkins 1996: 70-71; 1992: 78-79). Robertson sums it up with the phrase "identity [sic] is power"; self-presentation therefore can be a key part of the strategies of social actors in their interactions with one another (1992: 166; Burns 1992: 232).

Goffman's theory is, of course, not without its problems. One must also note, for instance, as Goffman does not, that it is not just that we present ourselves strategically, but that at the same time our self-presentation is being interpreted by, and incorporated into the strategies of, others (R. Jenkins 1996: 58). Oberg describes a tendency towards linking individuals' quirks with their ethnic groups, as witness Marsh's anecdote about Prime Minister Thatcher's 1989 visit to Germany, in which Chancellor Kohl made a strong effort to impress her with his Europeanness, but, despite this, she was heard to exclaim to an aide, "isn't he so German!" (Oberg 1960: 181; Marsh 1994: 45). The complexity of the relationship between multiple discourses of group allegiance suggests that there is more to it than simply the attempt to present oneself in the best light possible under the circumstances.

## Symbolism, Self-Presentation and Social Identity

Furthermore, anthropological studies of the use of symbolism (of which self-presentation can be said to be a specific form) suggest that symbols can be used to control and restrict discourses according to the needs of the dominant group. In his article "Symbols, Song and Dance" (1974), Bloch considers how symbols, rather than simply communicating concepts, evoke ranges of ideas and emotions which can be used in politics and organised religion to restrict a given discourse, and to prevent it from being led off into undesired areas (Ibid., 56, 68, 79). As Bloch puts it, "you cannot argue with a song," as the verses and choruses form a set pattern and cannot be deviated from without breaking out of the song; in religious and political rhetoric, similarly, the use of particular symbols restricts the discourse to the associations evoked by these (Ibid., 71). More recent examples of this can be found in the news broadcasts following the events of September 11th, 2001: by using the language of war to describe the action against the World Trade Centre, American politicians and journalists ruled out the mainstream interpretation of the actions as "terrorism" or even "freedom fighting." One might also note the adverse press reaction when the same politicians began insisting that captured Taliban fighters did not constitute "prisoners of war," suggesting that by breaking the discourse, the politicians were alienating their audience (see also Douglas [1970: 23, 55] for a discussion of symbolism as a Bernsteinian "restricted code"). Bloch thus indicates the uses of self-presentation in politics to control the way in which particular issues are discussed, and the ways in which this can be a double-edged sword. Strecker, similarly, explores the ways in which narratives, jokes and expressions of social allegiance can be used as tools of manipulation used to fulfil one's wishes without appearing to threaten the fulfilment of another's (1988: 74), or to establish dominance without engaging in physical conflict (172). This is achieved through the "multivalency" of symbolic discourses: that is, the ability of symbols to take on a variety of meanings, depending on the social context (see Sperber 1974). Studies of symbolism in the anthropology of politics and economics thus suggest that self-presentation may be a strategic tool which is used by various individuals and groups to control, even to shape, cultural discourses.

Symbolism also has strong applications in the formation of social identity. Although, for reasons described below, I shall be steering clear of in-depth discussions of the nature of social identity in this work, it is worth noting that, as Anthony Cohen argues, membership in social groups is defined by, and expressed through the use of, commonly held symbols (1985, 1994, 1987: 19). Although the interpretations given to the symbols vary from individual to individual, Cohen argues, key aspects of these interpretations are shared by all group members, due to their common experience of socialisation (1986: 9). Although Cohen's research was done among small-scale, traditional groups, his theory has been found to be generalisable to larger, more transnational groups: Hannerz, for instance, speaks of people surviving in transnational contexts through developing sets of "decontextualised knowledge," which can be recontextualised in different cases (1990: 246). Stack argues that "ethnicity" is a powerful force in contemporary world politics not only because it bypasses formal state authority, but because it operates on multiple levels, including the emotional level (1981: 6). The fact that symbols are used both in self-presentation and the formation of social groups thus means that symbolism and self-presentation play a major role in the development of social identity, and consequently in the way in which culture is constructed and developed.

*Transnational Groups and Self-Presentation*

While the work of Goffman, Anthony Cohen, Bloch and Strecker for the most part predates the ethnographic study of transnational business, the above works on self-presentation, symbolism and social identity have been demonstrated to have applications to global business settings. Head (1992), for instance, in his monograph *Made in Germany*, conducts a complex study of how the advertising campaigns of German businesses relate to the German national self-image at home and abroad, taking in positive and negative readings of adverts for well-known German products by UK consumers. Czarniawska's well-known study of narratives in organizations discusses how the personal narratives of employees can be used as ways of shaping and controlling the organization to a limited extent (1997). Kasmir, similarly, considers how the employees of the Saturn Corporation incorporate the company's discourses of advertising and marketing into their own self-presentations (2001). Goffman's theories of self-presentation, when applied to MNCs and other business organisations, suggest strong connections between the construction of MNCs as social institutions and strategic self-presentation.

Studies of non-business-related transnational groups, furthermore, demonstrate clear evidence that such actors do define and establish their positions through strategic self-presentation. In Baumann's account of the multiethnic English suburb of Southall, for instance, although both official doctrine and direct questioning of inhabitants suggests that the neighbourhood is made up of classic, symbolically bounded ethnic groups, observation of peoples' expressions of group allegiance suggests that these self-presentation activities come into play, not in defining boundaries, but in communication between actors in negotiating the interweaving of their different frames of reference (1996). Vertovec and Rogers, similarly, describe the ways in which Muslim European youth use fashion, music and faith to define themselves as products of both East and West (1998). In situations in which people are engaged with many continually changing discourses, such as when operating on the global level, the presentation of self becomes a means of establishing and continually redefining one's position within the environment.

It seems, therefore, that self-presentation can be continually altered to fit the social context in transnational situations. Banks speaks of the cross-culturally variable linkage of form and meaning with regard to popular press images: a particular photomontage is not read the same way in India as in the UK, and both it and its readings must be considered in context (1998). Gillespie's monograph *Television, Ethnicity and Cultural Change* discusses the role of television in "defining, contesting and reconstituting... identities" (1995: 2). Vertovec and Rogers' study also indicates that the self-presentation of the Muslim teenagers varies as they grow up and adjust into an "adult" role, and that they are at least to some degree conscious of this process (1998). Ulf Hannerz, who has done a number of studies of transnational elites in both Europe and Africa, describes identity in such situations as a kind of "toolkit," from which actors select to present themselves in the most positive light possible (1996, 1983). It is thus likely that the diverse allegiances to which actors can lay claim can be brought together through their day-to-day self-presentation, allowing them to incorporate links to diverse, even seemingly opposed, groups.

## Theoretical Premises and Objectives

The best way of considering the construction of culture in the context of transnational settings may thus be to see this as an ongoing process. R. Jenkins describes "social identity" as an ongoing dialectic between "our understanding of who we are and of who other people are, and... other people's understanding of themselves and others" (1996: 5). A sense of group affiliation, he argues, results from collective internal and external self-definition (Ibid., 5, 83-85). Hannerz describes the expression of group allegiance not so much as a monolithic "identity" as a repertoire of symbols, which can be selected from and mixed in different ways, and through which people view the world (1983: 348, 355; 1992: 65). Hannerz also discusses the case of actors with multiple group allegiances, or of subgroups within wider groups, in which the same symbols can be said to define both or all the groups in question, but with different interpretations (1992).

Douglas adds that there is an element of ascription as well (1983). Actors' allegiances thus change from context to context, and are informed by all the different possibilities for interpretation open to the actor expressing, and the actor(s) receiving, the symbols being used in group self-presentation (R. Jenkins 1996). Self-presentation in transnational contexts is thus not so much used to construct bounded, solidary "cultural identities," as they are to continually define and redefine the relationships between groups and/or individuals through changing the form and content of self-presentation.

The theoretical objectives of this work are, therefore, to address the question of whether "culture" in transnational business organisations is in fact a bounded trait which is the product of national, global and/or organisational influences, or whether it is more of a vague, continuously shifting process of self- and other- definition by businesspeople with various degrees of global and local affiliation. It will also consider the role of self-presentation in the global business world, and offer insights into the way in which national and organisational culture are actually experienced by the employees of multinational corporations. Finally, I will examine how my findings relate to those of earlier writers in this field, and build upon their theories to develop a tentative model of a transnational capitalist society. This book will thus focus on developing a new way of looking at culture in global business, and how it affects multinational firms and their staff members.

This monograph will thus consider culture from the point of view of individual strategy and agency, and how culture is actively used in business by international and local managers to negotiate between different social groups, ending with the proposition that it is not simply a matter of definite groups with particular cultures, but of continuous interaction within a globe-wide transnational capitalist society. We shall now briefly consider how best to approach this issue from a methodological point of view.

## Methodology: Ethnography and the MNC

In order to consider the ways in which culture is experienced within the organisation, I conducted an ethnographic study focused around the London office of a multinational German bank. The relative scarcity of ethnographic studies of business, plus the qualitative, experiential aspects of ethnomethodology, suggest that new insights into culture in business can be gained through adopting this particular method.

The material upon which this monograph is based consists of a pilot study conducted between August 1998 and April 1999 at the London branch of a German bank, and two more extended periods of fieldwork, one from January to June 2000 with the London office and Frankfurt headquarters of a second, larger German bank, and one from June to December 2000, which explored the wider German community in London as well as gathering additional material at the abovementioned Frankfurt office. This book is thus the product of nearly two years' cumulative fieldwork, not in a single community or physical location, but in and around a web of social connections loosely centred on London, England.

## Case 1: The Pilot Study

The pilot study consisted of a three-month period of participant observation at the bank's London Branch, in which I spent two to three days a week in the Trade and Commodity Finance section. For comparison purposes, I also spent one day apiece in two other sections, Information Technology (IT) and the Dealing Room. More formal interviews (following Fetterman's typology of "formal" and "informal" interviews) were carried out in January 1999 with the bank's seven German locally hired and expatriate employees (1998: 37, 11). Three auditors who visited the bank in November 1999 expressed an interest in participating; in the absence of time to conduct a formal interview, I prepared an open-ended questionnaire, which they completed in their own time. I also spoke informally with employees of other, mainly British, nationalities, and some German employees from other branches who spent short periods at the London office. In March and April I showed drafts of the study's writeup to my interviewees, feedback from which has also been incorporated into the current document. I also obtained impressions of the wider context through participant observation at the Goethe Institut London. I was not employed by the bank, but was answerable to its personnel director. This case study will not be featured directly in the work which follows, but material obtained during this time has been incorporated into the ethnographic chapters (Chapters 3-6).

## Case 2: "ZwoBank"

In the case of the second bank, more extensive participant-observation was carried out. To begin with, I was formally engaged by the bank as a researcher, albeit unpaid, the implications of which will be discussed below. I spent five days a week in the office, with access to a desk; the location of this changed three times over the six-month period, enabling me to observe activities in the IT teaching area, the Personnel and General Management area, and the Building Management area. I had access to the staff canteen and other such resources, as well as to meeting rooms in which to conduct interviews, and joined employees in informal social activities such as pub nights and leaving parties. Until August 2000, also, I lived as the flatmate of a British-born computer specialist employed by a non-German bank, who provided a certain amount of comparative data and information on the use of IT in the financial sector.

In the second fieldwork session, formal interviews (again, following Fetterman 1998), were conducted on a periodic basis over the course of the six-month participant-observation period. Follow-up interviews were also conducted with selected employees in the subsequent six months. The interviewees were for the most part junior and middle managers, with three members of senior management and two non-managerial staff members also participating. Of my interviewees, six were expatriate Germans, four were Germans living permanently in the UK, two were English who had lived in Germany, and three were English with no German connection. Formal interviews of this type were also conducted with five members of the personnel department and two managers from other divisions in the Head Office of the institution. These were conducted during three week-long trips to Frankfurt in April, September and October 2000, with follow-up contacts by e-mail (see Table 1.1).

Each participant was interviewed between one and four times, with interviews lasting roughly an hour apiece. Although a standard questionnaire was initially used, it was not normally adhered to once the interview was fully underway. Participants were given the option of being interviewed in English or German; although most at the London Branch chose English, and most at the Head Office chose German, no interview was conducted exclusively in one or the other language. Initially, all interviews were recorded; later, as I discovered that this practice often made interviewees nervous, I largely abandoned it in favour of shorthand, although, mindful of my limitations as a non-native speaker, I continued to tape and transcribe German-language interviews.

These activities were also complemented by informal interviews and conversations with some of the branch's employees. These were usually conducted over lunch or after work, and followed no set pattern, although I made certain to ask whether or not I could use the relevant part of the conversation in my work. All but four of the people who participated in formal interviews—in both offices—also engaged in informal discussions of this sort; in addition to these, I regularly had conversations with five Germans living permanently in the UK, six non-Germans who had lived in Germany, and nine non-German employees with no connection to Germany. Approximately two-thirds were junior or non-managerial staff, a fact which made up for the overwhelmingly managerial bias of the formal interviews. Finally, during my trips to Frankfurt, I stayed with a friend from the bank's London Branch (who moved back to Germany during my period of fieldwork), and was thereby able to observe and participate in life in a German transnational banking family.

As implied earlier, my position with regard to the second bank was as an outside consultant to the branch, brought in to gather data and formulate conclusions on the impact of a restructuring programme (discussed in greater detail in Chapter 5) on Anglo-German relations in the branch. I was expected to submit a report to the personnel director at the end of the six-month fieldwork period. It is therefore impossible to avoid an element of bias in my results, as my interviewees were aware of this situation and were no doubt on some level tailoring their responses. I have consequently tried to interpret and evaluate each interviewee's answers in the context of their position with regard to the extant situation in the bank. I also endeavoured to compensate for the fact that all interviewees had to be approved by the personnel office by asking individuals who showed an interest in the project to volunteer (although, if the contact seemed reluctant, I did not press the issue), and/or through conducting the abovementioned informal interviews.

**Table 1.1 Formal interview subjects at "ZwoBank"**

| Status | Gender | Ethnicity | Cohort (see Chapter 5) | Dept. | App Age | Branch |
|---|---|---|---|---|---|---|
| Manager | Male | German | Expatriate | Finance | 32 | London |
| Junior Manager | Male | German | Expatriate | Finance | 28 | London |
| Manager | Male | German | Expatriate | Finance | 30 | London |
| Manager | Male | German | Expatriate | IT | 55 | London |
| Manager | Male | German | Expatriate | Ops. | 40 | London |
| Manager | Female | German | Expatriate | HR | 31 | London |
| Manager | Male | German | Local Hire | Customer Service | 48 | London |
| Manager | Female | German | Local Hire | Sales | 55 | London |
| Front-Line Staff | Female | German | Local Hire | Sales | 28 | London |
| Manager | Male | German | Local Hire | Sales | 50 | London |
| Manager | Male | English | Germano-phile | Trading | 35 | London |
| Senior Manager | Female | English | Germano-phile | General Mgt. | 40 | London |
| Senior Manager | Male | English | Anglophile | Compli-ance | 64 | London |
| Senior Manager | Male | English | Anglophile | General Mgt. | 55 | London |
| Front-Line Staff | Male | English | Anglophile | Unknown | 30 | London |
| Senior Manager | Female | German | -- | HR/General Mgt. | 50 | Head Office |
| Senior Manager | Male | German | -- | HR | 45 | Head Office |
| Manager | Male | German | -- | HR | 32 | Head Office |
| Manager | Male | German | -- | HR | 38 | Head Office |
| Senior Manager | Female | German | -- | HR | 47 | Head Office |
| Manager | Male | German | -- | Invest-ment Banking | 34 | Head Office |

*Follow-Up Work*

Between June and December of 2000, I remained in peripheral contact with both banks, but concentrated on exploring the wider social context. During this period, I conducted formal interviews with a total of thirty-five key figures in London's German and financial communities, including representatives of the Bank of England, the Corporation of London, the German Embassy and the Deutsche Bank, as well as of five German business and four German cultural support organisations, three educational organisations and relocation agencies, and a total of six business think-tanks and consultancies (see Table 1.2). I also conducted several interviews at, and participated in two events hosted by, the Deutsche Schule London, more details on which can be found in Chapter 3. As before, some interviewees were re-interviewed, and follow-up work was done via e-mail. I also engaged in participant-observation between interviews, by conducting my writeups in the public areas of the Goethe Institut, the German Historical Institute London, the City Business Library and the Library of the Corporation of London; by going on field trips to Richmond, the area of London where most Germans are concentrated; and by attending occasional services of the German Lutheran Church. I also spent at least two afternoons per week in a pub, café or library in London's financial district, dressed in business clothing and observing the activities and behaviour of the people around me. Finally, I submitted a draft of the ethnographic chapters of this work to the banks for comment, and have incorporated some of the suggestions which I received into the final version.

In the summer and autumn of 2003, I conducted follow-up work on both banks. I researched what had happened to both organisations in the intervening period through newspaper clippings and press releases, and arranged interviews with those participants who were still available (many having taken other jobs in the meantime and proving impossible to track down). I also began a related research project with an Anglo-German manufacturing company, which has proved a useful source of comparative data in terms of the experiences of its members and the culture of the organisation.

*Ethical Considerations and Limitations of the Research*

In conducting my research, I have followed standard ethical practice, as described by the Association of Social Anthropologists, in terms of respecting the privacy of participants (ASA 1999). For confidentiality reasons, some details of the banks' location and operations have been changed and both the banks and their employees remain anonymous; where names have been used at all, they are pseudonyms, except in the case of such institutions as the German Embassy which it would be impossible to disguise in this way (and whose representatives were made aware that the organisation might be identified). In the chart below, think-tanks and institutions not identified in the text remain anonymous. In the following writeup, also, I have been selective in quoting interview excerpts, and have paraphrased

**Table 1.2  Interviewees in the City of London/Frankfurt**

| Organisation type | Gender | Ethnicity | Status | Appx Age |
|---|---|---|---|---|
| Bank of England | Male | UK | Executive Director | 50 |
| Bank of England | Female | UK | Regional Agent | 45 |
| Bank of England | Male | UK | Specialist | 50 |
| Corporation of London | Female | UK | Researcher | 30 |
| Corporation of London | Male | UK | Planner | 30 |
| Think-Tank 1 | Male | UK | Member | 30 |
| Think-Tank 2 | Male | UK | Member | 50 |
| Think-Tank 3 | Male | UK | Member | 52 |
| Think-Tank 3 | Male | UK | Member | 45 |
| Think-Tank 5 | Male | UK | Member | 55 |
| Think-Tank 6 | Male | UK | Member | 28 |
| Relocation agency | Female | UK | Owner | 48 |
| Language School 1 | Female | French | Teacher | 27 |
| Language School 2 | Male | UK | Teacher | 30 |
| Deutsche Bank | Male | German | Senior Manager | 55 |
| Deutsche Bank | Male | UK | Senior Manager | 48 |
| British-German Foundation | Male | UK | Director | 35 |
| British-German Foundation | Male | German | Member | 55 |
| German Embassy | Male | German | PR | 30 |
| German Embassy | Male | German | Diplomat | 55 |
| German Embassy | Female | German | Bureaucrat | 42 |
| German bus. support 1 | Male | UK | Partner | 45 |
| German bus. support 2 | Male | German | Director | 30 |
| German bus. support 3 | Male | German | Director | 55 |
| German bus. support 3 | Male | German | Member | 45 |
| German bus/ support 4 | Male | UK | Director | 60 |
| German cultural 1 | Male | UK | Director | 40 |
| German cultural 2 | Female | German | Volunteer | ?? |
| German cultural 3 | Female | German | Language teacher | 45 |
| German cultural 3 | Male | German | Manager | 48 |
| German cultural 4 | Male | German | Director | 50 |
| Deutsche Schule London | Male | German | Principal | 50 |
| Deutsche Schule London | Female | German | Board member | 45 |
| Deutsche Schule London | Female | German | Teacher | 40 |
| Deutsche Schule London | Female | German | Parent | 47 |

some interview material. Information obtained from publicity material from the bank has also been presented without citing references. In the case of all the interviewees cited here, some non-essential biographical data has been changed; the individuals in the "case studies" in Chapter 5 are all composites, that is to say that data from two or more similar people has been amalgamated under a single heading, although care has been taken to ensure that this does not interfere with the presentation of the data. With both banks, I drafted up a more or less formal agreement which included permission for interested participants to look over, comment on and, if it came to a dispute, veto, the material to be included in publications, in order to ensure the confidentiality of their clients and business divisions. In doing this, I am endeavouring to respect the need for privacy of my interviewees and fieldwork sites.

There were also more practical issues regarding my level of access. As a 25-year-old unmarried and childless woman, my ability to obtain firsthand information on the personal lives of people in other demographic brackets was limited (although I was able to learn more about the lifestyles of expatriates with children through my association with the Deutsche Schule London). Most of my socialisation time was spent with trainees and junior staff, although I also found that my gender and age meant that older employees, particularly male ones, were also quite willing to talk with me at lunch and in after-work gatherings. The social conventions associated with my gender also meant that older managers and think-tank members (who were almost universally male) were more relaxed when scheduling and conducting interviews with me than they would have been with a male interviewer of a similar age, whom they would have perceived as a potential business rival, and whose requests for assistance they could safely refuse without seeming unchivalrous. Although my social status did present some problems of access, it also opened up particular opportunities.

In light of the theoretical basis of my research, it is worth briefly considering my self-presentation as an ethnographer. Having discovered during the pilot study that most businesspeople were unfamiliar with (and slightly suspicious of) the idea of an anthropologist in business, I usually described myself during subsequent work as "studying German businesses" or "a business researcher" to casual inquirers, although I provided more detail to those people with whom I had to work on an ongoing basis. Also, the limited amount of time I was able to spend in Frankfurt meant that my perspective on the Frankfurt office is one of an outside observer, analogous, perhaps, to that of a London Branch employee whose job permits her some limited contact with Head Office. Both of these have undoubtedly affected my perspective on the organisation, but again, not necessarily to the detriment of the research.

Practical considerations have also limited the geographical scope of this project. It was unfortunately not possible, in terms of time, resources and access, to investigate the lives of transnational bank employees in any other "global cities" than London and Frankfurt. I have also limited my focus to German businesspeople, because to study every group which falls under the remit of the "transnational business elite" would be unfeasible. By limiting my focus to a single national group in a particular field in a particular global city, I am better placed to be able to examine the symbolic connections between local affiliation and transnational practices.

While I had of necessity to limit and modify my research activities in certain ways, I was therefore able to conduct a fruitful ethnographic study of German businesspeople in the United Kingdom. My investigations will therefore be able, if nothing else, to contribute to the understanding of the ways in which transnational actors use symbols to operate in a globalising environment.

**The Scope of the Present Study: Setting the Boundaries**

The work which follows is thus an exploration of the ways in which culture is used by German transnational businesspeople as they negotiate their relationships with others according to individual strategies of self-presentation. It also considers the origins and implications of the complexity of culture in transnational business, and whether or not this is causing the development of an entirely new form of social organisation which is neither "global" nor "local." In examining the uses of culture among transnational businesspeople of European origin, I will not only investigate the nature of social organisation in global business and the way in which transnational actors use culture as a strategic tool for success, but will contribute to our understanding of the impact of culture on business, and the implications for both researchers and practitioners.

In order to do so, however, I must necessarily limit the study to certain aspects of business culture: namely, "national" and "organisational" culture within a transnational organisation. Gender, for instance, although a significant factor influencing the culture of organisations, is too large a topic to be treated here, and has in any case been extensively dealt with in Part Two of *The Anthropology of Organisations* (Wright [ed] 1994, particularly the articles by Pringle and Kerfoot and Knights). The regional culture of Europe, and European policy, have also been the subject of other excellent monographs and collections (e.g. Whitley [ed.] 1992). Similarly, the problems of East German integration and of multiculturalism in Germany are being studied by other anthropologists, sociologists and historians (e.g. Borneman 1991, White 1997), and, since most of my interviewees were "white" West Germans, such issues seldom came up. While these gaps are significant, I maintain that by broadly limiting my conclusions to the two most visible discourses relating to national origin and global activity employed by my interviewees, I will be able to provide a more focused and detailed investigation of the ways in which they define themselves in cultural terms.

I also intend to avoid, as much as possible, the problematic term "identity." Although many earlier studies of culture in transnational situations has focused on the definition of national or ethnic identity, researchers in this field have increasingly found the term problematic, as "identity" is not so much an object which a given individual or group "has," as it is a nebulous series of discourses relating to age, class, gender and so forth (see Banks 1996). Furthermore, one can, for instance, "express Germanness," or "be German," without necessarily expressing or belonging to a particular "German identity." This is complicated by the fact that "identity," aside from a few superficial uses of the term in companies' promotional literature, has generally been subsumed into the concept of "culture" in business studies (see, for instance, Anthony 1994; Deal and Kennedy 1988), making the finding of common ground between the disciplines rather difficult. In acknowledgement of these developments, I shall here avoid the term except when quoting sources which use it. The work which follows is thus focused on the use of culture in an organisation, with specific reference to national and organisational culture, and will leave the problematic issue of "identity" to the side for the most part.

## Outline of the Work

This monograph takes a case study of a particular German bank with a large branch in the City of London, and draws from it issues which are of relevance to other groups involved in transnational business. Initially, I will briefly give the background to my study, first defining and exploring concepts relating to globalisation, transnational activity and the way in which culture is developed and expressed, to set the scene for later exploration. In particular, I will examine the utility of the home-country, host-country, and Leslie Sklair's "transnational capitalist class" (2001) models for describing culture in transnational places. Chapter Three then sets the scene by introducing the German transnational business community in London, their history and their institutions, examining how they use these, not to define themselves as a detached transnational elite of the sort described by Sklair, but as tools for networking and negotiating with other groups. Chapter Four will situate the Germans in the City of London, Europe's main financial centre, and consider the ways in which "culture" is used by different groups in this setting, again with regard to whether the Germans form a detached, solidary transnational elite or something more complex and strategy-based. Chapters Five and Six will consist of a case study of culture in a particular German bank. Chapter Five explores the question of whether there is in fact a sharp cultural division between "British" and "German" business cultures in the bank by considering employees' reactions to a recently-instituted restructuring programme, and how the failure on the part of both London and Frankfurt managers to acknowledge cultural diversity in the organisation caused problems with the restructuring. Chapter Six takes this further to discuss the role of communication within the organisation, and whether it is a tool for cultural dominance and resistance activities on the part of elite and subaltern groups, or of negotiation between diverse social entities. Chapter Seven, finally, will return to the earlier models of culture in business and consider how they can be redefined in light of the evidence which we have seen to reflect the role of culture in transnational business more accurately. I will then, building upon Sklair's "transnational capitalist class" model, speculate on the development of a "Transnational Capitalist Society" incorporating a diverse variety of global and local elements. Through using Goffman's theory of strategic self-presentation and applying it to the case of a particular German bank in London, I will thus consider the ways in which global and local culture interconnect through the personal activities of transnational businesspeople.

The volume's key objectives are, therefore:

- To examine the validity of the current definition of "culture" in international business studies;

- To discuss the ways in which the concept of "culture" is exploited by both individuals and groups to further their own strategies for success;

- To examine the problems which can result from the failure to take a realistic view of culture in MNCs, and to take the abovementioned exploitation into account;

- To consider the role played by the personal strategies of self-presentation of individuals in defining and altering the cultures of organisations and social groups;

- To consider the implications of the possibility of the development of a new form of culture, incorporating both global and local aspects and in continuous development, in transnational business.

This book will thus be an invaluable source for both researchers and businesspeople, as its unusual methodology yields startling new insights into the roles of local and global cultures in the operation of multinational corporations: not as concrete objects defining a particular group, but as strategic resources by which globe-trotting businesspeople further their individual ambitions, and through this, develop new forms of interaction uniquely adapted to transnational business.

The monograph which follows is thus based on an ethnographic study which aims to address one of the main deficiencies in anthropology and business studies: that both fail to consider the nature and complexity of culture in transnational business settings. Using Erving Goffman's theory of strategic self-presentation, I will argue that "culture" is not so much a matter of bounded, self-contained groups both "global" and "local," but of complex, constantly changing connections between different groups of varying degrees of global and local affiliation.

## Conclusion

This volume builds upon such classic works as Hofstede (1980) and Whitley (ed. 1992), adding to them the theories of culture developed by anthropologists working with transnational economic groups and recent work on the construction of culture in multinational corporations, to explore how the concept of "culture" is used and exploited by transnational business managers to further their own ambitions and their companies' strategies for expansion, in the process causing the development of new globe-spanning social forms and transnational connections. We shall now consider the theoretical background to this study, with particular reference to studies of globalisation, culture and multinational corporations.

# Chapter 2

# Transnational Culture's Consequences: Theorising the Global and the Local

## Introduction

In order to understand the cultural situation of German transnational businesspeople in London, and before we can formulate theories about the form of social organisation in the global business world, we must first consider the impact which the concepts of globalisation, transnationalism, "the global" and "the local," have on the operation of business in general and MNCs in particular. To this end, I will examine the idea that national cultures retain an overwhelming significance in global business, and the counterargument that business is becoming dominated by a "transnational capitalist class." This overview will provide the background for a more balanced assessment of the influence of local and global culture on transnational business, and how individuals and groups use the concept of "culture" in strategic ways, ultimately developing transnational social connections through their strategic self-presentation activities.

## A World Apart: Theories of Globalisation and Transnationalism

The proposition that a globe-spanning, business-focused elite is currently rising to prominence has its basis in another theoretical discourse, which revolves around the idea that the world is presently in what is known as a period of globalisation. We shall here consider some of the key theoretical positions and debates surrounding globalisation, transnationalism and the formation of culture.

### Globalisation: Definitions and Themes

Globalisation is defined by Waters as a "process in which the constraints of geography on social... arrangements recede" (1995: 3). Most writers on the subject define this phenomenon as characterised by the rise in importance of four things: namely, advances in electronic communication and transportation, which "compress" time and space and have an impact on the importance of the nation state (Ibid., 35; Schein 1998); the "freeing" of capital, which leads to a 24-hour global financial market in which the state plays a minimal role in regulation (Leyshon and Thrift 1997: 46-47); the rise of a "flexible" workforce, which could potentially lead to a "jobless" society in which few have permanent employment

(Sassen 1991: 295; Castells 1996: 264-268); and, finally, a positive valuation of capitalism (Portes 1998: 4). From these have arisen certain social processes relating to interconnections and interdependencies between groups which may be geographically separated, and different ways of viewing time and space (Tomlinson 1999a: 2, 4; Harvey 1989). We shall thus refer to the changes in communications, transportation and economics as the "processes of globalisation," and define globalisation itself in broad terms as the impact of these processes on human interaction and social behaviour.

"Transnational" groups, by contrast, can be defined for the purposes of this monograph as those which have arisen from the transformative effect of the processes of globalisation upon national boundaries. Vertovec, more specifically, defines them as groups possessing "multiple ties... linking people or institutions across the borders of nation states" (1999: 447). Although the concepts of globalisation and transnationalism are frequently conflated, it should be noted that transnationalism is a slightly different concept, as it is predicated on the continued existence of nations and borders in some form where globalisation need not necessarily refer to these. Transnational groups are distinguished from earlier, "international" ones in that their cross-border ties form a conduit along which people, goods and information are constantly flowing, and which enable simultaneous communication between localities; "international" implies the crossing of borders, but without the element of simultaneity (Waters 1995: 18, 27; Portes 1998: 18). We shall thus consider transnationalism as a concept related, but not identical to, globalisation.

Although the existence and form of premodern types of globalisation remain the subject of debate (see Held et al. 1999: 16-20), the present period of globalisation traces its origins to the 1970s and 1980s. This period saw rapid advances in communications technology, including the development of personal computers and the Internet (Ibid., 342-346). This was coupled with a series of economic changes, including a crisis over oil prices and the termination of the Bretton Woods agreement, which placed world currency rates officially in free-fall (Ibid., 183, 199-201; Thrift and Leyshon 1994: 305-6; Chandler 1977: 491-500). These events have brought about a world in which people can communicate with each other in real time, travel faster and more cheaply than ever before, and in which currency rates do not reflect a predetermined economic hierarchy of nations, but a continuously changing world economic situation in which sharp and drastic changes of fortune are likely (Held et al. 1999: 201-220; Castells 1996: 434). Most writers thus seem to agree that the processes of globalisation exist, have been operating at least since the mid-1970s, and continue to operate today.

Where writers differ, however, is with regard to the nature and extent of the processes of globalisation, and what exactly their effects, if any, have been upon human social behaviour. Held et al., in their seminal book *Global Transformations*, identify three broad stances on globalisation: the *hyperglobalisers*, the *sceptics* and the *transformationalists* (1999: 2). We shall here consider each of these positions in turn.

*The Hyperglobalisers*

The *hyperglobalisers*, first of all, take it for granted that the processes defined above are bringing about a new era in which nation-states are decreasing in importance, the old "North-South" divisions are being eroded in favour of a new, more egalitarian economic system and the hybridisation of cultures is celebrated (Ibid., 3-5; see also Ohmae 1990). Furthermore, they argue, people are becoming more globally aware and inclined to think in global, rather than local, terms; again, they seem to regard this as a historical novelty rather than a norm or established phenomenon (see Iyer 2000). The hyperglobalist stance thus holds that the processes of globalisation are bringing about a new era which differs categorically from any which has come before.

Out of the hyperglobalist position has emerged a model of globalising social activity which could be of great value in considering such groups as transnational businesspeople: Appadurai's concept of "global landscapes." In his 1990 essay "Disjuncture and Difference In The Global Cultural Economy," Appadurai argues that the best way to consider the present, "globalising" world is not in terms of nation states, however interconnected they may be, but as "global landscapes," existing as imagined concepts which link particular sorts of activities or interest groups across the globe (Ibid., 296). The "ethnoscape," for instance, consists of all activities taking place worldwide which are related to ethnicity: so, for instance, that the world is not seen in terms of "Ireland" and "Germany" but "Ireland/the Irish diaspora," "Germany/the German diaspora/former parts and colonies of Germany" and so on (Ibid., 297). More important from the point of view of studying global business activities, however, is his concept of the financescape (Ibid., 298). This involves what can be broadly called the "world economy"; that is, global activity as it relates to financial and commercial transactions (see Mickelthwait and Wooldridge 2000: 104-105; Castells 1996: 60). The "global landscapes" concept not only allows for the acknowledgement of social activities which take place across borders and boundaries, but also for the unequal and uneven nature of globalisation. India, for instance, is a fairly small player in the financescape, but a titan in the mediascape. The "global landscapes" model, and in particular the concept of a "financescape," could thus be a useful way of conceiving of the world when studying transnational socioeconomic activities.

The idea of a global financescape is one which has a good deal of support among people who study transnational business. Pryke and Lee (1995) suggest that economic activity is a social and cultural process which does not simply relate to particular local cultures but exists as something above and beyond them. Castells describes economic activity as a kind of world-spanning web running between the three "triad" regions of NAFTA, the EU and the Asia Pacific area (1996: 100). Amin and Thrift, similarly, argue that the seemingly increased localisation of the finance industry—as more and more businesses concentrate themselves in the City of London, New York and Tokyo—is in fact an artefact of increasing transnational contact-building and information-sharing, as such cities become nodes in wider social networks (1992). This idea also informs McDowell's descriptions of a world in which a new, mobile professional class concentrate themselves in particular financial and political centres at the same time as they move internationally through their firms' international labour markets (1997b: 2). In a later article, Thrift develops this further, presenting the City of London as a site of knowledge transference and information dispersal in an informational and relationship-driven global financial system (1994). Leyshon and Thrift, finally, make the premise of their book *Money/Space* the idea that financial activity has its own geography, distinct from actual physical geography (1997). Writers in several disciplines thus seem to take the idea of the existence of a financescape, above and beyond actual physical landscapes, for granted.

*The Sceptics*

The *sceptics*, however, provide a challenge to this viewpoint. Sceptical writers, most notably Hirst and Thompson, argue that there is nothing new about the processes of globalisation, if indeed they have the impact which the hyperglobalisers claim for them. Hirst and Thompson note that similar phenomena occurred in the 1300s and the 1870s, suggesting that the present period is less unique than the hyperglobalisers claim, and that the Gold Standard period saw a more interlinked economy than that of the present time (1996: 19, 36). They also note that there continue to be marked inequalities between countries, with the USA financially and militarily hegemonic, suggesting that globalisation has had little impact upon social order (Ibid., 14). Finally, they argue that economic union need not bring about social or political unity, and that recent financial developments could herald the collapse of the so-called "global" economy (Ibid., 1996: 167). In this, they are supported by others: McDowell, for instance, suggests that the recessions of the 1990s have led to an abandonment of "flexibility" in favour of a renewed focus on social boundaries in the City of London (1997a). It is thus possible that the social phenomena of recent years will have no lasting effects, and that the rumours of globalisation are greatly exaggerated.

There are, however, social scientists who, while they agree that the processes of globalisation do not have the radical effects claimed by the hyperglobalisers, nonetheless argue that one should not therefore assume that they have no significant impact on present-day society. Yeung (1998) proposes that while it is not true that social and geographical boundaries have become obsolete, the processes of globalisation do exist and are having an impact on most if not all states and societies. Tomlinson says that globalisation does not mean the development of a global monoculture, but that people, even though their actions may be confined to particular areas, consider the world as a whole as they act (1999a: 10). An increasing number of writers argue that the processes of globalisation are having a transformative effect on society.

Other social scientists take the fact that similar processes have occurred before as a point of interest rather than as a reason for discounting their significance. It has been suggested for instance, that the possibility that globalisation has been the historic norm rather than the exception means that we should reconsider our views of human history (Held et al. 1999: 77-82). Foner's study of Italian migrants in New York in the early twentieth century (1997), and Mickelthwait and Wooldridge's journalistic account of "globalisation" in the British Empire (2000: Chapter 1), both make interesting comparisons between the earlier and present-day phenomena, to suggest how the concept and nature of globalisation has changed, and what causes societies to become more and less "globalised" over time. These studies also suggest that the fact that communication today is instantaneous rather than near-instantaneous has meant certain qualitative differences between modern and past periods of globalisation, as global interactions can take place today in real time, rather than over hours or days (Vertovec 2001: 22). Some writers thus take a more middle-ground stance, accepting the sceptics' critiques but still arguing that globalisation has effects which should not be ignored.

*The Transformationalists*

The sceptics' critique that the processes of globalisation are causing the "West" to become richer at the expense of developing countries (see, for instance, Fröbel et al. 1980), is similarly challenged by middle-ground writers. Mickelthwait and Wooldridge point out in exhaustive detail that, contrary to Hirst and Thompson's claims, not all of the "losers" of globalisation are in "Third World," developing countries (2000: Chapter 13). Portes (1998) notes that international inequalities have not prevented workers from "developing" countries from operating transnationally. The likelihood that globalisation may be widening the gap between rich and poor thus provides an argument for, rather than against, the increased study of globalisation. The middle-ground writers thus acknowledge some advantages to both sides of the debate; they argue that the social formations of past times are not being swept away by the processes of globalisation, but are being transformed.

David Held et al. have given this middle-ground stance the name *transformationalism* (1999: 7). Transformationalists generally hold that the processes of globalisation are reshaping the social order of the world, and that the contemporary form of globalisation is unprecedented in terms of its speed and extent (Ibid.). However, they also argue that these effects are historically contingent, and remain sceptical that they will lead to some form of new, egalitarian global order. Rather, they suggest that they are in fact producing new patterns of power (Ibid., 8); while borders and nations remain important, it is in a different form to earlier eras (Ibid., 9). They also eschew the faintly utopian stance of the hyperglobalisers (in some cases to the point where Sparke accuses them of setting up a "straw man" [2001: 173]). Castells, contemplating the hyperglobalisers' scenario of a near-fully-globalised world as a possibility, argues that the diminishment of the nation state and the rise in importance of transnational communications would ultimately lead to an end to (or at least, a diminishment of) the welfare state, increased surveillance, less secure jobs, and rising economic imbalances (1996). Mickelthwait and Wooldridge are not reticent in discussing the social difficulties which would follow in the wake of the processes of globalisation

(2000: Chapter 13). The less dogmatic transformationalist theory thus appears to provide a balance between the two earlier viewpoints.

To the transformationalist hypothesis outlined by Held et al., however, I would add Tomlinson's observation that globalisation is not geographically universal, and that global activities link in with local ones in different ways (1999a: 84, 130-1). Hannerz's Central African *sapeurs* may regard Parisian clothes as prestige items, but the items of clothing which they consider status symbols would not be regarded as particularly indicative of distinction by the Parisians (1996: 132). Some groups are still, either by choice or due to the action of the market, relatively isolated: Castells presents a grim description of how the processes of globalisation have bypassed post-Soviet Russia and large parts of Africa (1998: 28, 92). We will thus here broadly adhere to the transformationalist view of globalisation as a social process which is changing, rather than eradicating, local actions and social formations, but also emphasise that the effects of the processes which cause globalisation are not universal, and have different impacts in different areas.

Some transformationalists have also built upon this to suggest that the relationship between the global and the local is one of "mutual embeddedness." Yeung, for instance, points out that nations, far from being superseded, are in fact engaged in globalisation, and Tomlinson speaks in terms of dialectics between global and local practices (Yeung 1998: 299; Tomlinson 1999a: 25). One might cite as evidence the case of the government of the Philippines, which actively facilitates its citizens' economic migration (Anderson 2001a). As well as involving the local interpretation of global practices, then, engaging in globalising activities seems to involve the continual definition and redefinition of the concepts of global and local vis-à-vis each other.

It thus seems that it might be best to consider the relationship between the global and the local in terms of Tomlinson's "complex connectivity" (1999a: 2), mentioned briefly in Chapter 1, in which "global" and "local" cultures are defined not as concrete entities, but as having meanings which are largely dependent on the context. The sceptic Smith's argument, for instance, that the increasing interdependence of states binds people closer to the local, speaks less of a globalising or localising world than of many different kinds of relations between individuals and global processes, as "the local" seems to refer as much to regions and ethnic "homelands" as to national entities, and indeed people can find themselves claiming a connection to several localities simultaneously (1995: 159, 60). Balibar describes local boundaries as "vacillating" under globalisation, which "does not mean that they are disappearing," but does suggest that we consider them in different ways than formerly (1998: 220). It thus appears that the relationship between the local and the global is contextually defined, and subject to redefinition.

It seems, furthermore, that engaging in globalising activities involves a continuous process of negotiating between particular local and global cultures. Some writers have described groups engaged in globe-spanning activities whose resources flow, not just between the home and host countries, but throughout their social networks (e.g. Portes 1998). Hannerz notes that there are different degrees and kinds of global engagement; there are, he suggests, "people for whom the nation works less well as a source of cultural resonance," but others for whom it is still important (1996: 29, 88, 90). It thus appears that there is no single way of relating global systems to physical localities, but an infinite number, as individual actors negotiate between the global and local components of their social environments.

Referring again to the financescape, then, we may therefore revise Appadurai's original concept to one which more strongly resembles Castells' "networked" description of global economics (1996: 96, 171). The financescape should not necessarily be seen as a "global landscape" which takes place in some realm divorced from other sorts of social and physical geography, but one which involves global and local components which are continually constructing each other and redefining their relationships, and in which the degree of embeddedness of all actors and practices is variable (see Tomlinson 1999a). The situation may thus best be seen in terms of Yeung's locally embedded capitalism, in which the processes of globalisation intersect and reinforce each other in complex ways (1998: 303, 299), and which consequently takes into account connections to global entities and local ideas about globalisation. We shall thus here consider the financescape, not as a detached "global landscape," but rather as an extended, business-focused network encompassing particular localities and the globalising activities which connect them.

The best way of approaching the question of how transnational business cultures operate may thus be not to think in broad, theoretical terms, but to take an in-depth look at how a particular group negotiates between global and the local components of the financescape, and to consider, not what general form these interactions take, but what can be learned from the diversity and types of activities in which it engages. Rather than try to address the relationship between global and local in general and abstract terms, then, we shall see what conclusions can be drawn about it from examining the sort of interaction which goes on in and amongst particular "transnational" groups.

It thus seems that the recent changes in communications, transportation and economics have had an impact on human societies, but this has not incurred the total abandonment of local practices. The transformationalist thesis, which argues that globalisation refers more to the transformative effects of these processes on societies, is thus the one which seems to best fit the actual situation, given that one also accepts that these effects are different in different areas in terms of intensity and impact (see Held et al. 1999: 7-10; Vertovec 2001). Globalisation, at least as far as the business world is concerned, is not a matter of all or nothing, but of the uneven effects of certain technological and economic practices upon social activity. As suggested by the discussion on "third cultures" discussed in the previous chapter, then, studies of globalisation suggest that culture in transnational business is more of a vague, shifting, strategy-based thing than was previously thought.

**Business Twenty-Four Seven: The Cultures of Multinational Corporations**

The globalising social formation which is most relevant to us here, and on which we will consequently focus, is that the multinational corporation or MNCs, sometimes, erroneously, referred to as "transnational corporations" or TNCs (see Sklair 1995: 52).[1] In this section, I will describe MNCs and consider whether their cultures are really focused on particular national influences, or are something more diffuse and globally-engaged.

*MNCs and Globalisation: Overview and Definitions*

MNCs can be defined as corporations with physical or conceptual bases of operations in two or more countries simultaneously, of which at least one is in a "global" city, with each of the branches and the centre linked to each other by lines of communication and trade (Bartlett and Ghoshal 1993: 78; Tugendhat 1971). According to Chandler's definition, still employed by many in business studies, the MNC is distinct from the traditional, localised business, and the later hierarchical organisation with many different operations, in that MNCs are decentralised, with multiple divisions and functions being spread across the world (1977: 14, 1, 480). One might add to this, in light of the present period of globalisation, that MNCs increasingly rely on so-called "flexible" employment, and, as their hiring-and-firing policies are determined by central office policy rather than local markets, their presence frequently forces people in the locations in which they set up branches into more job flexibility than they had anticipated (Augar 2000). While most of the theoretical discussion has focused on the large, Western MNCs, Stopford notes that small and non-Western companies exist that also fit this paradigm (1998/9). We shall thus consider MNCs as transnational social formations with a business focus.

As such, MNCs draw their genesis and continued existence from the processes of globalisation. Such corporations reproduce their structure and carry out their functions through the use of rapid communications (Egelhoff 1993). Furthermore, it is due to the geographical "flexibility" of work that MNCs settle in diverse parts of the globe in order to obtain the most economical source of labour, and due to the global nature of the market that they are able to do this at all (Fröbel et al. 1980; Beaverstock 1996b, c; Beaverstock and Smith 1996). In their turn, MNCs contribute to the processes of globalisation: on one level, they make similar products available all over the world; on another, the flows of capital directed through them perpetuate the global financial system; and finally, their concentration in certain areas facilitates the development of "global cities"

---

[1] Although the term is often used as synonymous with MNC, Bartlett and Ghoshal (1992) argue that in fact, for a corporation to be "transnational" involves more than simply having operations in diverse countries, and indeed that "transnational corporations" as such do not actually exist, as much as corporations exist with transnational aspects. For a fuller discussion, see Bartlett and Ghoshal 1992.

(Castells 1996: 380; Sassen 1991). MNCs are thus inextricably linked with the political, economic and social processes of globalisation.

The organisational cultures of MNCs are also of a form which is more compatible with border-crossing activities than with those which relate to the interests of specific nations or local groups only, being networks with "component parts... [which] are both autonomous from, and dependent upon, [their] complex system of relationships" (Vertovec 1999: 452-453). Castells notes that the self-sufficient company appears to be a thing of the past; instead one finds networks of producer companies, consumer companies and so forth, all dependent upon one another (1996: 191). MNCs thus take a dynamic, networked form, linked to outside entities as well as internally divided along the lines of the interests of their component groups.

## MNCS and Other Transnational Social Formations

As a result of this distinctive social form, MNCs do not exist as bounded, solidary cultural entities, but have links to other transnational social formations. One such formation which MNCs are both affected by, and strongly resemble, is the ethnic/cultural diaspora (see R. Cohen 1997). Robin Cohen cites Safran's definition of diasporas as expatriate minority communities which have been dispersed from an original centre to two or more other regions, who retain an idealised collective memory of the "homeland," to which they hope to return; remain separate from the host community, although this may not always be voluntary on the part of diaspora members; and maintain group consciousness (Ibid., 23, 19, 26). MNCs and diasporas have a number of common features: leaving aside the fact that both are difficult to define, both have complex, "triadic" links with home, host and transnational cultures (Vertovec 1996a: 14; Clifford 1994: 310). Both are flexible, with diaspora members blending in more or less with their surroundings depending on the situation (Borneman and Peck 1995). Both have complex relationships with the processes of globalisation: while Robin Cohen notes that present-day telecommunications have made it easier for diasporas to maintain cohesion, it has also been said that the processes of globalisation are responsible for the continued dispersal of diasporas (1997: 169; see van Hear 1998 for a more extensive discussion).

MNCs do not only resemble diasporas, however, but individuals may belong to both groups at once. Robin Cohen cites several "occupational" diasporas with direct relationships to transnational business practices, such as the Chinese (1997: 178). One might also, like Portes, draw a parallel between Sassen's international executives and Portes' own Dominican entrepreneurs (Sassen 1991; Portes 1998: 8). Furthermore, MNCs intersect not simply with diasporas in general, but with several distinct sorts of diaspora; Cohen notes that the category "labour diaspora" includes groups as diverse as Chinese "astronauts" (1997: 93) and Jewish and Lebanese "pariah capitalists" (101). Furthermore, MNCs also draw on the casual labour networks, refugees and other sorts of transnational social formation which space does not allow us to describe in detail, in order to make up the flexible workforces described by Castells which make it possible for MNCs to be active economic concerns (1996: 264-68). One cannot therefore speak of MNCs as single, definite entities, possessed of particular cultures, but rather as involved, not only with diasporas, but with several quite distinct transnational social formations, between which the boundaries are difficult to discern and whose cultures intersect with each other.

Finally, it is difficult to pinpoint, in the case of MNCs, where the global social formation ends and the local social formations begin. The (seemingly localised) nation state often has a stake in the furtherance of multinational corporations (Held et al. 1999: 274-275; 276-278). The Bank of England, a seemingly local financial organisation whose aim is to protect UK interests, also engages in transnational finance and education programmes (Bank of England 2000: 43-44). Many of the subsidiaries forming part of the multinational corporation described by Kristensen and Zeitlin are, in fact, local companies which were acquired by the larger group, which in some cases continued to operate for the most part as if they were still local companies (2004, Chapter 1). Doz et al., more recently, have proposed the emergence of the "metanational" corporation, which operates indiscriminately across the globe, acquiring and making use of knowledge wherever they find it rather than simply focusing on the transfer of knowledge between the head office and the overseas branches (2001). Multinational corporations thus not only have local connections, but it is in some places difficult to draw the line between their local and global engagements.

MNCs thus have a multifaceted culture consisting of engagement with, not a single "community," but several social formations both local and global, to the point where the boundaries between MNCs and associated groups become indefinite. Furthermore, they are not single entities, but are made up of a variety of different subgroups with their own interests. It thus cannot be said that there is a single paradigm which defines multinational corporations, nor that transnational social formations in general can be characterised as specific entities in isolation from each other and from other types of social formation both transnational and locally-focused. The social forms which have sprung up under globalisation, and in particular multinational corporations, cannot be considered in the traditional way as isolated cultural units, but should rather be seen as networked entities with many different sorts of internal and external connections. Much as the nature of the relationship between local and global must be contextually determined, then, it seems that a single theoretical model of transnational social formations is of less value than an examination of the nature and types of engagements possessed by these groups.

MNCs are thus globalising social organisations par excellence, being engaged with, and deriving from, the processes of globalisation, and having a complex, networked structure. Furthermore, they are not single, solidary entities, but the locus of strong dialectics between global and local social forces. It is thus worth considering what form culture takes in a complex environment such as a multinational corporation, and the impact of this on the relationship between the global and the local.

## Dealing with Culture's Consequences: Nationally-focused Theories of Culture in MNCS

As discussed in the previous chapter, "culture" tends to be defined in business studies as a unified, solidary property of groups, organisations and individuals. This approach also persists in the study of global business, with most theorists arguing that the culture of MNCs is most strongly influenced by particular national cultures. More recently, it has been suggested that it might be better to think of corporations as influenced by a *transnational* culture, that of the globalizing business elites who are the dominant group in many if not all MNCs. While this viewpoint does allow us to consider culture less as a static entity and more as a shifting, changing concept, it remains to be seen whether it can truly capture the complexity of national, organisational and global influences on corporations.

Writers who prioritise national influences on MNCs tend to fall into three camps: the "country-of-origin" (or "home country") the "national business systems" (or "host country") and the "third culture" approaches. Those who argue for the first theory, the "home-country effect," believe that the strongest influence on a given organisation is the country in which the company originates. This perspective can be seen most strongly in early studies of multinationals and expatriates, which tended to argue that MNCs exported the culture of the home country to their branches, by virtue of the fact that their primary economic interests lie within the home country, that most of the company's policies are dictated from Head Office, and that the bulk of expatriates occupying key positions in branches have tended, in the past, to come from the home-country culture (Bergsten et al. 1978). In the 1960s and 70s, it was frequently argued that the culture of the corporation's home country was the most dominant factor, particularly with regard to whether American MNCs were vehicles for American economic colonialism (e.g. Behrman 1970; Bergsten et al. 1978; see also Wade 1996). This approach has, however, been called into question by many who point out that the bulk of employees in MNC branches are in fact local (Tugendhat 1971), that branches have to cooperate with local laws and regulations (Ghoshal and Nohria 1989) and that, as expatriation grows increasingly complex, we have to take into account the fact that many are "third-country nationals," i.e. coming from a country other than the home country of the corporation (Janssens 1994). The "country-of-origin" effect" thus does not cover all the complexities of culture within MNC branches.

Proponents of the "national business systems" approach (e.g. Whitley 1992), by contrast, prioritise the influence of the branch's host-country culture over that of the home country on its makeup. Taking Hofstede's classic study of cultural differences between employees of the branches of a single MNC, *Culture's Consequences*, as a starting point, supporters of this view argue that branches are socially disparate parts of the wider organization, which bring local expertise to the corporation as a whole (Hofstede 1980; Mueller 1994: 408; Andersson et al. 2001: 1014). Several countries either have, or have had, policies promoting the hiring of locals; the most extreme—and telling—example is that of Nazi Germany, which banned all non-German companies (Beaverstock and Smith 1996: 1390; Tugendhat 1971: 39). Tugendhat argues that MNCs "try... to assume a local character" for strategic reasons (Ibid., 200): Bergsten et al. cite the case of Opel advertising its products as triumphs of German engineering, although the firm was owned by an American company (1978: 47). One should thus consider MNCs less as single entities, and more as collections of groups with diverse needs (Hofstede 1980: 381).

This approach has, however, come into question, as other studies have demonstrated that in fact the culture of a corporation's head office can be a major influence on its branches *at the same time* as it experiences influence from the host country (Mueller 1994: 408); although the scope of his study did not permit him to develop this, Hofstede himself acknowledged that there were other influences on branches than simply the culture of the host country (1980: 105). McSweeney, furthermore, has written an article detailing a number of fundamental flaws with Hofstede's study, chief among them being that Hofstede fails to take into account the interplay of home-country, host-country and corporate cultures within the branches, simply prioritising national culture above everything (2002). Subsequent writers defending the "host-country approach" have similarly glossed over the influences of other sorts of culture, and have frequently, through their efforts to develop a counterargument to the "home country" stance discussed above, focused their arguments more or less exclusively on branch culture to a sometimes unrealistic degree (Mueller 1994: 407). Many researchers today thus feel that branches possess a "third culture," which is a mix of home and host country influences.

However, in taking this approach, they continue to prioritise national cultures above other possibilities. It has also been recognised, for instance that a corporation is affected by its members' interests and social connections (by, for instance, Torbiörn 1982; Douglas 1987; Boden 1994). Morgan notes that the concerns, aims and interests of its managers affect the practices of a company; Cyert and March's study of corporations concludes that firms are not single entities, but are the sum of their employees' individual and collective interests (Garth Morgan 1997; Cyert and March 1992). The dynamic between different groups in the corporation, for instance management and staff, affects the organisation as a whole (Jackall 1988: 17-74; Schwartzman 1993: 18). A multinational corporation is therefore a cultural entity which is constantly being redefined, and which blends into other social groupings.

It thus seems that theoretical approaches based primarily on national culture, while they go some way towards explaining the social and cultural composition of MNCs in the global financescape, are insufficiently complex and do not take the transnational nature of MNCs' structures into account. We shall now consider a theory explicitly formulated to consider business from a global, rather than a national, perspective.

**Businesspeople of the World Unite: The Transnational Capitalist Class**

Recently, a school of thought has emerged which holds that organisations are increasingly being influenced not by national cultures, but by an emerging global business culture. This can best be seen in LSE sociologist Leslie Sklair's work on what he calls the "transnational capitalist class." This term refers, broadly speaking, to a transnational elite with connections to business. Sklair is neither the first nor the only social scientist to have described such an elite; however, we will use his terminology because his work is probably the most extensive and comprehensive to be written on this type of transnational actor. It might thus be fruitful to consider MNCs not in terms of national business cultures, but as participants in an emergent transnational elite business culture.

## *Definition of the Transnational Capitalist Class (TCC)*

According to Sklair, the TCC (to borrow his abbreviation) consists of "those people who see their interests... and/or the interests of their countries of citizenship, as best served by an identification with the interests of the capitalist global system, in particular the interests of the transnational corporations" (1995: 8). He defines the origins and ideology of this group through four propositions: firstly, that "a transnational capitalist class based on the multinational corporation is emerging that is more or less in control of the processes of globalisation." Secondly, that "the TCC is beginning to act as a transnational dominant class in some spheres." Thirdly, that "the globalisation of the capitalist system reproduces itself through the profit-driven culture-ideology of consumerism." Finally, he proposes that the transnational capitalist class is "working consciously to resolve... the simultaneous creation of increasing poverty and increasing wealth within and between communities... and.... The unsustainability of the system (the ecological crisis)" (2001: 5-6). We thus get an image of the globalising world as being dominated by a bourgeois class which is concerned with global financial and ethical issues. In keeping with the discussion above with regard to the relationship between global and local in the financescape, Sklair acknowledges that this group does have local links. However, his arguments that some local businesses share the TCC's globalising interests and that most elites, even local ones, are becoming globally conscious to some degree suggests more that local groups are increasingly being recruited, as it were, into the TCC than that there exists a genuine global/local social interplay (Ibid., 18). Given the fact that MNCs operate across different national cultures within the global financescape, then, it may be that it can be best understood in terms of cultures whose hegemonic voices are a global capitalist elite with local links, which operates within the financescape and promotes a globalising ideology.

The TCC theory also does not limit members to a single culture, corporate, national or otherwise. According to Sklair's two books on the subject, the TCC consists of four broadly defined groups (1995: 72; 2001: 17):

1) The corporate fraction: MNC executives and their local affiliates
2) The state fraction: globalising state bureaucrats

3) The technical fraction: capitalist-inspired politicians and professionals (in 2001: 17 modified to "globalising professionals")
4) The consumerist fraction: consumerist elites (modified in 2001: 17 to "merchants and media")

These groups, taken collectively as the TCC, share four common points with regard to transnational engagement (1995: 71; 2001: 18-22):

1) Their economic interests are increasingly globally linked
2) They seek to exert economic control over the workplace
3) They take outward-focused global, not inward-focused local, perspectives on most issues, considering themselves "citizens of the world"
4) They share similar lifestyles, especially with regard to consumption and valuation of a cosmopolitan ideology

The transnational capitalist class thus consists of four interconnected groups defined by common practices and values; the business fraction, which we will consider here, consists of businesspeople with an increasing focus on globalisation, including the employees of multinational corporations. As such, these individuals are said to transcend both national and corporate cultures.

Sklair also briefly notes that resistance by other local and global groups to the TCC's increasing domination has been limited (2001, p. 18). Although this has more recently proven not to be the case, with the rise in anti-capitalist protests and the activities of international terrorists, one might observe that the resistance has proven to have, often ironic, connections to the elite. As many a journalist has pointed out, most of the anticapitalist protestors at WTO meetings are the children of this global elite, and are less anticapitalist in deed than in word; they use the Internet, own commercially-manufactured mobile phones, and drink imported coffee at the same time as they decry global capitalism, multinational corporations and sharecropping arrangements. The TCC's own environmentalist ethic causes them to support groups and individuals opposed to global capitalism (see Sklair 2001: 200). During the Afghan conflict, US forces seized a number of Western-made laptop computers from al-Qaeda headquarters and cave complexes; even a group ideologically opposed to Western capitalism apparently sees little wrong in using its products (www.ananova.com 2002). While the events in the wake of September 11, 2001 might seem to have overtaken Sklair's analysis of the resistance to the TCC, it would appear that he is correct in arguing that such activities do not provide a particularly counterhegemonic voice in practice, and indeed, they may simply demonstrate the broader efficacy of the social formation in including within it dissenting voices.

*Support for the TCC Theory*

Support for this position can be found in the works of other writers on the subject of transnational business and MNCs. Castells, for instance, speaks of a business elite with a cosmopolitan lifestyle, whose environment consists largely of transnational social spaces—airports, international hotels, "global cities" and so forth (1996: 417). Although he believes that there is no such thing as a global labour force, elite or otherwise—it being still constrained by institutions, culture and borders—he argues that there is an increasing tendency towards *interdependence* of the labour force on a global scale (1996). Ong, in an article on cosmopolitanism and Chinese business, quotes a banker as saying "I can live anywhere in the world, but it must be near an airport" (1998: 157). From the mid-1980s (which Leyshon and Thrift [1997] characterise as the period in which various economic processes coalesced into a 24-hour, more or less global, financial system) onwards, Beaverstock charts the emergence of a group of high-waged labour migrants, due to the needs of MNCs for a labour pool of individuals with particular skills who could interpret company policy—i.e. reproduce the company culture—in the local context (1991; 1994; 1996a; Beaverstock and Smith 1996: 1390; see Torbiörn 1982). People with these skills were rewarded with high pay and "fast track" careers, and thus "must be internationally mobile if they wish[ed] to climb the corporate ladder" (Beaverstock 1996b: 427, 430). These migrants came to form a transnational network with nodes in the "global cities" (422), characterised by particular skills, a particular lifestyle, and a more or less common ideology in which transnational practices are strongly valued (Beaverstock and Smith 1996; Beaverstock 1996b: 427-430; Westney 1993: 64). One may note the popularity of "intercultural training" among MNC employees, and the large number of books and articles intended to instruct them in using cultural differences to their own advantage (Delacroix 1993: 111, Dahlen 1997; I recommend Horovitz [1980], Hickson and Pugh [1997], Hunt [1998], and Trompenaars and Hampden-Turner [1994], as good examples of the genre.). There is thus support from other social scientists for the concept of a transnational capitalist class, in the form of an inward-focused, globally-engaged elite, which interacts with the local only inasmuch as it serves its economic purposes (see Fig. 2.1).

In addition, the TCC model has made it into more popular accounts of the globalisation of business. A pair of journalists, Mickelthwait and Wooldridge, write at length on the subject of "cosmocrats" (2000: Chapter 12). While theirs is a broader definition than Sklair's, encompassing globetrotting academics, artists and people who work on or with the Internet as well as the expatriate employees of sprawling MNCs (Ibid., 230-1), their description of the capitalist-related fraction of the "cosmocrats" is very close to the above formulation of the TCC. Like Sklair, Castells and other social scientists, they define this elite "by their attitudes and lifestyles rather than just their bank accounts," these being "cosmopolitan in taste and usually Anglo-American in outlook" (Ibid., 230, 229). Mickelthwait and Wooldridge argue that "global habits" are developing in this elite, with increasing dependence on communication, reverence for intelligence and sharp anxieties about change (Ibid., 233, 240ff). Two economic journalists thus also make an argument that the social organisation of elite transnational businesspeople takes the form, more or less, of a TCC. There is therefore much to suggest that it might be fruitful to apply the TCC theory to MNCs as a way of understanding their cultures.

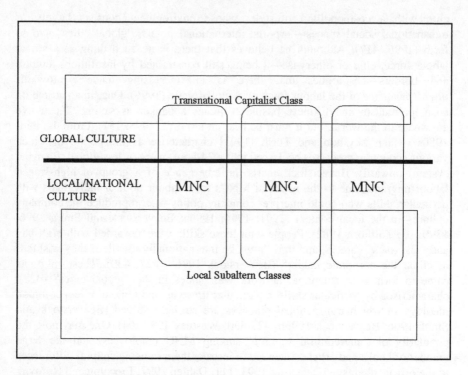

**Figure 2.1  The transnational capitalist class**

*Limitations of the TCC Theory*

Unfortunately, however, this position has a few weaknesses. The TCC model defined by Sklair has much the same problem as those focusing on national cultures: namely, that it defines culture as a monolithic entity, of which groups can only "have" one, and does not consider it as a dynamic concept subject to continual change. Writers discussing the TCC for the most part treat it more or less in isolation from other groups, both transnational and more localised; they seemingly assume a lack of engagement with any of these on the TCC's part. Sklair very seldom refers in either of his books on the subject to the engagement of these capitalists with the local; his article about the executives of tobacco companies makes a nod in that direction, but only a slight one (1998b). The question of the relationship of the TCC with less globally-focused groups is thus seldom directly addressed by Sklair.

Other sources, furthermore, suggest more in the way of complex engagement between the TCC and local groups. The *History of Deutsche Bank* discusses the involvement of the corporation and its management with local affairs both in Germany and elsewhere over the years (Gall et al., eds., 1995). All of the monographs on the global business elite discussed above show them to, at some point in the study, claim allegiance with some particular cultural background or other. It is significant that in Goodman's study of the children of Japanese transnational businesspeople, his subjects were not urged to reject local roots, but to take "the best" of both their Japanese family background and of the cultures in which they had spent part of their childhoods (1993: 137). Far from being an aloof elite dominating a local group of subalterns, then, the TCC seems to have a number of local connections which have not been considered by most writers on the subject.

Many social scientists, furthermore, appear to consider the TCC as lacking in contact with other sorts of transnational social organisations. While this would seem a pretty incredible feat simply on paper, there is also considerable evidence to the contrary even within the works on the subject. Members of the TCC are also by definition members of other sorts of transnational social formations, be they expatriates sent abroad by MNCs or wealthy members of an ethnic diaspora, or even both. Furthermore, they have contacts and connections with less obvious transnational social formations: the expatriate managers of MNCs, for instance, are engaged with anticapitalist demonstrators, if only to refute their claims, both local and migrant workers (Roberts et al. 1992), Internet-related organisations and consumers all around the world (Miller and Slater 2000: Chapter 6). In addition, transnational businesspeople receive their collective attitudes, disciplines and values from the writings of such groups as travel journalists and popular academics, transnational elites in and of themselves (e.g. Barley 1998). Most writers thus fail to consider the engagement of the TCC with other transnational groups.

In addition, while some (including, significantly, Sklair), do acknowledge variation within the TCC, there is also a tendency to treat it nonetheless as a unit. While part of this is simply a drawback of the fact that he is using sociological rather than ethnographic methodology, as the former is much better at extracting quantitative rather than qualitative data (Mitchell 1983), Sklair does not consider the possibility that the four segments he cites have different sorts of relationships with the global and with other groups. A quick comparison of different sorts of transnational capitalist elite also suggests much variation: Goodman's (1993) Japanese "international youth" have a different sort of lifestyle to Ong's Chinese "astronauts" (1998), and Hannerz's West African "beentos" (1996: 139). All of the groups discussed above thus fit Sklair's criteria, but live quite different lifestyles and take different views of the world. While the TCC approach has its advantages, then, the global financescape seems to be too complex for it to satisfactorily explain.

It would seem, then, that, while the TCC theory is better for understanding culture in the financescape than earlier hypotheses, it lacks the necessary complexity to fully explain the social operation of MNCs. What is needed is a more multilayered approach to studying transnational business than simply looking at "cultures," whether in isolation from each other or as the product of diverse interaction. It might, for instance be worth looking at transnational business cultures in terms of its members' networks, their interactions with other groups, and how its members consider their position in terms of global landscapes.

It might also be worth considering how interactions with other groups, "global" and "local," affect transnational businesspeople, not to mention the other groups in question. One should also look at what anthropologists call "indigenous categories" of social organisation as well as ones which are more clear to external observers; that is to say, one must consider how transnational businesspeople socially construct themselves and the financescape as well as how the researcher views these (see Sperber 1974: Chapter 2). Finally, the question of the role of individuals and their self-presentation, discussed in Chapter 1, must be taken into account. A more organic, dynamic, internally-focused view of transnational businesspeople, such as the transnational capitalist society hypothesis, thus might provide a means of filling one or two of the extant gaps in research, and developing the utility of the TCC theory.

In sum, then, culture in transnational business is not a matter of a dominating influence from a particular national or global source, nor is it simply a matter of different cultural influences acting on an organisation. Rather, it seems to be the product of dynamic social interaction between individuals and groups in the transnational business sphere, through which social identities are formed, supporting the hypothesis that culture in transnational business should be viewed as a shifting, continually-redefined concept, and social organisation as a globe-wide, dynamic network of connections.

## Conclusion

The case of MNCs and their employees operating under conditions of globalisation would thus seem to be one with particular relevance to the theories of self-presentation and the development of culture discussed in Chapter 1. The fact that globalisation encourages transnational activity and the development of social forms based on networks rather than on bounded geographical locations means that groups are likely to be strongly dependent on symbolism and self-presentation to express their allegiances and social identities; furthermore, the fact that, as Held et al. note, globalisation involves the continual transformation of the relationship between local and global social entities opens up the possibility that the continual negotiation between, and self-definition of, particular groups and individuals through self-presentation plays a key role in this environment. Much of Sklair's definition of the TCC, significantly, has to do with the presentation of particular attitudes and group allegiances. For groups under globalisation, therefore, strategic self-presentation takes on a particular significance in terms of demonstration of allegiances and definition of culture.

It would thus seem that culture under globalisation is not a matter of solidary, static groups subject to particular national or global influences at the expense of others, but that such entities as multinational corporations are dynamic, third-culture networks whose culture is subject to continuous negotiation through strategic self-presentation. While Sklair's "transnational capitalist class" theory goes some way to explaining the action of culture in such situations, it requires further development into a more flexible, dynamic, society-based theory if it is to be truly useful. We shall now consider one such transnational business group, German businesspeople in the City of London, and how they develop and present their culture, and those of their corporations, through particular strategies for self-presentation.

# Chapter 3

# Community, Interrupted:
# The German Businesspeople of London

## Introduction

German transnational businesspeople have a long history and a clear, if tacit, presence in London. Today, they appear to present themselves in ways suggesting a single, solidary transnational group, possessing a unified culture and defining themselves in total opposition to local groups and to other members of the German diaspora, in line with the nation-based theories of culture in the global financescape and Leslie Sklair's formulation of the transnational capitalist class. However, a significant degree of engagement, both with local people and with other Germans, appears to take place at other levels and in different ways, suggesting that in fact, the situation is more complex, vague and shifting, and involves a number of social connections with other, related transnational capitalist groups. In this chapter, I will consider the history and present situation of German transnational businesspeople in the UK, and the influence of national cultural institutions, political organisations, educational institutions and business networks on the culture of the community. I will then consider how these form a site for the development, not of a single, unified transnational culture, but of complex, linked, cultural networks with local and global components.

## Defining Germans: the Cultural Symbols of "Germanness"

Before we discuss German businesspeople in London, however, we must first, in line with the theoretical objectives of this book, briefly examine the ways in which Germans define and present themselves as a cultural group, and how flexible this self-presentation is. Considering the theories of symbolism and social identity discussed in Chapter 1, we shall look in particular at three symbol complexes by which Germans define themselves: *Blut und Boden* (literally, Blood and Territory) and language, money and business, and *Ordnung* (order and efficiency), and consider whether they are used by German businesspeople to define a definite national culture, or to develop a flexible culture adaptable to any situation and connected with other groups.

## Germany: History and Present-day Structure

The question of what constitutes "Germany" has been debated for at least the past 150 years. At the time of the nationalising movements of the Enlightenment, Germany remained a collection of diverse states (Weidenfeld 1983: 24). The unification of these in 1870 did little to define what it is to be "German" (Watson 1995: 48). The aftermath of the Nazi period has left Germans at once eager to define themselves as a nation, and afraid that to do so is to express a potentially dangerous nationalism (Bruhn 1994: 66; Elias 1996: 16). Shortly after I finished my fieldwork, I was introduced to an elderly German former journalist making a brief visit to England, who, upon hearing that I was writing about "German identity," said ruefully, "Hitler has taken away our identity." This sentiment is echoed by Forsythe's 1989 study, tellingly entitled "German Identity and the Problem of History," which argues that Germanness in the 1980s was strongly defined in opposition to those symbols which had been used to present it during the Nazi period. Following WWII, the debate on what constitutes "Germanness" was also complicated by the fact that there were at that point two lands with equal claims to being "Germany" (Borneman 1992). Since reunification, the debate continues to be problematic, albeit in different ways. While Henrich's observation that Germany is still characterised by regionalism may be correct, this has taken on new dimensions in the context of, first, the rhetoric of unity of the immediate post-reunification period, and, second, the subsequent East-West rivalry (1993: 65; Weidenfeld and Korte 1991: 201). Habermas' description of Germans as an ethnic community (*Volksgemeinschaft*) rather than a legal community (*Rechtsgemeinschaft*), similarly, reflects the controversy over the official acceptance of the current German borders (1994: 129, 132). For most of the past hundred and fifty years, then, Germany has been "something beyond nation and instead of nation" (Watson 1995: 16; see also Best 1993). To be "German" is thus not so much to belong to a particular national group as to present oneself using particular symbols of culture.

One of the things contributing to the difficulty in defining what it is to be German is the presence of a strong German diaspora. As well as maintaining a presence in Eastern Europe and in North and South America, Germans have also had a lesser-known historical presence in Northern Europe, including Britain (Bade [ed.] 1992; Panayi 1995). Germans maintain an awareness of these offshoots, possessing a host of terms for Germans in different areas (Vertovec 1996b: 384; a comprehensive list can be found in Amiraux [1997: 251]). The presence of these contributes to the definition of Germany as a diffuse, even global, social formation (Bade 1992: 19). Due to this diasporic consciousness, Germanness may be best seen as a subjective continuum, or, in Räthzel's words, a "pecking order of 'Germanity'": Forsythe's West Germans saw themselves as the "most German," Easterners as less so, the European section of the diaspora less again, and so forth (Räthzel 1990: 41; Forsythe 1989: 143). White, also, says that today German citizens, even ethnic Germans (i.e., persons of German descent born outside Germany), can be deemed "foreign" by other Germans under certain circumstances

(1997: 760). Therefore, to be German is not to belong to a single cultural unit, but to participate in an association of groups (who may or may not live in Germany") engaged in various individual and collective discourses on what it is to be "German."

## *"Blut und Boden" and Language*

One of the most familiar ways of defining Germanness is *"Blut und Boden,"* blood, or German ancestry, and territory, or (a claim to) German land. *Blut* is a long-standing powerful discourse defining what it is to be German: Forsythe says that diaspora Germans prioritise *deutschstammigkeit*, German "genetic" origin, as the most significant aspect of their self-definition as German (1989: 143). Many people, both German and non-German, with whom I discussed my research were puzzled as to why someone with no German blood relatives would have an interest in studying Germans. By virtue of their German *Blut*, ethnic Germans receive German citizenship, even if they have no knowledge of the language, and Amiraux says that they consider themselves German (1997: 252). The concept of *Blut* thus appears to sharply divide the German from the non-German.

However, on closer inspection the discourse appears more problematic. Forsythe says that whether ethnic Germans such as the ones Amiraux describes will be accepted as having a claim to German social status, as opposed to citizenship, by native Germans is less certain (Forsythe 1989: 153). Most people accepted my German relatives by marriage and prior residence in Germany as justification for my interest. White notes that, although Turkish *Gastarbeiter* (literally, "guest workers," the descendents of non-German migrants to Germany in the postwar period, who are not permitted full citizenship under German law) have usually been seen as "foreign," they are increasingly viewed as "not foreign" compared to East Germans (1997: 761-2). Furthermore, the German government has made moves during the past few years towards revising the citizenship requirements, culminating in an attempt to change the constitution around the turn of the millenium (Vertovec 1996b; Darnstädt et al. 1999). *Blut*, then, does not define a single way of being German, but has different connotations under different circumstances, and in different parts of the German continuum.

*Boden* is equally problematic. The concept usually manifests itself through the concept of *Heimat*, which, although usually translated as "homeland," has other associations. Certainly, land is crucial to the idea: the *Heimat* discourse stems from the writing of the Enlightenment philosopher Johann Gottfried von Herder, who argued that the culture of a people (*Volk*) was linked to their territory (von Herder 1969; see also Borneman 1991: 14; Dumont 1994: 84, for discussions on Herder's impact on German philosophy). Several of Borneman and Peck's German Jewish interviewees insisted on returning to Berlin, despite their experiences of persecution, because they considered it their *Heimat* (Borneman and Peck 1995: 93). However, like *Blut*, *Boden* is not easy to pin down, particularly given the shifting of Germany's borders. The notion that Germany should include all European regions with a claim to Germanness was one of the keystones of the Nazi endeavour, and continues to inspire at least some right-wing Germans (Bruhn 1994: 48). In contrast to Borneman's experience, many of the German Jews interviewed by Goltz in Argentina had very mixed feelings as to the definition of *Heimat* in light of the fact that the Nazis frequently used the symbol in question to justify their persecution of Jews (1998: 2). Also, one cannot ignore the fact that *Heimat* is as much about belonging to a particular region as about being German, although evidence exists that regional consciousness may be less important for business expatriates (Applegate 1990: 65; Borneman and Peck 1995: 215). Although linked to notions of actual physical territory, then, *Boden* is mostly made up of less definite discourses.

Furthermore, the concept of *Heimat* is more complex than a simple reference to a particular territory. Borneman and Peck render it as "a... sense of belonging, familiarity and security, which might be located in a feeling, a landscape, or even an idea" (1995: 184). Greverus, in a seminal book on the concept, describes *Heimat* as evoking a sense of normality, of *Welt in Ordnung* ("world in order"; see below), and speaks of diaspora Germans constructing a "*Heimat* of homesickness" (*Heimat des Heimwehs*) implying that *Heimat* takes different forms for different groups of Germans (1979: 116). Most feeling about *Heimat* seems these days to be sustained by the *Heimatsfilm* cinematic genre, not by a particular piece of land (Mai 1993: 74; see Buruma [1989] for a discussion of the original *Heimatsfilm*, Edgar Reitz's *Heimat*). The word also has connotations of being where one's ancestral "roots" are, where one was born or grew up, thereby making it problematic whether *Heimat* is more of a *Blut* or a *Boden*-related discourse (Weigelt 1984: 15, 19). *Boden*, like *Blut*, is thus a powerful symbol, but one whose meaning varies depending on the context, and as such, one that incorporates numerous different discourses within itself.

Another *Boden*-related symbol which has recently been adopted in some circles as definitive of Germanness is *Weltoffenheit*. This term, literally meaning "world-openness" but more generally translated as "cosmopolitanism," refers to a sense of multiculturalism and of having a positive orientation towards intercultural contact (Vertovec 1996b: 394-5). Vertovec discusses the term in an article entitled "*Berlin Multikulti*" which focuses on a number of recent initiatives in Berlin aimed at encouraging Germans to think of Germanness as a state of mind rather than an empirical category, and Germany as a multicultural (hence the term "*multikulti*") country of immigrants (Ibid., 389-393). While Vertovec describes these as an innovation aimed at counteracting xenophobic tendencies, it is also becoming adopted as a "German characteristic," perhaps a little hopefully, by the elite; in the pilot study of this project, most elite Germans listed "*Weltoffenheit*" as a German national trait (Ibid., 383-4; Moore 1999). An ethos of *Weltoffenheit* is strongly promoted as an alternative to nationalism, among the German business elite if not elsewhere in the nation.

The positive attitude towards the European Union on the part of many elite Germans (attested to in Forsythe 1989: 153 and Engelmann 1991: 56) can be seen as an aspect of this *Weltoffenheit*. One of my German interviewees (a London resident with Eastern European German relatives), who was otherwise very anti-

European, said that the one benefit she could see to European unification was that it would prevent a recurrence of Nazism in Germany. Ardagh, similarly, describes how the concept of Europe is held up to Germans as a positive focus for identification (1995: 445). *Weltoffenheit*, and in particular a positive orientation towards other European cultures, is thus a symbol of present-day Germanness among elite Germans.

Once again, however, this is a discourse which is not uncontested, and which has many variations. It has already been noted, for one thing, that the majority of Germans may not feel quite as open to the world as the elite bracket might believe or wish (Mehr and Sylvester 1992). *Weltoffenheit*, it must be said, is also a bit of a paradoxical symbol of a national (or at any rate nationally-based) group, as it refers to the regional or the "global" rather than the national. There also seem to be different variations on the *Weltoffenheit* discourse, with my interviewees using it to refer to an external love of travel and interest in foreign cultures, while the social scientists whose works I consulted used it instead to refer to an internal acceptance of multiculturalism in Germany itself (e.g. Vertovec 1996b; White 1997; Kosnick 2001). Not all Germans, furthermore, are pro-Europe, even among the more liberal demographic (König 1994). *Weltoffenheit* is therefore not just a simple, straightforward way of presenting Germanness, but one with a variety of interpretations.

Another symbol of Germanness of at least as long a standing as *Blut und Boden* is that of the German language. Nineteenth-century philosophers took language as an important marker of what it is to be German, as witness the Grimms' work on German dialects (von See 1994: 135-137). Bade notes that for expatriates, speaking German is an important way of expressing Germanness (1992: 19). Engelmann refers to it as a defining marker of Germanness, quoting a nineteenth-century epigram: *"Lernt Deutsch, ihr Jungling, dann ihr seid deutsch!"* or, loosely translated, "learn German, young people, and then you will be German." (1991: 58). However, as with *Blut* and *Boden*, things are not that simple: Forsythe notes that while all German-speaking lands may be viewed by Germans as *deutsch*, they are not necessarily seen as *Deutschland* (1989: 140-1). The importance, and the connotations, of the German language as a symbol of Germanness thus varies in different contexts and at different times. *Blut, Boden* and related discourses are not so much ways of presenting oneself as belonging to a particular culture, as flexible ways of instigating discourse on what it is to be "German" in different contexts.

### Money and Economics

More recently, economic symbols have begun taking hold as a common means of expressing Germanness. Today, many Germans emphasise the "economic miracle" (*Wirtschaftswunder*) of the 1950s, which is seen as having brought a "new order" to a devastated Germany, as instrumental in the nation's self-definition (Henrich 1993: 167; Watson 1995: 153; see Mikes [1953] for a contemporary discussion of the impact of the *Wirtschaftswunder* on postwar Germany). Corporate slogans such as Audi's *Vorsprung durch Technik* have become symbols of national pride—a trend satirised by Engelmann, who proposes writing an "economic anthem" to replace the national anthem (1991: 227; Head 1992: 105). Head, whose 1992 monograph on Germany is tellingly subtitled "The Corporate Identity of a Nation," argues that the goods-mark "Made in Germany" is a symbol of national pride; a 1995 report on the relevance of this mark to German businesses says that it is linked to "a range of identity issues" for Germans (Wolff Olins Identity Research 1995: 3). Many Germans feel a similar sort of national pride in the *Mittelstand*, this being the German term for (mostly) small-to-medium-sized, family-owned corporations with ties to particular regions of Germany (*The Economist* 1995; Viehoff 1978). The reunification of 1990 was, for Borneman's interviewees, symbolised by the flow of consumer goods from West to East as well as by the "greeting money" (*Begrüssungsgeld*) given to Easterners as they came over (1991: 174, 51). Biermann's book of essays on German society is called *Über das Geld und andere Hertzensdinge*: loosely translated, "on money and other beloved things" (1991). Weidenfeld and Korte sum this up with the phrases *Wirtschaftspatriotismus* (economic patriotism) and *DM-Nationalismus* (Deutschmark nationalism) (1992: 149, 154). Economic symbols are thus significant ways in which Germans represent their Germanness.

However, the use and meanings of these symbols are not uncontested. For one thing, not all Germans view business in the same way, as when Sorge remarks that most Germans do not have a strong work ethic, but feel compelled by "social rules" to seem industrious (Sorge 1996: 77). The *Vorsprung Durch Technik* slogan in particular, as well as defining Audi as a company, also evokes images of Nazism for many non-Germans (Head 1992: 113). The impact of the Euro, furthermore, is still something of an unknown quantity, as has caused Germany to have the same currency as other countries in Europe and therefore will have associations with these countries as well; the possibility exists that a *Euro-Nationalismus* is arising, but in that case it would be linked in with the debate over the relationship of German to European affiliation (*Spiegel* 1998b). Again, then, the economic symbols of Germanness are used in numerous discourses, and are not associated with Germanness alone.

*Ordnung*

The concept of *Ordnung* is also worth briefly considering. While a more complete discussion may be found in Hoecklin (1996, 1998), we shall note here that while the word can be literally translated as "order" (as opposed to chaos), it also has connotations for Germans of cleanliness, structure and morality (Hoecklin 1996: 26, 36). Borneman quotes a children's rhyme: "*Ordnung muss sein/Das weisst man schon von klein*" which can be translated as "There must be order/one knows that from when one is small" (1992: 8). Hoecklin notes that the discourse is related to notions of Germanness, linking in with ideas of Germanness as involving order and efficiency; she suggests that Germans greatly value structure and logical organisation (1996: 36, 53; see also Lawrence 1980 for a discussion of the impact of this on German business). However, again this discourse is problematic; Boll, in a 1949 essay, satirised pride in "German efficiency" (1992 [1949]). Similarly, in articles on Germany, the image of the *Ordnung*-obsessed German comes across as a bit of a self-deprecating national stereotype, rather along the lines of the stiff-upper-lipped Englishman (Scheuermann 1997). *Ordnung* is thus not a straightforward discourse, but one which can be used to indicate narrow-mindedness or demarcate a stereotype as well as define a group.

*Analysis*

As well as being open to interpretation depending on the context, all of these symbolic discourses tend to blend into each other. Bruhn points out that notions of *Blut* and *Boden* inform each other; Applegate defines *Heimat* as a means of expressing national and regional affiliation simultaneously (Bruhn 1994: 94; Applegate 1990: 244). Altmann describes *Heimat* as incorporating discourses on kinship and industry; Rovan adds to this the notion of language (Altmann 1984: 220; Rovan 1983: 236). *Weltoffenheit*, similarly, relates to the discourses of *Blut und Boden*, as it involves a redefinition of Germanness which tacitly alludes to the fact that territory and blood are strong symbols of it: the idea that non-white people can also be "German" is still a definition based on folk genetics, as it extends rather than challenges the definition of "Germanness" based on physical characteristics (see Vertovec 1996b: 390). Given the association of German interest in other lands with the actions of German MNCs, *Weltoffenheit* does also relate to the economic discourses of Germanness (Engelmann 1991: 60). The flexibility and diversity of ways in which German culture is defined and presented thus means that no symbolic discourse can be isolated from others.

Furthermore, the symbols which are used to present Germanness can be used to express other sorts of allegiances. *Weltoffenheit*, for instance, is a discourse of cosmopolitan openness to other cultures with particular relevance to the German situation. The concept of *Heimat*, as we have seen, can also be reformulated to allow people to acknowledge other *Heimats* than those located in Germany, or to see it as a kind of nebulous concept of "home place" (Goltz 1998). The seemingly essentialist concept of *Blut*, also, allows people to continue to consider themselves "German" at the same time as they acknowledge allegiances to a non-German *Boden* (Blaschke 1992; also Applegate 1990: 170; *Spiegel* 1998c). *Ordnung* also relates to particular multinational corporations, as their success is thereby explained through discourses relating to an alleged national characteristic (Boll 1992 [1949]; Head 1992: 51; Lawrence 1980: 12). The association of German pride with particular multinational corporations of German origin also means that discourses of Germanness can relate to the corporations themselves (Head 1992). The speaking of German, finally, can also indicate, as well as German origin, a cosmopolitan interest in German culture or membership in a global diaspora. Due to the flexibility of the practice of self-presentation, they combine, not only with each other, but with outside discourses of Europeanness, corporate affiliation, cosmopolitanism and so forth.

The presentation of self as "German," then, is not just a matter of a single group defining itself as a culturally unified entity, national or transnational, through the use of a definite set of symbols. Instead, the nature of strategic self-presentation means that the concept of Germanness incorporates many subgroups adhering to different cultural discourses, some in harmony and some at odds with each other. These discourses, like the Germans themselves, both appear to be divided from and combining with each other in many different ways depending on the circumstances, and to have links to other cultures and nations. We shall now consider the specific case of German businesspeople in London, with particular regard to whether they form a single, solidary transnational culture or a more complex, diverse transnational society.

## Another Nation of Shopkeepers: The History of German Businesspeople in London

German and German-speaking businesspeople have been a visible group in London since the eighteenth century, and arguably as far back as the eleventh (Panayi 1995: 29; Mann 1993: iii), a fact which influences the way in which they relate to other groups in the UK. In this section, I shall briefly outline what is known about the historical German business community, with a view to contrasting it with the modern situation in this and subsequent chapters.

### 1: The Middle Ages (1000-1579)

According to Borer, "London's foreign trade during the 11th and 12th centuries had been mainly with the Germans, Flemish and French, but by the 12th century the Germans were predominating in the City [of London—i.e., London's business and financial district], as elsewhere in Western Europe.... [I]n addition to [importing] German wine, metal work and coats of mail, and boatloads of grain at times of poor harvest in England, they were entrepreneurs for the produce of the East" (1977: 89). Following a period of rivalry between the Cologne traders and those from further east, the Germans combined into the Hanseatic League, which by 1282 had a house on the present-day site of Cannon Street Station (Ibid., 89). The League were granted privileges by the crown, despite objections from local merchants, because England at the time did not have sufficient shipping capacity to engage in international trade, and because of the revenue and loans which they provided for the crown (Ibid., 90). However, as the years passed their presence caused more and more resentment; by the time of Edward VI, when the English shipping industry was in a better position, their privileges were revoked, and in 1579 Elizabeth I ordered their expulsion.

## 2: The Hanoverians (1750-1914)

Following a gap of about 150 years, the next major wave of Germans came to London after the House of Hanover gained the British throne in the mid-eighteenth century (Mann 1993: viii). At first many were musicians, sugarbakers and unskilled labourers, but by the nineteenth century an influential economic and cultural elite had developed (Holmes 1988: 43-44). Germans have been associated with banking and finance in England since the mid-nineteenth century, when such figures as Rothschild came to London to start up financial operations (Panayi 1993: 113-114). Most of the institutions which they founded, such as Reuters and Schroeders, have since become regarded as "domestic" (Farrell 1990: 5). In addition, there existed a small number of German banks with London branches from 1870 through 1914, partly, as today, for the purposes of information acquisition and networking, but also to obtain access to trade within the British Empire (Pohl and Burk 1998: part I; correspondence available in the Deutsche Bank Archives, 1870-1914). From 1812 to 1914, the Germans were a visible group, expressing their presence as a community through common areas of residence and membership in German clubs (*Vereine*), some of which became quite powerful (Holmes 1988: 43-44; Panayi 1995: 183-190). The second major wave of German immigration thus bore recognisable similarities to the present one, the main difference being that its members were more visible than their modern equivalent.

## 3: The World Wars and their Aftermath (1914-1999)

WWI, significantly, marked the end of German visibility. In the years leading up to WWI, anti-German sentiment, often tinged with anti-Semitism, was rife (Firchow 1986; Wraight 1991:42). The Deutsche Bank Archive has in its possession documents and letters chronicling the creation and progress of the Anglo-German Conciliation Committee, founded in 1905 by prominent German and UK business figures in response to the demonisation of Germans in the UK media, for the promotion of good political and social relations between the two groups; the initiative appears to have failed sometime after 1906 (Deutsche Bank 1905a, b, Anonymous 1905, see also *Morning Post* 1908; *Berliner Lokal Ausaiger* 1912). During WWI persons with German surnames were physically attacked and sometimes killed, and in both world wars they were interned (Panayi 1993: 114-115; Wraight 1991:42). The assets of all German businesses were confiscated at the outset of WWI and not returned (Anonymous 1916, 1919). Many ethnic Germans, including the British Royal Family, changed their names and disguised their origins; the prewar practice of ethnic Germans self-identifying as German fell into disuse (Panayi 1993: 114; Farrell 1990: 5-7). After WWII, the numbers of Germans in the UK again rose, with most of the new émigrés being either refugees, the wives of servicemen, or exchange students and au-pairs (Mann 1993: 143; Berghahn 1988; Breitenstein and Hommerich (eds.) 1976). Of the three groups, however, only the first retained any form of visibility, and that mainly on the basis of shared religion rather than shared nationality. There thus exist sharp discontinuities between the pre- and postwar German communities, even though some of their members are the same.

Until the twentieth century, then, the Germans of London formed a more or less conventional economic immigrant group, albeit one with a higher proportion of elites, entrepreneurs and businesspeople than is usual (see Holmes 1988), and appear to have presented themselves as a single, solidary culture. In recent years, however, they have become less of an obvious presence: while they have not necessarily lost power or influence within the London financial world, they are far less visible than formerly. We shall now take a more in-depth look at the shape and culture of the present-day German community.

## The Invisibles: Germans in Present-Day London

German transnational businesspeople, while they may be difficult to identify as a group, nonetheless possess a strong sense of solidarity and of membership in a particular expatriate culture. In this section, I will look at how they achieve this solidarity while still, at the same time, blending in with other groups in London, through the use of complex symbolic self-presentation.

### The Germans: An Unseen Community?

Today's Germans form something of a non-community in London. When I asked about the "German community," I was repeatedly told that it did not exist. At the same time, however, most of the Germans whom I knew had acquaintances in common, belonged to the same professional associations, sent their children to the same school, and many at least knew of each other. My own research bore out Panayi's observation that, while the modern German community does not congregate in one area as the older ones did, it does focus around institutions such as schools, clubs and churches (1993:16)—although for businesspeople, clubs and churches did not seem to figure strongly, aside from the smattering of families, mainly ones with small children, who regularly attended the monthly services of the German Lutheran Church. The Germans can thus be said to be a community, but one which relies on subtle network connections rather than the displaying of obvious membership traits.

Richmond, the area of residence for most of London's elite German population (particularly those with children, due to its proximity to the German-language school, known as the Deutsche Schule London or DSL), does not immediately show signs of hosting a visible German community. Wandering around the area, it is difficult to find evidence of a German presence: the supermarkets stock the same food as those elsewhere in London, and, aside from the presence of a small German-language section in some bookshops, there is no real German mercantile, religious or cultural presence. The district is an attractive, upscale one, with large houses with gardens, prominent luxury-goods shops and wide, tree-lined, well-tended roads; several famous cultural sites are in the area, and jazz festivals are held in the summer. In this it is no different to many other districts in London whose inhabitants are well-to-do; one might compare the area with others which are fashionable among British business elites, such as Islington and Kingston. The Germans are thus not particularly visible within Richmond.

However, a closer inspection reveals more subtle signs, for instance a group of German teenagers, too young and well-groomed to be backpackers, having a picnic on the riverbank; families of Germans shopping for household staples in the supermarket; the local bus company advertising regular services to the DSL with a German-language placard. The local museum, while it had no exhibits on the German population and portrayed WWI and II very much in the standard patriotic vein of received British history, was on my visit staffed by an elderly German volunteer who was quite happy to tell me about the Germans in the area. The German community may have a geographical focus, but this is only discernable through subtle, almost tacit, acts of self-presentation.

*German Transnational Businesspeople*

Within this non-community, there was a sizeable group which fell within the Sklairite, if you will, definition of a transnational business elite given in the previous chapter. Its members are involved with the globalisation of capital, have a cosmopolitan mindset, and share similar consumption patterns with each other and with transnational elites from other countries. As we have seen, they also share common patterns of residence and similar jobs. The Germans of London thus seem to form, if not a "transnational capitalist class," certainly a solidary transnational elite focused around business activity.

Within the German business world, however, transnational businesspeople associated with finance and banking have less visibility than others. Most interviewees of whatever nationality, asked to name a German company, were much more likely to name Siemens or Bosch than Deutsche Bank. While discussions with the managers of manufacturing corporations suggested that there are fewer German transnational businesspeople in manufacturing than in the financial services industry in England, most people, both English and German, seemed to take manufacturing companies as the "unmarked" category (as defined in Banks 1996: 159) of German MNCs. Furthermore, the financial wing distinguished itself from other Germans in subtle ways: the managers, particularly the top managers, at all of the German banks in London knew each other, in some cases personally. Even front-line staff, who tend to drift between banks, often maintained relations with ex-colleagues at their previous places of employment, and employees who had left one bank for another tended to come back occasionally for social events. Top managers and specialists share membership in—often nationality-based—professional organisations. Finally, acquaintanceships are frequently maintained through encounters with colleagues on the Stansted-Frankfurt air service, known in London's financial community as the "Bankers' Express" (Anonymous 1994: 130). Although my research with German manufacturing companies is more limited, there seem to be different patterns of association, with expatriate German managers defining themselves in terms of their corporate affiliation and the products with which they are associated, and developing networks within their particular MNC rather than with colleagues in the same industry. Despite the apparent solidarity of the group, there is a visible, if subtle, difference between German transnational businesspeople in the financial and manufacturing industries.

Most of my German interviewees in the financial industry, furthermore, tended to describe themselves in culturally mixed terms. Many of those who were permanently settled in England were in relationships with someone from the UK, and defined themselves in terms of this. Others, including those who were only in the UK for a year or two, described themselves in terms of mixing English and German culture; one manager, who had attended the University of Manchester, half-seriously described himself as "the Manc from Frankfurt." While many of the more settled Germans encouraged their children to "discover their heritage," and maintained a number of German cultural markers (for instance, bread and cheese for breakfast instead of more traditional British foods), they also spoke with pride of their and their children's abilities to get on in a UK environment (one recently-emigrated interviewee proudly announcing that he had taken to eating cereal in the mornings). This self-description, focused on cultural mixing, may fit with the idea of a globe-trotting, business-focused elite class which values cosmopolitanism, but it also shows the Germans' ability to engage with the local culture at the same time as maintaining their transnational links.

When describing Germans in the UK, German transnational businesspeople tend to exclude the historical dimension. Most were not aware of the long history of German banking in England; one young staff member, upon being told, exclaimed in surprise, "I wish somebody would tell the English about that!" Only one interviewee spoke of the German connection to the old UK banks, and he was in fact an Englishman with a German wife, prior residence in Germany and a strong interest in the culture. However, neither he nor the first interviewee were particularly interested in spreading the information. This fits with the idea that an orientation towards transnational business and away from national cultures leaves little room for interest in history other than as a personal quirk, and the focus on modernity, simultaneity and the present is in keeping with the fast-paced, postmodern ethic of a transnational elite. However, there is a particular, strategic dimension to this avoidance: if one acknowledges the prominent role of Germans in nineteenth-century London, one must then ask what happened to change their position, which leads one to the problematic question of the events of WWI and WWII. The historical depth of the German community thus did not figure strongly in German transnational businesspeople's views of London, but, it seems, less from a desire to remain detached from the local than from a need to engage with local discourses about German history.

Similarly, the Germans defined themselves in implicit opposition to other elements of the German diaspora in the UK. While they cannot totally be unaware of the presence of refugees from Nazi persecution in the country—aside from the fact that the German Lutheran Church was founded by refugees, the

*Sozialberätungsstelle* (Social Advice Office; see below) run by the German Consulate was originally set up to help such people and, although it now caters to other elements of the diaspora as well, many are still regular patrons of the office. However, I did not find out about the refugees except through Berghahn (1988), and through acquaintances in the German Lutheran Church. One German bank employee who self-identified as having few ties to Germany, and to whom I had sent a portion of a news article which quoted a London German Jewish community leader complaining about anti-German feeling in Britain (Appelius 1995), responded with the words, "that's *her* opinion" Again, this fits with the association which Sklair draws between the "transnational capitalist class" and the corporations for which they work. German corporations wish to forget the Nazi past as much as possible; it goes virtually unmentioned in all the corporate promotional material which I collected (including, interestingly, that of corporations which were shut down during the Nazi period and thus could not be said to have political skeletons in their closets), apart from cases in which the company has established a reparations programme (*Financial Times* 1999). The primary reason for this silence is, of course, that reviving the Nazi past creates a bad image for present-day German corporations; however, the refugees, for obvious reasons, wish the war to be remembered as much as possible (see Appelius 1995). It could be equally bad for business, furthermore, for Germans to be seen as refugees or in need of charity and assistance. Consequently, the German bankers dissociate themselves from the former refugees, partly because of their different position vis-à-vis the Nazi past, but also because of the negative economic implications.

More complicated is the relationship between German transnational businesspeople and the German students and tourists who come to London. Again, German transnational businesspeople tended to distance themselves from such groups. The symbolic connotations of these social formations run broadly counter to those which a transnational business elite might embrace; both tourists and students are seen as naive and in search of education or simple entertainment, as opposed to the more sophisticated world-openness of bankers (Hannerz 1996: 104). Finally, as noted above, these groups take quite different views of history, culture and landscape to businesspeople. However, all of the German transnational businesspeople with whom I spoke were (and, in the case of those who were trainees, still are) students at some point, and many, given the prestige value of study abroad among transnational businesspeople, were international students. Similarly, the boundary between tourist and businessperson is often a vague one: businesspeople go on holiday at least once a year, and it is a common thing during business trips to engage in a certain amount of tourist activity. The Germans thus distance themselves from these groups when they act as a transnational capitalist class, but when they adopt other roles, they may be less distant from them.

German businesspeople in London do not present themselves simply as a solidary, detached transnational culture, but in a variety of ways reflecting strategic responses to other groups' self-presentations. The tendency to view history purely in aesthetic terms and the dislike of tourists probably owes much to contact with English colleagues, and in particular, the "German tourist" jokes which circulate in the English media. Furthermore, the dissociation of themselves from other groups of "foreigners" may stem from an awareness of the place of WWII in English stereotypes of Germans (see Chapter 6, this volume). The self-presentation of the German population of London is thus not merely down to their being a transnational capitalist elite, but also to influence from the local culture's presentation of Germanness.

Similarly, their self-presentation is also affected by discourses of national identification in Germany itself. With a few exceptions, studies of the German diaspora seem to be fairly limited in Germany itself; most of the scholarly—and popular—interest seems to come from British and New World ethnic Germans (Grass 1990: 120). Furthermore, the German media also tend to dissociate modern Germany from the refugees of the Nazi and post-Nazi periods. Finally, as before, the ways in which the community is defined are also affected by those used by groups viewed as outside of it. The Germans with whom I spoke were aware of other groups of Germans in London, and implicitly defining themselves in opposition to these. Consequently, they present themselves in different ways to the other groups, and reject the modes of self-presentation used by these. Again, German transnational businesspeople in London are influenced in their self-presentations as overseas Germans by the way in which this group is defined in Germany and elsewhere, rather than simply existing as a detached cultural group.

The way in which Germans present themselves, moreover, is not down to any one engagement but to engagements with many groups in diverse ways. Their particular take on Anglo-German history, for instance, is partly down to the culture of the London financial community, partly to local attitudes to German history, and partly to German attitudes to their own history (see Forsythe 1989; MacDonald 2001). Individuals within the German population take on different roles over their lifetime; the same person can be a student, a tourist and a businessperson at different stages of their life or even at the same time. Additionally, a German transnational businessperson may have different degrees of global and local engagement at different times, for instance when studying, working abroad, taking time out to have children or reaching retirement age. This affects their position relative to the way in which the group presents itself; an individual with school-age children, for instance, might focus more on local history than a bank employee. The self-presentation of transnational businesspeople thus does not only not take place in a vacuum; it takes place at a variety of different levels at different times.

The German transnational businesspeople of the City of London are therefore a non-community of sorts, whose members present themselves as economically engaged, transient and cosmopolitan, and emphasise the discontinuity with other segments of the German diaspora in London. However, this process of strategic self-presentation does not take place in a vacuum, or without reference to other sorts of Germans or transnational businesspeople, varies over individual and group life-cycles, and is shaped by the present-day Anglo-German social and political context. The German community thus has no fixed, definite "culture," but a vague concept of themselves and their social attributers which is under constant negotiation according to the strategies of individuals and groups inside and outside the community. We shall now look at how Germans make use of dedicated cultural and business institutions to reflect a mixed, subdivided and shifting culture rather than a solidary, definite one.

## Joining the Club: German Institutions in London

In this section, I will look at German transnational businesspeople in the context of the institutions with which they are associated. A comprehensive discussion of all German-focused institutions in London is impossible, for reasons of space, logistics, access and relevance. Furthermore, by focusing on a few pertinent examples, we can throw the behaviour of German transnational businesspeople in this area into sharper relief. I will therefore aim to present a sample of German institutions rather than a complete overview. I will thus focus on four specific cases, each relating to a different aspect of German life in London: the Deutsche Schule London (an educational institution); the Goethe Institut (a cultural institution); the German Consulate (a political institution) and the German-British Forum (a business networking institution). Through focusing on specific cases, then, I shall give a general impression of German transnational businesspeople's self-presentation through the use of particular institutions.

### Educational Institution: The Deutsche Schule London

The German School, or Deutsche Schule London (DSL), is a cultural institution which plays a distinctive role in the lives of many German transnational businesspeople. As well as encapsulating a complex of symbols of Germanness and transnational affiliation which adults can use as a means of self-presentation, the DSL also serves as a means of socialising the next generation of future German transnational businesspeople, whether as a solidary culture or as more a diffuse social formation.

The DSL, which is housed in a donated building named "Douglas House" in Richmond, was founded in 1971 for the children of German, Austrian and Swiss Embassy staff and of the occasional business expatriate. Since then, the numbers of children of transnational businesspeople has increased greatly; while the Embassies still have a presence, the bulk of pupils appear to be the children of executives doing a three to five year stint in the UK. In either case, however, most of the students at the DSL are there because of a temporary absence from Germany, such that their parents do not wish to take them out of the German school system for the duration. The data in this section is based on interviews with four parents (three of whom were associated with the school's *Vorstand*, of which more later) and two teachers, one being the head teacher of the school, comments from other interviewees who had children, and participation in some of the school's events; time, resources and the scope of the project have meant that a more in-depth study of the school was not feasible.

The DSL's main source of funding is the German government, but recent cutbacks have meant that at the time of my fieldwork alternative forms of support were being sought. The staff are a mixed group; in 2000, fourteen of them had been sent by the government to serve a two to six year term. The others, some thirty-six or so, were *Ortskräfte*, locally hired teachers; in many cases these were the spouses of expatriates who had left their jobs to join their families in England, and were turning their hand to teaching as an alternative (Deutsche Schule London 1998). There are about 680 pupils, between 5 and 19 years of age. Of these, 80% are German, 11% are Swiss or Austrian, and the rest are children of other nationalities whose parents want their children educated under the German system for one reason or another; the most usual reason is because one parent is German and wants the children to grow up bilingual and/or bicultural. The children are thus for the most part members of a transnational elite who are seemingly encouraged to maintain connections with the "homeland" through their schooling.

One interesting aspect of the DSL, however, is the degree to which parental social life is organised around the school. As well as the abovementioned *Ortskräfte*, the school's governing body, or *Vorstand*, is also staffed mainly by the spouses of expatriates who have given up their jobs to come to London; as the *Vorstand* are unpaid, one member dryly commented that they have the best qualified parental volunteers of any school in the district. The *Vorstand* is a managerial committee which effectively runs the school, arranging its finances, sorting out the allocation of resources, approving personnel selection and the curriculum (to which the German government gives final approval, but this is largely a formality). German transnational businesspeople thus have a lot of influence on the running of the school, if only through their spouses.

The school has a number of events every year which are, again, largely organised by parents, including such familiar German festivals as *Oktoberfest* (a harvest festival involving traditional songs and dances as well as the consumption of much beer, bread and sausage) and *Osterbrünnen* (an Easter party in which wells, or facsimiles of wells, are decorated with flowers). Adult sports clubs and social activities are also organised around the school; there are groups to help welcome and orient new expatriates and their spouses, and the Parents' Association produces the only formal guide to life in the UK for German expatriates which I have seen (Friends of Douglas House 1993). The DSL thus not only educates the children, but also provides both a focus for social activity and a means of self-presentation and network formation for their parents.

This was visible at the two events which I attended at the school: a *Frühschoppen* (a traditional German spring event in which crafts and secondhand goods are sold by children) and a Christmas fair (*Weihnachtsmarkt*). These were held on the ground floor of the school, in the corridors and a few commandeered classrooms; it was also possible to go upstairs to the first floor, to view displays of art by the older students. Participation of all members of the family was evident: the merchandise on sale—handpainted silk scarves, Christmas ornaments, clothing and accessories, and so forth—at the Christmas fair was all made by parents, and most of it was of startlingly high quality. Children and teenagers sold crafts and toys, ran games of skill (one group at the Christmas fair organising a version of "Who Wants to be a Millionnaire/*Wer Wird Millionär*," a quiz show popular in both England and Germany) and, under supervision, cooked and sold food. Members of the family who were not directly involved with the staffing of booths or administration of the event could also be seen talking with friends, playing games on the lawn or otherwise enjoying themselves. The Germanness of the institution was also made plain on several levels: while one or two of the booths at the Christmas fair emphasised the school's origins openly, others did so in a more subtle way, by offering for sale German foods and toys (which were emphasised by my interviewees at all levels to be the items which most reminded them of Germany and their own Germanness). Most of the manufactured goods being raffled off at the Christmas fair had been donated by German companies. At the *Frühschoppen*, a Bavarian-style oompah band was present to play a mix of traditional German music and contemporary hits; at the Christmas fair, the school band performed the same function. School events thus present the Germanness of the institution and its members both through obvious and traditional means and through more subtle, domestically-focused symbols.

The DSL also encouraged a less formal sort of German self-presentation. Parents at school events would pass on information to each other regarding German bakeries, delis and bookshops; such businesses frequently advertise in the DSL's publications as well as donating goods and services to its events, ensuring that parents are aware of their presence. The DSL's networking function also extends to Germans with no obvious connection to the school, as parents spread the word about these cultural resources to single or childless colleagues. The DSL thus facilitates the informal networking between Germans in the UK which centres around access to such cultural symbols as food and books.

All of the people with whom I spoke, both at the DSL and in the banks, agreed that German social life in London is closely linked with the school, suggesting again a solidary German transnational social formation which is in opposition to local groups. It was when the school was discussed that bank employees abandoned their usual stance that no German community existed in London. One *Vorstand* member, Frau A, when I was introduced to her as someone here "to study the German community," rather than, as I expected, responding with the usual facetious comment about the lack of one in London, said "you have come to the right place for your study, there is quite a German community here!" Significantly, however, she then added, "that is, if you have children, it is a German community." It is worth noting that one of my business-expatriate interviewees, a middle-aged woman who "did not see" herself as "part of the German community," sent her children to a British "public" (i.e., not state-run) school. It is significant that it is a school which plays this role; people with children are interested in instilling and reproducing culture in their children, and consequently give a good deal of thought as to how this culture is transmitted (see Pelissier 1991: 82). The presence of the DSL also encouraged the perception of Richmond as "German space": interviewees whose children were at the DSL had a greater tendency to identify Richmond as a locus of German activity than those without children at the school. The DSL thus seems to be a strong focus of German solidarity for transnational German businesspeople, or at any rate for those with children.

The building of a German transnational community was also present in the day-to-day administration of the DSL. The school's educational philosophy emphasises and prioritises the teaching of the German language, literature and history, and operates on the assumption that the pupils will be going back to Germany later, although the headmaster and teachers acknowledged that an unknown percentage do go on to UK universities. At DSL events German is spoken more or less exclusively; people spoke English to me because I was an outsider, and a few people visibly identifiable as local spouses (English-speaking adults with a German-speaking child or two in tow) could also be seen speaking English to each other. The DSL thus defines itself as a German institution through the use of language, curriculum and educational style.

The DSL is also strongly engaged with the German state school system. The German government officially endorses its curriculum, and consequently has at least a theoretical influence over what the pupils learn. Although some of the *Vorstand* spoke of making a break with the state, the school was started partly on a government initiative, and the Embassy presence is visible. The DSL is also part of a government-run network of overseas German schools; Frau G, a member of the Embassy staff, spoke of how her son had lived in four separate countries without a noticeable falling-behind in his studies, as he could simply "plug into the Deutsche Schule" of the city to which the family had moved. Additionally, parents and teachers to whom I spoke described the school as "German, because [it is] in the German [school] system." Significantly, however, these explanations ignore or pass quickly over the strong differences in style and curriculum which exist between German states, much as the DSL's definition of "German" touches only lightly on the differences between German regions and, indeed, German-speaking countries. The DSL is thus engaged with the German state school and social systems; however, it also erases the regional differences in these, thus apparently defining a pan-German enclave in London.

The DSL also appears to distance itself from local schools and educational practices. One teacher spoke of English schools as isolationist, in that they do not emphasise the learning of a second language; due to the requirements of ERASMUS and other European student exchange programmes for a second language, she said, the English become culturally isolated, and do not learn about any place other than England. The DSL thus defines itself as German in opposition to English local schools.

The parents also describe the relationship between the DSL and local schools in a similar way, as witness these responses to the question of whether or not they had considered sending their children to an English school by two Embassy staff members:

1.      The British school system isn't bad, but it is different. If you want the kids to continue in the German system, you put them in the German school. We

have one daughter who is seventeen and one who is fourteen, and so it would not be good for them to be taken out of the system at this time. From a learning point of view we would have preferred an English school, but the systems were not compatible. (Herr F, diplomatic staff, late forties)

2.          **Frau G:** (bureaucratic staff, mid-forties): I could send [my children] to British school, but then they wouldn't be able to come in to the German system. Socially, we would rather send them to British school.

**Interviewer:** Why not?

**Frau G:** Because I really want them to learn at a German school where the primary language is German... but at a German school you don't have the contact with the British. It all depends on the contact with the British how much you use German and how well you interact cross-culturally.

The reasons both individuals had for sending their children to the DSL were thus focused both on maintaining symbolic ties to Germany, through language use and through remaining in the "German school system." It is interesting that both, as well as the woman who sent her children to a UK public school, felt that sending children to a local school would encourage them to integrate into the British system. The use of the DSL thus seems to involve the maintenance of a solidary German culture overseas.

However, the above extracts also show a certain degree of flexibility. The parents interviewed *did* want their children to have contact with the other educational system, whether it is British or German. The mother who sent her children to public school said that by speaking German to them at home, she ensured that they did not become insular. Other parents, both those with children at the DSL and those with children at other schools, said that the main reason why they would send their children to a UK school would be for them to speak English properly, which, as well as suggesting the development of connections with English culture, implies a desire for them to learn the "global language of business." All parents want their children to have connections with diverse groups both local and transnational, rather than to simply "be German," or to become detached from the local.

The DSL does also have connections with the local public schools. Sports and other intramural activities are coordinated with the public schools in the district, rather than the state ones. Contact exists between the DSL and local schools, albeit sometimes in negative fashions: the DSL recently experienced a case of racist bullying which was reported on both the BBC and on Köln Radio 2, in which pupils from other local schools had beaten up some DSL pupils, calling them "Nazis" (there was another case around this time in which a German exchange student in Cornwall underwent a similar racist attack by local teenagers; see Irwin

[2000]). More positively, there were also exchange programmes with other public schools elsewhere in London. The DSL also had a member of the local council on the *Vorstand* at the time of my fieldwork, although I was given to understand that this was not always the case. There are thus connections between the DSL and local schools.

In addition, the DSL has in some ways come to resemble British public schools. Like these, the DSL had a networking role, both in terms of the child's future career and its parents' personal career development. Although I do not have direct confirmation of this, a certain amount of personnel movement between German corporations appeared to take place partly due to conversations at DSL events. Furthermore, the rationales of most interviewees for sending their children to the DSL tended to resemble those of their English colleagues for sending their children to high-prestige public schools: getting them a "good start," teaching the importance of networking, and introducing them to the mores of their social group. It is worth noting that the parents with whom I spoke who had not sent their children to the DSL had all chosen to send them to public schools, and that the DSL's booklet aimed at parents moving to London from Germany recommended public over state schools (Friends of Douglas House 1993: 20-23). The possibility of officially turning the DSL into a UK public school in the case of its governmental funding being entirely withdrawn was actually being discussed by the *Vorstand* at the time of my fieldwork. The DSL thus associates itself with symbols through which the local business elite presents itself.

Consequently, German transnational businesspeople do at first seem to be defining themselves as a solidary culture through the use of the DSL. However, they are defining themselves through local British symbols of elite status and cosmopolitanism, for instance through adopting a public-school discourse to describe themselves. The school's "cosmopolitan" reputation largely depends on the fact that the school's linguistic and geographical focus is seen as "foreign" by local standards; in Germany, its curriculum would not be seen as quite so cosmopolitan. To put this phenomenon in terms of Bloch's hypothesis (discussed in Chapter 2), they are redefining the discourses of their elite status to fit with those employed by the local, non-German, area (Bloch 1974). German transnational businesspeople thus were presenting an elite transnational self-image, but through local symbols.

In addition, the DSL is a forum for teaching children how to present themselves strategically as German transnational elites. Firstly, it gives them a repertoire of symbols for use in self-presentation in later life; secondly, however, the fact that the community is focused on transnational business means that they are learning the particular modes of self-presentation of the German business community. "Germany" and "German education" are treated largely as a unit. The DSL thus teaches students how to present themselves according to the norms of transnational business; its multiple links and student diversity are therefore significant.

The DSL's pupils in some ways resemble the Japanese "International Youth" described by Roger Goodman, these being the children of Japanese expatriates who spend part of their childhood abroad, are encouraged to attend special schools, and who frequently grow up to become transnational businesspeople themselves (1993). Much as Goodman's students appear to be learning, through their international experiences and subsequent special education, how to use the positive associations of being both "Japanese and international" to their own social and business advantage, the DSL students learn how to use their experience to define themselves strategically (Ibid.). Like Goodman's "youth," the German children learn ways of existing in two or more cultures, and balancing between them (1993, esp. p. 137). The teachers quoted me a range of between 10 and 50% of pupils remaining in England every year after they do the *Abitur* (university qualification exams). Asked about the effect of having to move every couple of years on the students, the teachers acknowledged that it had a negative impact on lasting friendships, but added that the children are "very sophisticated," and often very skilled in making new friends, as a result of their frequent moves. The teachers describe the students as very *Weltoffen* as a consequence of their experiences. One teacher called them *"multis"* (recalling Vertovec [1996b]'s interviewees' use of the term *multikulti*): "they are global and are German; they do not choose between them" (*die sind globales und sind deutscher; keine Entscheidung*). The students are also, according to their teachers, adept at making use of the opportunities afforded them by their education, often going to elite universities and taking jobs with top firms. Like Goodman's Japanese youths, the German students are expected to have difficulties as a result of their frequent moves, but in fact benefit actively from these experiences (1993: 159-169).

Unlike Goodman's youths, however, there is generally not much fuss, positive or negative, made about these pupils; their experiences are seen as being good for them, but there is no real sense that they are particularly different to locally-focused Germans of the same social status. The acquisition of cosmopolitanism is openly encouraged by parents and teachers as a means of getting on; one parent, asked why she was eager for her children to learn English, said "English is very important today; very, very important for international success." However, there was no sense that these students were necessarily privileged above those who had learned English in school without leaving Germany, and there seemed to be no fear of them becoming "less German" as a result of their education. Students thus learn to treat their Germanness and their overseas experiences as strategic resources, rather than as the definition of a new global business elite.

It is worth observing, however, that the uses and interpretations of these resources again varied from actor to actor. Frau F described her three children's adaptation to England: while all had experienced difficulties at first, the middle child now uses English as a default language, even with German friends. However, the eldest and the youngest prefer German. One teacher noted that the pupils pick up English more from neighbour children, television and pop music than from formal lessons. The pupils thus learn the same symbols for self-presentation from their experience in England but, like their parents, they use them in different ways.

The DSL thus is used on one level to define and transmit a particular, transnational-business-focused version of Germanness, through the curriculum and through the possibilities for networking on the part of parents and children. The DSL serves as a symbol of elite businesspeople and diplomats, and of a globe-trotting, cosmopolitan lifestyle, at the same time as a strong sense of belonging to a German overseas community. It seems to define people very like Pico Iyer's "Global Souls," presenting themselves selectively with reference to what they see as "the good bits" of the multiple cultures to which they can claim allegiance (2000). Furthermore, like Iyer and his interviewees, they also enable themselves to claim a kind of "neutral status" as people travelling between cultures, or who emphasise different allegiances depending on the context in which they find themselves. German transnational businesspeople thus, through the education of their children, define themselves as a detached global elite culture.

However, in doing this, the DSL has to engage with local groups. In order to define itself as a German school, it must forge social ties with the local system; the school cannot operate in a vacuum. At the same time, also, it has to have connections to the German state; the assumption of the teachers, however justified, is that their pupils will return to Germany at some point. Even were it to become an English public school, it would be impossible for it to free itself of its German connections, if only because the pupils in their final year would have to write the *Abitur*, which is set by the German Ministry of Education. Similarly, the elite in question may emphasise its cosmopolitanism, but it is also a German elite; it is only here, in a setting more associated with cosmopolitanism than most, that the Germans will acknowledge the existence of a German "community" in London. At the same time as its uses of the DSL define them as a global elite, German transnational businesspeople are also connected with diverse localities.

Furthermore, this suggests that there are diverse ways of being global and local within German transnational business culture. Some German businesspeople do *not* in fact send their children to the DSL, for reasons which are equally to do with presenting Germanness as those cited by their colleagues who made the opposite choice. Also, the DSL caters to many diverse, overlapping groups: Embassy staff, businesspeople from the financial and manufacturing sectors, academics, people in mixed marriages, and others. In all cases, the symbols involved in their self-presentation are the same, but they are interpreted, received and used differently. For Embassy staff, sending your children to the DSL can mean seeking cultural continuity for a child who moves every two years; for a German in a mixed marriage, it could be a way of encouraging the child to learn about its heritage. For the children, also, it presumably evokes a number of other associations which are relevant to them. The same symbols are used by all groups to present themselves, but which are most important depends on the group and the context.

The DSL thus involves multiple modes of self-presentation as "German" which are engaged with local English perceptions of nationality, participate in discourses of globalisation and allow the mediation between social allegiances through strategic self-presentation. While the DSL may be a German transnational institution, it does not define a "German" or "transnational" culture, but links different sorts of self-defined Germans together through engaging with Germany and with local institutions. The DSL thus does not so much define a solidary group, but a contains many different elements within itself, and has links to other social formations rather than simply catering to one body of elite business expatriates. We shall now consider whether the same holds true for cultural institutions.

## Cultural Institution: The Goethe Institut

The German cultural institution in the UK which is most visible to non-Germans is arguably the Goethe Institut London, part of a worldwide network of German cultural institutes. My means of investigation consisted partly of attending a conference hosted by it, partly of interviews with two staff members (one a teacher, one an administrator), partly of interviews with businesspeople, and especially of visiting it repeatedly on random afternoons from June through December 2000 and observing attendees in the cafe, art gallery and library. As such, I was able to gain both an outsider's and an insider's perspective on the organisation.

The Goethe Institut was founded in the 1950s by the German government, largely as a postwar public-relations exercise. By emphasising the German language and high culture (through promotion of classic German literature, classical and avant-garde music, and art film), the government hoped to present an alternative image of Germany to counteract that developed during the Nazi period. The Institut has a staff of 43; all but three are German, and most are locally hired. The exceptions are a small group of administrators who are rotated back to Germany every four to six years; they originate largely from the Foreign Service, and are said to be focused mainly on a diplomatic career. The Goethe Institut thus looks to the German Embassy for its origins and structure.

The Institut's London branch is currently located in Kensington, a well-kept central London area containing a large number of museums and cultural institutions, near Imperial College London and Hyde Park. During the time of my fieldwork, it boasted an art gallery, a cafe, an auditorium, a library and a teaching section; in mid-2000, the art gallery was closed and the rest of the building extensively refurbished. The building which houses it is furnished in a sparse, 1970s-modern style; the walls are stark white, with posters on the walls advertising past exhibitions and display cases on the landing housing books and pictures of relevance. Upon entry, the visitor is confronted with a rank of leaflets advertising cultural events in London, particularly those with a German connection (a Brecht festival, for instance, or a new German film at the National Film Theatre). The next immediate area is the cafe and art gallery, which are sparsely furnished and decorated, again in a spare, minimalist, black-and-white motif, with rubber tiling on the floor and metal-and-plastic chairs. Most new visitors are directed first to the library, which is the central focus of the Institut and the most welcoming area of it, decorated with wood panelling, carpets and comfortable chairs. Off the central area (containing the reception desk, a bulletin board, lockers for visitors' bags and coats and more posters) are rooms devoted to newspapers and magazines, videos and film, reference books and computers, and, largest of all, the main library, with desks, high ceilings and balconies. In an alcove at the back of the room is the multimedia area, with a full-screen television (receiving German television on satellite) and video and audio equipment to allow visitors to play the Institut's collection of films, dramas and educational programmes.

The Goethe Institut London maintains visible connections to Germany. Many of the books on offer are in German; the Institut has two televisions which receive German channels on satellite, or else are available to watch its collection of German or German-oriented videos. The art gallery focuses on young German artists. The computers, similarly, have a German keyboard and German-language interfaces on most programmes; the bookmarks on the web browsers in September 2000 included guides to German television and radio and a German-language online comic based on the legend of the Nibelungen. Theoretically (if not always in practice), users are supposed to confine their searches to German-language websites, or those of relevance to German studies. All the cultural materials on offer are thus of German interest if not actually originating from Germany.

The people who use the Institut include many German transnationals. Leaving aside the staff, there are always a few German pensioners about, and the bulletin board in the foyer will, at any given time, contain several advertisements for exchange students or au-pair placements (mainly German expatriate families looking for German gap-year students). Most of the English people who take language lessons there appear to have a German connection: many are students hoping to go abroad, or are the English spouses or half-English children of Germans. The Institut thus has at least some connection with Germans in London.

However, of the Germans who use it, very few are actually from the business community. The proportion of recognisably German businesspeople (as ascertained by virtue of their being in business dress, with relevant accoutrements, but speaking German or with a German accent) was small compared to that of other groups. Admittedly, some businesspeople may have come to the Institut dressed in casual clothing; however, it is equally likely that some of the patrons whom I saw in business suits may have had non-corporate jobs. These demographics may have resulted partly from the building's location; the Goethe Institut Toronto, situated at the time between the business and theatre districts, attracted a higher percentage of obvious businesspeople. It is significant that, while the Goethe Institut did host a conference on German business in 1998, most of the participants were in fact teachers, who, when asked, said that their reason for attending was to find out about job opportunities for their students. While the Institut does have contact with German transnational business, it maintains a certain amount of distance from it.

In addition, the Institut is overtly focused more on non-Germans than Germans. While it does run joint cultural events with other institutions, for instance co-sponsoring film festivals with a German focus, the main activity which the Goethe Institut showcases is its language lessons. The greater part of Institut users seemed to be non-German university and secondary-school students, taking language or art courses with a German focus. The bulk of the Institut's resources thus are focused less on events of interest to Germans, and more on encouraging an interest in Germany in non-Germans.

  This situation, however, is not inevitable. The Goethe Institut could have a lot to offer German businesspeople, for instance by hosting conferences, or running programmes catering to homesick or lonely expatriates. However, it does none of these things. One Goethe-Institut freelance teacher, who had worked in business beforehand, described it as "untransnational" (by which she seemed to mean that it was German-focused, rather than that it was truly a non-transnational institution) and strongly linked to the social life of the German Embassy. She also noted that the Institut's reputation among businesspeople of her acquaintance is of being conservative and irrelevant to business. German transnational businesspeople thus ignore or reject the high-cultural image of the Goethe Institut.

  Despite this, however, connections with the business world exist at other levels. One Goethe Institut teacher surprised me in an interview by saying that she did not see herself as having contact with the German community, as she had remarked only a moment before that most of her pupils are businesspeople who work for German companies. As noted, the children and partners of German transnational businesspeople do involve themselves with the Institut. Businesspeople themselves make a perverse kind of use of it, by setting themselves up as culturally in opposition to it; their avoidance of it thus indicates their interest in business issues above cultural and educational ones. I had myself initially assumed that the use of German cultural institutions would be a strong symbol of Germanness for transnational businesspeople, based on the history of Germans in London, and on my knowledge of the German community in Toronto (see Panayi 1995). While links exist between the Institut and the business world, these mainly take the form of businesspeople symbolising their allegiance to the global financescape rather than to parochial national cultures by openly avoiding the Institut.

  However, the fact that such institutions are avoided means that they do on some level figure in an actor's self-presentation. The expatriate employees of German banks with whom I spoke commented on the lack of a "*deutsche Klub*" in London: one, who had spent time in Japan, contrasted London with Tokyo, where one spent one's free time in the "German pub" with other business expatriates. All of them agreed that this lack was because England was "similar" enough to Germany that one did not feel the need for such institutions. Since this does not always follow—as the presence of businesspeople at the Goethe Institut Toronto suggests—the avoidance of such institutions may have enabled them to display an appreciation for the local culture. The fact that such a club reportedly exists in Hong Kong and Japan, but not in London, further suggests that the expression of Germanness is contextual, and that the symbols used to present it are different in different contexts. It also implies that the same ways of presenting Germanness take on different meanings in different contexts; visiting a German institution is not the same act in Hong Kong as it is in London. Again, then, the businesspeople whom I interviewed may be German, transnational and business-focused in all locations, but their ways of presenting this—and its strategic significance—vary from context to context.

Furthermore, the nature of the groups which do use the Institut allows German transnational businesspeople's acts of avoidance to fit in with their self-presentation as such. The people who use the Goethe Institut, for instance, tend to be students, the elderly, and UK-born Germanophiles, all of whom are groups against which German transnational businesspeople define themselves. Embassy employees, who form a visible part of the Institut's hierarchy, also are one of these groups. The avoidance of cultural institutions allows German transnational businesspeople to define themselves against other groups; the German transnational businesspeople's existence, therefore, depends at least in part on the presence of other sorts of German transnationals.

It is also worth noting that in some situations, it is acceptable for German transnational businesspeople to use the more overtly cultural institutions. It is, for instance, acceptable to have contact with the Goethe Institut if one is (or has recently been) a student, if one's company provides charitable support for their activities, or if one meets a representative of the institution at a business conference. The Deutsche Schule London, to which many executives send their children, makes frequent use of the Goethe Institut. German transnational businesspeople thus, whether they admit this openly or not, maintain social connections to other German and transnational organisations.

One might also consider the case of the Goethe Institut advertising pamphlet which was placed on a staff bulletin board at the MNC branch which is the focus of Chapters 5 and 6, ZwoBank London. This might at first seem an odd place for it, since the employees of this branch did not appear to have much interest in cultural institutions. However, the presence of the pamphlet did have other uses. Most obviously, it could be taken as an indication that the branch's management wish employees to take an interest in German high culture. Additionally, as this bank was then encouraging its English employees to take German lessons, it may also have been placed there with this in mind. However, since both messages would be aimed at non-German rather than German employees, the use of the pamphlet can be seen as a way of defining the place of non-Germans and Germans vis-à-vis German institutions: non-Germans can participate in Germanness, but only in particular ways and contexts. In this case, a normally-rejected discourse of Germanness is embraced and used to signify Germanness—but this Germanness is of a particular sort, and not one used in the self-presentations of German transnational businesspeople.

The German transnational businesspeople did not, therefore, appear to use any institution which expresses Germanness alone, but only those, and in those ways, which allowed for strategic connections with other groups. It is not so much that the Goethe Institut was not seen as a symbol of Germanness as that it was one which did not fit with my interviewees' self-presentation as bank employees and cosmopolitans. Inasmuch as institutions can be symbols of Germanness, then, their use defines not so much a boundary as several discourses combining with each other in ways which allow the expression of more than one affiliation through the same act of self-presentation.

## Political Institution: The Embassy

It is also worth considering the case of the Embassy of the Federal Republic of Germany (usually referred to as the "German Embassy"), in that it has dealings with all Germans in the United Kingdom culturally and bureaucratically. Despite this, it is treated much like the Goethe Institut by German transnational businesspeople: not as a means of defining oneself as German or transnational, but as a form of Germanness and transnational culture to define oneself *against*.

The Embassy is located in the central-London Knightsbridge district, within walking distance of the Goethe Institut, in a pleasant and attractive area containing a number of other embassies and consulates. It is of moderate size and distinguishes itself mainly by the presence of a large German flag over the main entrance. I was able to make three visits to the Embassy and speak with two official representatives; through the Deutsche Schule London, I was able to interview two other employees in a more private capacity. The Embassy's main function is in the political realm; however, it does engage with the general public with regard to the dispersal of information about Germany, immigration issues and so forth. The Embassy does therefore have contact with German transnational businesspeople.

Despite this, my interviewees at ZwoBank described the Embassy as detached from German transnational business. This impression was borne out by my reception at the Embassy: although employees were polite and friendly, I could find few willing to speak with me in their official capacity. Frau F said that Embassy employees are very segregated from the local area, with only those in the passport division having much to do with the British or with Germans in the UK. The Embassy thus appears to have little to do with German transnational businesspeople.

However, some sections of the Embassy do have undeniable contact with the corporate sector. Individuals requiring a passport or other immigration-related documentation do have to contact the Embassy; it is safe to say that none of the Germans in my sample had not had some contact of this sort (although this contact was also the subject of jokes and complaints among the businesspeople, allowing them to distance themselves from the Embassy even as they use it). In addition, the presence of the Embassy makes the location of German corporations in the UK legally possible, and its promotion of investment in Germany to local entrepreneurs helps to maintain transnational links with the UK. There are thus more connections between the Embassy and the business community than either will admit.

As well having contact with businesspeople as through the passport office, the Embassy also houses the German Social Advice Office *(Deutsche Sozialberätungsstelle)*. This was founded in 1952 at the initiative of the German ambassador. Its mandate is to offer support and advice to anyone of German origin. Significantly, it employs the folk-genetic definition of "German origin"; users do not need a passport to qualify for assistance, but must be able to prove that they have "German blood." It focuses mainly on problems arising from the differences between the bureaucracy and the judicial system of the UK and that of Germany, which are of relevance to at least some German businesspeople. Finally, the *Sozialberätungsstelle*'s representatives also emphasised the generous charity support given to it by German businesses in the UK. One section of the Embassy thus has contact with German transnational capitalism in many ways which are seldom discussed by either group.

The Embassy thus seems to perform a similar function to the Goethe Institut as a means of self-presentation. A locally-hired German senior manager at a German bank which was outside my sample, whom I had asked for advice before starting my fieldwork, summed up the social division between expatriates and local hires at his bank by saying that the expatriates "spend all their time down at the Embassy." Businesspeople at ZwoBank tended to speak of the Embassy as a kind of "other," through jokes and stories which distance the Embassy symbolically from themselves. At the same time, however, all made use of the Embassy in some form or another at some point in their careers. As with the Goethe Institut, the avoidance of the Embassy is used as a part of strategic self-presentation, meaning that contact with it on some level is a required part of transnational business.

My interviewees, therefore, seem to define themselves as transnational businesspeople by rejecting an association with the Embassy. However, this process of rejection is complex and involves, on many levels, acceptance of the institutions' presence as transnational actors, the acknowledgement of, and association with, other groups of transnational Germans, and even, in some contexts, use of the rejected institution. The other images of Germanness and transnational business expressed through the use, or non-use, of cultural institutions thus connect with and influence those of the German transnational businesspeople, suggesting diverse but linked German, transnational and/or business-focused groups rather than a simple, solidary globalising culture.

*Business Institution: the German-British Forum*

The German-British Forum (GBF) was founded around 1995 by a group which included two consultants, a German studies professor, and an economist. In the course of my investigations, I interviewed two of these, along with several members of the organisation, attended one of the GBF's conferences and kept up with its online activities, of which more below. Its mandate is to promote German business, and Anglo-German business cooperation, within the UK, supported by a number of prominent politicians and diplomats in both countries.

The initiative to launch the organisation was sparked by the infamous "Chequers Report" of the early 1990s, in which a media leak revealed that Prime Minister Thatcher and some of her aides, in a private conference, had described Germany as a crypto-Nazi entity with designs on the rest of Europe (Watson 1995: 290). The initial object of the GBF was thus to counteract what they saw as a predominantly negative perception of Germans in the UK. Its representatives say that there has been a substantial improvement, but still cite the maintenance of the perception of a good relationship between the two countries, particularly as regards business, as their main role. The organisation today exists mainly in the form of mailing lists and websites, with the committee being the only conventionally organised part of the institution. One committee member described it in a formal interview as having "no members, no [membership] list, no office even—we're a 'virtual organisation.'" As such, then, the GBF is an organisation whose entire existence is largely an act of self-presentation, with a particular strategy and a direct focus on transnational German business.

The main activity of the GBF is the holding of conferences, the function of which is ostensibly the promotion of good Anglo-German relations, with talks on relevant topics, and awards being given to individuals and groups who have promoted Anglo-German relations, including a "wooden spoon" award for the person or institution who has done the worst job at fulfilling this requirement for the past year (the first recipient having been Mrs Thatcher). Speakers come from the Anglo-German global elite, including Gerhardt Schröder, Tony Blair, and Edward Heath. The GBF thus focuses on people from, and issues relating to, German elites with transnational (if only as it relates to Anglo-German business ventures) connections.

The conference which I attended in the autumn of 2000 was also a very elite affair, with the lowest-priced ticket costing around £150; this allowed the participant to attend the conference and the pre-conference reception, but not the post-conference drinks or the dinner, which was reportedly the highlight of the occasion and at which the awards were given, and which cost about £75 more per person. It was held in one of the most prestigious hotels in London; representatives of at least the major German multinationals were present, as were many German diplomats, and members of academia and the media with a German connection. As the theme of the conference was "Europe and the Internet," most of the speakers were members of IT companies or writers on the subject; however, several were UK or German politicians or retired politicians, who were given the most prominent spots on the programme. The focus of the conference thus appeared to be on the presentation of elite German transnational business.

The main function of the conferences, however, seemed to be the development and maintenance of participants' social networks, rather than the definition of a German community. All in all, the conference was fairly brief (lasting from late afternoon into the late evening); the speeches were largely political ones, with little actual information imparted or problems raised. Most of the time allotted was taken up not with the speeches or panels, but with the receptions and dinner. Attendees include many without an obvious Anglo-German connection; at the conference which I attended, I spoke with Poles, Indians, Koreans and Americans as well as Germans. Most of these said in conversation that they were present for the opportunity to network with businesspeople. The conferences are thus largely networking events, and as such are focused on self-presentation; they therefore reveal links between German transnational businesspeople and other groups.

The GBF also uses symbols of Germanness in ways which suggest connections with diverse groups of varying degrees of Germanness and transnationalism. Its conferences are on general themes such as the Internet (2000), Europe (1999), and transatlantic connections (2001), which can be interpreted as having a German or a more general focus, depending on how one wants to define the topic. The choice of "celebrity" guests suggests a focus on local affairs as well as global. Their publicity materials are attractively produced, resembling those of large corporations. The self-presentation of the GBF thus reveals, again, that the organisation cannot define itself as German without engaging with other groups.

The situation of the GBF is thus in some ways the mirror image of that of the cultural institutions discussed above. In this case, the institution in question is actively embraced by German transnational businesspeople, particularly for its German connections. However, rather than defining an exclusive class, it is also characterised by diverse sorts of links to other groups on many, sometimes unspoken, levels. Once again, the German transnational businesspeople use a German organisation to connect with other groups, German and otherwise, through the act of self-presentation.

In the case of German-focused business organisations, we see a reversal of the trend shown with regard to the cultural and political institutions discussed earlier. Where these institutions were outwardly ignored and made use of on other levels, here German transnational businesspeople make active use of the business organisations, but seldom according to their stated purpose. Conferences are attended less for the presentations than for the networking opportunities. The way in which the organisation presents itself as German is through ways which also connect it to other social groups. The organisations are thus outwardly used to define a group of transnational German businesspeople, but in many cases this focus is less significant for members than the possibility of using them to obtain useful contacts.

It is worth noting, also, that the membership of the "German" organisations also includes non-German employees of German corporations. By using "German" institutions, Britons can present a connection with Germany: an employee can be English, and yet have "Deutsche Bank" on his/her nametag. S/he can also indicate a German connection by taking up a post or position within these organisations; most were run, if not founded, by Germanophiles as well as Germans. Furthermore, these same positions can be used to accumulate social capital within the City of London. The organisations are thus also used by non-Germans, suggesting again that boundaries between German transnational business and other groups are difficult to discern.

By contrast, actual German expatriates, despite having a more direct connection to Germany, seldom attended events organised by German business institutions. I never saw an expatriate from ZwoBank at any of these conferences, although I frequently ran into German acquaintances with a more long-term connection to London. As expatriates will not be staying in the City of London for long, however, it is more useful to them to cultivate contacts within the foreign branches of their institution than to engage in external networking. Again, the outside organisations do not have equal significance for everybody who falls under the general remit of "German transnational businessperson," suggesting that this definition does not cover a single class so much as diverse interest groups.

These different interest groups can even be embodied in a single actor. The General Manager of the UK branch of a German industrial MNC, whom I interviewed, is not only a German transnational businessperson and a member of his company, he is also a keen supporter of charity initiatives, an active member of the committee of several German business organisations, and through these has Embassy connections. The same individual, through the organisations, can be seen as belonging to several diverse sorts of German, transnational and business-focused cultures at once. These organisations also affect other people in the City of London: bank employees who do not make use of these organisations are usually aware of them on some level, and a good part of their discourse about "national business styles" and what they constitute originates from lectures and discussions at the organisations' conferences. Again, rather than defining a single class, these organisations are used in a variety of ways by different actors.

This suggests that not only are there diverse sub-groups within German transnational business culture, but that these are mutually engaged through their uses of German-focused business institutions. The top management, rank and file, Germanophile Britons and expatriates connect with these organisations in different ways, suggesting that the use of such institutions is a strategic act of self-presentation. A junior staff member brought along to a GBF conference by a senior manager will have different aims in attending it than does the senior manager, and possibly will be allowed to attend different portions of the event (as a junior staff member might be considered out of place at the gala dinner). The organisations also include people who have German and transnational connections, but are not German transnational businesspeople. Again, there are not only diverse groups within German transnational capitalism, but these groups link into other organisations.

The role of the German business organisations is thus not only to emphasise a particular image of Germanness, but to develop local connections and create social links with different localities, and diverse forms of global engagement. The organisations thus promote German solidarity at one level and encourage outside links at another, suggesting that German transnational businesspeople actively prefer outside connections than defining themselves as a solidary class. Consequently, like the cultural institutions, they do not define a transnational capitalist class so much as they do an amorphous set of allegiances, some more German and business-focused than others.

*Analysis*

The ways in which German social, cultural, political and business institutions are used, or not used, by Germans in their strategic self-presentation appears at first glance to define a solidary transnational group with particular national and occupational connections, as in Sklair's theory. As in other areas of the lives of

German transnational businesspeople, however, the use of these organisations suggests a much more complex, diffuse social formation, a fact which is reflected in the way in which the nature of transnational life is defined in and around the institutions in question.

From what we have seen, the ways in which the institutions are used suggests a group of German transnational businesspeople defining themselves against other, more local groups by the pattern of which institutions they patronise or do not patronise. Through the networking function of the business organisations, the German transnational businesspeople make contact with international clients; social networks are built and maintained through attending conferences and other events. Similar networking activities take place at the DSL. My interviewees' choice of institutions thus seemingly defines a particular group of globally-focused businesspeople with a particular unified culture.

However, this impression is something of an oversimplification. The relationship of businesspeople to cultural institutions is not just a simple matter of using or not using the organisations in question, but involves using and rejecting them simultaneously on multiple levels. There are links between the Goethe Institut and German business through charity initiatives, English employees taking German lessons and retired German businesspeople taking teaching jobs. Similarly, many German transnational businesspeople do *not* make use of the German business institutions. Again, we have here not so much the definition of a single group as a complex pattern of acceptance and rejection of cultural and business institutions, with different uses conveying different messages and furthering different strategies on multiple levels.

One might also consider the case of the Embassy. Embassy staff are German, transnational and, arguably, capitalists; Sklair's definition of a transnational capitalist class includes civil servants (2001: 17), and Embassy staff spoke of their transnational activities as "part of the job" in much the same way as the business expatriates did. They share certain symbolic markers of Germanness with businesspeople, including the use of the DSL as a school for their children and a social centre for themselves. However, at the same time their position on German transnational business is not that which is experienced in the City of London; the Embassy's main focus is on business as it relates to government. It is also not focused on one specific company or sector, but on all German business in the UK, and then only as they relate to the bureaucratic procedures of their locating and remaining where they are. Embassy staff are, therefore, for transnational businesspeople, *like* them but *not* them. As the Embassy staff are undeniably German, transnational and (to some extent) business-focused, and yet are equally undeniably distinct from German transnational businesspeople, then, so different German transnational groups may define themselves as culturally distinct from each other at the same time as they present themselves using exactly the same symbols.

This carries over to the other groups. Each of the institutions considered here is in and of itself a transnational social formation, which more or less directly relates to transnational business; they connect with other German transnational groups with varying degrees of connection to business, such as students or Embassy staff, in diverse ways. The organisations are thus part of German transnational capitalism in some ways, auxiliary to it in others, and linked in with a variety of other groups at the same time. The German transnational businesspeople and the organisations discussed here thus all form part, not of a definite solidary group, but of a more diffuse social formation, in which there are diverse but overlapping ways of presenting Germanness and of relating to the local and the global.

Furthermore, one must also consider the fact that the most important German social institution in the UK appears not to be a formal one, but rather the informal information network which spreads through peripheral contact between conationals. As noted above, Germans in the UK compare notes and trade information as to where to obtain the best German food, books, toys and so forth. Additionally, small-scale, ad-hoc trading networks existed in the businesses which I studied; people going to Germany would take orders from friends and workmates for foodstuffs, sweets or videotapes which were unavailable in London. The most important social institution through which German transnational businesspeople present themselves may thus, appropriately, be a non-institution: a flexible, informal and seldom-acknowledged social network, connecting most if not all members of the community.

This multiplicity and flexibility also comes across in my interviewees' images of globalisation. As an example, in a discussion with a representative of the German-British Chamber of Commerce on whether a firm can be global and German, he brought up the case of Coca-Cola, saying that it is said to be a truly global company and product, but that it is also seen as truly American. He then turned the question back on me, asking whether there really is a global market, or just one in which American culture is now so universal that it *appears* global. While this sentiment echoes a debate which has been raging in both the popular and academic presses for a long time (see, for instance, Krauthammer 1999; Hirst and Thompson 1996; and Tomlinson 1999b), it also casts light on how globalisation is experienced by transnational businesspeople. By raising this question, my interviewee evoked images of global and local elements blending into each other so that it is somewhat difficult to tell which is which; Coca-Cola can be American, it can be global, and it can also be a particular product or corporation. It also raises the question of where the relationship between local and global begins and ends. Globalisation and being global are thus defined in the business environment as a process which includes a variety of linked local and global components, and a variety of ways of relating to these.

Interviewees in business also define what it is to be a "global individual" in a similar way. Over and over in interviews on the subject of cultural institutions, German businesspeople said that they valued being global, but retaining and recognising your own culture. Their image of the ideal global person comes across as one with multiple links of varying degrees of importance; they define themselves not only as Germans in the UK, but as Germans who have also been to Hong Kong, Germans from particular regions, and many other ways of presenting themselves as German and transnational. People thus recognise different connections between local and global and between different localities; they then express these as part of their presentations of Germanness and cosmopolitanism. Significantly, in these presentations, the two are not mutually exclusive, as they appear to be for Forsythe's German interviewees (1989), or for Mrs Thatcher (Watson 1995: 290), suggesting that the accommodation of multiple allegiances is possible within their self-presentation. German transnational businesspeople thus define their existence as a state of multiple allegiance, rather than of being *either* global *or* local.

It is thus possible to claim that there is a transnational business elite of German origin in London, discernable through Germans' uses of particular institutions. However, to see it as a unique, bounded entity is to overlook the multiple ties, and diversity of subgroups, which are made possible through my interviewees' self-presentation. We thus have here a case of diverse groups within a single, broadly defined transnational social formation, rather than a unique, solidary German transnational or national cultural group. These groups possess many engagements with outside groups, both global and local; it is not so much a case of "us and them," as of varying degrees of us and them.

When dealing with outside institutions, German transnational businesspeople give the impression of being not so much a solidary group with a definite culture, national or transnational, as a diffuse array of actors with diverse agendas and outside connections. Furthermore, it seems that they present both localising and globalising concepts in similarly diffuse, context-dependent ways. It thus might be more fruitful to consider them as a diffuse, complex social group with a number of internal divisions and external connections, both local and global.

## Conclusion

An examination of the history and social structure of the expatriate German community in London thus suggests that, outside of their workplaces, German transnational businesspeople do not form a solidary, united and visible national and/or organisational culture (as the nation-based theories of culture would suggest), nor do form a particular transnational social stratum (as the TCC theory suggests) but that they link into other groups and incorporate diverse interests through their strategic self-presentation as German and as businesspeople, forming instead a "society" of groups with social connections of varying degrees of strength. Furthermore, different groups within the German community employ different strategies for success, and, while using the same symbols—language, business, a relationship to territory and genetic origin, a fondness for "order," etc.—to present themselves, do so in strikingly different ways. From this examination, it is possible to formulate the hypothesis that within the firms for which they work, culture will similarly be a shifting and mutable process of self- and other-definition, with links to a variety of other national and organisational groups, and also incorporating a diversity of ways of being "German" and "transnational" within the same broad self-presentation.

The case of the German community considered here thus suggests that in London, there is no single "culture" of German transnational businesspeople, but a variety of groups, each with different ways of presenting German and global affiliations, under a single, business-focused, social aegis. Furthermore, it suggests that German transnational businesspeople do not exist in a vacuum, but have links to a number of other groups of varying degrees of global and local engagement through the act of self-presentation. We shall now consider how the Germans fit into the business-focused environment of the City of London, and whether the same pattern of using the same symbols to present very different takes on national and global affiliation holds true in business as it does in private life.

# Chapter 4

# A Financial Utopia:
# The "Global City" of London

## Introduction

In the UK's main financial enclave, the City of London, German transnational businesspeople construct a social environment suitable for their global financial activities through strategic self-presentation. Although this process may seem to define a solidary business culture based on particular connections to their home and host countries, however, a closer examination reveals that not only is there more of a degree of transnational affiliation between them, but that it is impossible for them to define their culture through strategic self-presentation without engaging with those of other groups, or without acknowledging elements of cultural diversity among German transnational businesspeople themselves.

Global cities, such as London, are recognised by many (including, among others, Sassen 1991, Castells 2000, and Beaverstock and Smith 1996) as the social focus of transnational businesspeople, such as the Germans described in the previous chapter. Global cities are the key nodes of Castells' transnational networks, and as such are increasing in importance, both symbolic and physical, in the processes of globalisation, as more and more transnational actors concentrate themselves in such cities (2000). Furthermore, as noted in the last chapter, the German presence in the UK has historically been focused on the City of London (Panayi 1993, 1995). Finally, if, as Sklair suggests, an understanding of the transnational business environment is essential to an understanding of the concept of the transnational capitalist class, one must consider the cities in which the most transnational financial corporations have branches, and London outstrips New York and Tokyo in this regard (2001: Chapter 3; Rose 1994: 43). In order to investigate the nature of culture in transnational business environments, then, we shall examine the global city in which the German transnational businesspeople operate, and the ways in which they define it through strategic self-presentation.

## Hiring a Cocker Spaniel: The "Global City" of London

The City of London, the financial enclave in which most of the German transnational businesspeople interviewed for this project carry out their daily business, is essential to their self-definition as a transnational social formation. The way in which the German transnational businesspeople whom I interviewed described the City of London appears at first to be consistent with the self-definition of a transnational capitalist class with a definite culture associated with particular national cultures; however, closer investigation in fact reveals not so much a process of defining a group, as of shifting, multiple engagements with local and global social entities.

## The City: History and Structure

The City of London (also known as "The City" or "The Square Mile") is an area of approximately one square mile roughly in the centre of London, the political and economic capital of the United Kingdom. While its physical boundaries are marked by statues of silver dragons, the City's emblem, its symbolic boundaries are somewhat vaguer, as a number of "City" banks and institutions in fact have their offices in Knightsbridge (a high-prestige area further west), and, while this was still seen as a sort of exile or hinterland as late as 1996, an increasing number are establishing positions further east in Canary Wharf (Augar 2000: 18). Furthermore, many connections exist between the City and the wider governmental structure of the United Kingdom (most notably with regard to the Bank of England), with top financial experts frequently going on to more or less formal careers in politics (Stockdale 1957, Kynaston 1995). In conceptual terms, however, the City is a transnational business enclave which is symbolically if not physically located in the centre of London.

While the area which comprises the City of London has been occupied since Roman times, the City's government, the Corporation of the City of London, dates from the ninth century (A. Jenkins 1988: 6; Dyer n.d.: 1). As the Middle Ages progressed, the City area became increasingly mercantile, and trade associations, known as Guilds, became the dominant power, headed by the Lord Mayor (Dyer, n.d.: 1-3; Borer 1977: 70ff.). The City was largely trade-focused up until the founding of the Bank of England in the seventeenth century (A. Jenkins 1988; Anonymous 1994:17); the next major boost towards financial specialisation came in the eighteenth century, with the founding of Lloyds' Insurance House and the invention of stockbroking and financial speculation (Winchester Group n.d. [1990?]; Plender and Wallace 1985). The City's period of glory is said by many historians to be the years 1810-1914, as it covered both financial and mercantile functions, supported by Britain's position as the dominant economic and military power of the time. After WWI and II, and the consequent fall of the British Empire, the City became more financially specialised (Courtney and Thompson 1996: introduction; Rose 1994). The City of London thus has an extensive history of participation in international trade and financial activity.

Today, the City is distinct both legally and socially from the rest of London, to say nothing of the rest of United Kingdom. It is still governed by the Corporation of the City of London, which is housed in a building called the Guildhall and headed by the Lord Mayor, along with the Aldermen and the Court of Common Council, who are elected by residents and businesses of the City (Corporation of London 2000a; www.corporationoflondon.gov.uk). In addition, the City Guilds elect some of the officials and nominate the candidates for Lord Mayor

(Corporation of London 2000a: 7-9). While the Guilds still retain some aspects of their medieval form and function, today their role is partly as networking associations, partly as charity organisations, partly as lobby groups vis-à-vis the government of the United Kingdom (A. Jenkins 1988: 8). The Lord Mayor, while less powerful than during the Middle Ages, is still the Chief Magistrate of the City, and "within the square mile of the City the Lord Mayor still gives precedence to none except the sovereign of the realm" (Borer 1977: 298; A. Jenkins 1988: 16). Less officially, however, the dominant force in the City consists of the, mainly American, global financial corporations which operate there. The City of London is thus a distinct financially-focused area within London.

The City's "global" status is easily visible to anyone walking through the area. The architecture is a bewildering mix, with streets of elegant Georgian houses (now mostly housing think-tanks and small consultancies) standing alongside glossy glass-and-concrete towers. The streets are narrow and winding, but are cleaner and better-lit than those in most other parts of London. The City boasts several Georgian and Victorian churches, all attempting to draw in the business crowds with signs advertising lunchtime concert recitals and "lectures on modern issues" rather than sermons. The people in the streets are all dressed in near-identical suits, and accents from the Southeast of England dominate; however, a visible—and audible—number are from other countries. A Canadian friend who had come to London to visit me remarked that he had identified five separate languages on the short journey between London Bridge and St Paul's. The City's financial focus is also to be seen everywhere: while there are few of the LED stock-market quote displays which characterise the financial districts of New York and Frankfurt, nearly every building bears the name of a financial firm and boasts at least one security guard on reception. Even the City's architecture and population indicate its distinct status.

Furthermore, the area is visibly one in which few people actually live (*The Economist* 1962). Unlike in the rest of London, City pubs and shops close on Saturdays and Sundays. While the City contains a number of sites of historical and cultural interest, tourists tend to restrict themselves to the area immediately around St Paul's Cathedral and the Museum of London, except during the peak of the season in mid-August. Shops tend to cater to a specialised and non-local market, with luxury-goods retailers, clothing stores and gift and electronic emporiums dominating over the more usual supermarkets and retailers; many of the firms, such as the sandwich chain Prêt-A-Manger, advertise their global-philanthropist ethos prominently (see Sklair 1998b; 2001: Chapter 6). The physical boundaries between the City and the rest of London are visible: to the east of the silver dragons, the streets narrow, the tower blocks peter out, the buildings become Victorian tenements and modern council houses, and the population become the Bangladeshi immigrants and working-class English of Brick Lane, while to the west the businesses are replaced by the fashionable shops, galleries and theatres of the West End and Soho.

City people cite three main factors as drawing companies to the area. The first is gossip and/or the networking potential of having an office in the same area as other corporations in the same field (Beaverstock and Smith 1996: 1379): one think-tank member remarked that even in these days of instantaneous global communication, "'buzz' counts for a lot." This is also reflected in the use of coffee shops and pubs by many as supplemental offices, where meetings can be held, projects discussed, and contacts at other corporations met. The second is, as one put it, credibility: for all financial corporations, having a London office is a status symbol. The third is the large and mobile pool of skilled labour which the City boasts, which in turn creates a snowball effect, as companies come to London for the labour pool, causing people with the appropriate skills to come to London for the jobs, and so forth. Interviewees who were more financially knowledgeable pointed out a fourth reason: that since the "deregulation" of the mid-eighties the City has had more lenient tax laws and a much less strict regulatory system than the rest of the UK, and indeed than many countries, including the USA (Augar 2000: 49; Plender and Wallace 1985: 2-3). All of these factors cause the City to be dominated by foreign financial corporations.

These factors also combine to make the City one of the principal "global cities," to use Sassen's phrase: that is, cities, such as London, New York and Tokyo, which have as many ties to places around the world as to their host countries (1991). Most of my interviewees described the City as culturally "closer" to New York and Tokyo than to the rest of the UK; asked the question "Is the City English," all of my interviewees responded in the negative, some adding that while it was *in* England, it was not *English*. The ethnic and cultural diversity of the City aside, the nature of financial activity requires people to be actively connected and communicating with other cities around the world in real time. London also trades in all major currencies, including the dollar and the Euro (Corporation of London 2000a: 14). The City's bookshops have unusually extensive travel and map sections, and numerous City service companies exist which specialise in intercultural training, expatriate relocation and foreign-language lessons (see Dahlen 1997). In a sense, the City can be described as a financial Utopia, both in the sense of being an ideal state for financiers, but also in that the original Greek word "Utopia" literally means "No Place," and is thus a fitting designation for a place located at one remove from the country which is its host (see Leyshon and Thrift 1994).

Popular histories of the City frequently claim that the City has "always" been a financial Utopia, even though this specialisation is actually less than a hundred years old (Courtney and Thompson 1996: xiv). Merriman and Visram insist that "London itself was founded by people from overseas and the Roman town was cosmopolitan" (1993: 3). Borer similarly describes the medieval town as a global financial centre; all the writers mentioned ignore the fact that in both contexts London was a small-scale operator and that it is doubtful that at the time it was at all "cosmopolitan" or "global" in the modern senses (1977: 41). Following WWII, the City remained dominated by old English merchant banks, and like them was conservative and wedded to a paternal-capitalistic ideal; Augar likens the atmosphere of a merchant bank in the 1970s to that of an Oxbridge common room of the 1950s (2000: 20, 35). Although internal sources claim great antiquity for the City as a cosmopolitan and global entity, this state of affairs has in fact been present for less than thirty years.

1986 looms large in both books about the City and in its denizens' personal narratives as a year of transformation, the dividing line between the "old" and the "new" City, although this date, being the official year of the adoption of deregulation and of the "Big Bang," actually refers to a series of changes beginning in 1983 and cumulating in the Barings scandal of 1992 (Courtney and Thompson 1996: 218). Deregulation brought in the distinctive regulatory status of the area, making it easier for foreign companies to locate there and compete for human resources and market share with the older merchant banks. The Big Bang, more dramatically, saw the computerisation of all major City institutions; this made face-to-face dealing unnecessary, putting many firms out of business and causing a shift away from the old, slow-paced capitalist ideal to a faster, more globally-focused one (Anonymous 1994: 124-5; Augar 2000). This change was also symbolised by a shift in dress styles from a formal one characterised by the wearing of dark three-piece suits, top hats and bowlers, to the present preference for bare heads, brightly-coloured shirts and two-piece suits among City men (Courtney and Thompson 1996:190ff.) The stock market crash of 1987 further exposed weaknesses in the established traditional structure (Augar 2000: 4); furthermore, as the foreign banks tend to scale back and expand their London offices congruent with gains and losses in their domestic spheres—and as the local merchant banks were forced of necessity to adopt similar "hire-and-fire" policies—the City as a whole developed a transient ethic placing little value on paternal capitalism (Ibid., 168). Lewis, in his personal account of City life in the mid-1980s, quotes a trader who left his bank for a more lucrative job elsewhere as saying "You want loyalty, hire a cocker spaniel," a phrase which has since passed into the mythology not only of the City, but of global business in general (1989: 242). The early nineties saw the steady collapse of the old merchant banks, with one or two notable exceptions, and the replacement of the familistic, hierarchical ethic with a more egalitarian but less loyalty-driven system (Courtney and Thompson 1996: 158; Augar 2000).

The present-day City is described by those who work in it as fast-paced, egalitarian and globally engaged, with a strong emphasis on flexibility and of the pursuit of personal gain. While one can still find examples of the "old City man," they tend to be self-employed or retired, and to be most often found in the City Business Library, tracking their own stocks with the aid of the *Financial Times*. People in the modern City tend to change jobs every couple of years and believe company loyalty to be a thing of the past (Courtney and Thompson 1996: xxvi-xxix). Lewis' cocker-spaniel joke was echoed by numerous City people in interviews, as witness this exchange with a young, male English manager of the "New City" type:

**Manager:** Ask the first question any human being ever asks.

**Interviewer:** "Why"?

**Manager:** "What's in it for me?"

While the City can be described as having become more meritocratic in that it is now dominated by people from working-class backgrounds and state schools, and is no longer chauvinistically English, ethnic minorities and women are still rare and frequently face prejudice; women adopt a different dress style to men, favouring brightly-coloured two-piece or contrasting trouser suits with scarves or jewellery over the abovementioned dark two-piece and coloured shirt (Ibid., xxviii). Furthermore, there is a fairly anti-intellectual tone to the City; one of Courtney and Thompson's interviewees cynically remarks that the City has gone from a public school clique who wouldn't hire anyone who wasn't an Old Etonian to a grammar school clique who won't hire anyone who didn't go to a grammar school (Ibid., 167). Nick Leeson, the "Rogue Trader" whose insider-trading activities were blamed for the final collapse of Barings, is celebrated in City stories and jokes (an example which was circulating during my fieldwork ran: "have you heard that Nick Leeson was seen walking by the river? He fell in the water—the bank collapsed") (see also Leeson 1996, Beaverstock and Smith 1996: 1382). The modern City thus is seen by the people who work in it as meritocratic, flexible and globally engaged, and yet this state of affairs is also a recent and traumatic development.

*German Views of the City*

The German transnational businesspeople whom I interviewed tended to describe the City in ways fitting with their image as an elite, German, business-focused culture. Most people, as noted above, spoke of the City as "not English"; Germans looking for "real Englishness" went to Oxford, Stratford-upon-Avon or Cornwall, or to tourist sites elsewhere in London such as Buckingham Palace or Kew Gardens. Local aspects of self-presentation, such as the class tension within the City, went largely unmentioned; it seems that the Germans were not unaware of it, as several, mainly trainees, expressed puzzlement at the lack of emphasis on university qualifications in the City, but for the most part it was not discussed. On the other hand, they also tended to define the City in terms of its English or "Anglo-Saxon" business culture, as opposed principally to the German one. Interestingly, however, this Englishness can paradoxically be seen as a way of expressing a more global allegiance, given that English is seen as the "global language" of business (see Chapter 6, this volume) and American business culture remains the hegemonic form. In keeping with the TCC's orientation to the financial and transnational aspects of the City rather than its engagement with the local, the Germans thus have an image of the City as "Utopia"; *in* England but not *of* it.

Their descriptions of the City, furthermore, emphasised its cosmopolitanism, in the sense of maintaining a "world-open" attitude. Most interviewees set up a paradigm in which the UK is presented as narrow and occasionally racist, but the City as cosmopolitan and open. German bank employees in particular remarked on the City's ethnic diversity. Interestingly, however, this discourse did not take into account the fact that the City is in fact *less* diverse than many other areas of London, or acknowledge the possibility that other forms of cosmopolitanism might exist. Additionally, it was never remarked upon that the openness to other cultures was fairly selective; in eighteen months in the City, for instance, I never once saw a woman in a headscarf. German transnational businesspeople thus present the City as cosmopolitan, but only in the particular ways most relevant to businesspeople.

The City was also described using symbols of finance and financial speculation. Its distinctive tax and regulation systems, discussed above, figured heavily in interviewees' accounts. Political aspects of the City, for instance the Guildhall, were for the most part ignored, likely because these did not feature heavily in bank employees day-to-day lives. Symbols of consumption also featured prominently in descriptions of the City: Lewis attributes the popularity of London as a location site for American banks to "its time zone, its history, its language, its relative political stability, its large pool of dollar-hungry capital and Harrods (don't underestimate the power of shopping opportunities in all this)" (1989:184). Most of my German interviewees similarly focused on the consumption possibilities afforded by the City's location, whether luxury-goods retailers such as Harrods or, especially among the trainees, bargain-goods areas such as Petticoat Lane. Virtually all visitors to the bank went out to a West End musical and/or shopping on Oxford Street as part of their visit, both of which were regarded as *de rigueur*. Again, the German transnational businesspeople used symbols of elite consumption and trade, of particular interest to a transnational business elite, to define the City.

The historical depth of the City was also described in a way which fit with the priorities and interests of a transnational business elite. History figured in Germans' descriptions of the City, but primarily from a practical or aesthetic standpoint; for the most part the historical buildings and churches were talked about as objects of beauty, or places to go to for a bit of peace and quiet at lunchtime. 1986, more curiously, did not seem to be of much concern to the Germans; while English people at ZwoBank referred to it continually, only one German interviewee even mentioned it, and he had been in London for over thirty years and had worked for English and American banks prior to working for a German one. It cannot be the case that the Germans were unaffected by the change, as the English employees who mentioned it did so in terms of their (German) bank's reactions to deregulation and the subsequent crash. Images of the history of the City are thus also restricted to those of interest to a German transnational capitalist class.

This definition of the City, however, is not developed in a vacuum or without engagement with other groups. The fact that two-thirds of the employees of even the most German-focused bank branch in the City are English, mainly of the "new City" type, would suggest that the Germans had quite a bit of contact with this group; few bank employees outside of top management had contact with "old City" people, employees of the Corporation of London or think-tank members. This fact explains the focus on the financial and consumption aspects of the City, and the lack of emphasis on its politics. Furthermore, it is not in the interest of the "new City" people to delve too deeply into the history of the City, as this would suggest that the dominance of the "new City" type is recent and precarious; hence, while the age of the City is acknowledged, this is done through aesthetic interest in the buildings and through stylised displays of history such as the floats and displays representing Dick Whittington (Lord Mayor of the City of London in 1397, 1406 and 1419, and the subject of a well-known English children's story) and other semi-mythological figures which are sponsored by Guilds and companies in the City's annual festival, the Lord Mayor's Show. This fact also explains the Germans' relatively low concern with class structure, as it is in the "new City" people's interest to emphasise modern meritocracy over traditional hierarchies. The representations of local people thus shape Germans' portrayals of the City, rather than them developing it on their own as a group.

Similarly, popular works on the City are very much read by Germans as well as English; Courtney and Thompson, Lewis, and Augar were all recommended to me by interviewees. Books on comparative national business cultures, such as Trompenaars and Hampden-Turner's *Seven Cultures of Capitalism* (1996) were familiar to everyone in the City; if they had not read them themselves, in most cases they had heard the contents summarised by intercultural trainers (see Dahlen 1997: 79ff; Moore 2003). The Germans' definition and construction of the City thus is not wholly the product of a transnational capitalist class, but is influenced by a variety of local and global factors.

In addition, London's German transnational businesspeople are influenced by the local culture of Germany, even while they are resident elsewhere. The lack of emphasis on 1986 may quite likely be because it is eclipsed, in most Germans' minds, by the events of 1989 (see Watson 1995). The ignorance of the class system also suggests influence from Germany; while there exists some social stratification, at present Germany lacks England's hereditary class structure (Panayi 1995: 255). Similarly, the patterns of consumption and the knowledge of what to consume in London seem to be learned from travel guidebooks and from Germans who had been to England. Finally, even a relatively homogenous part of London may seem cosmopolitan and multicultural to Germans who, despite initiatives aimed at raising awareness, largely view multiculturalism as something which happens in other countries (Vertovec 1996b: 383). My visits to Frankfurt gave me the impression of a financial district with much less visible diversity among the population than the City, and virtually all the buildings had been constructed within the past thirty years. Local influences from Germany thus affect the way in which the City is defined.

Furthermore, the City is also defined in terms of what it is *not*. Behind the descriptions which German interviewees gave of the City, there seemed to be an implicit contrast to Frankfurt; Frankfurt is smaller, newer, less aesthetically pleasing in their eyes, contains less ethnic mixing (although, despite the lack of visible non-Germans in the financial district, it is debatable whether Frankfurt as a whole is less ethnically mixed than London), and contains less in the way of high culture and shopping opportunities. The other implied contrast was with other groups of Germans in London, such as tourists and students; St Paul's, viewed by most City Germans mainly as a nice place to have lunch, would be seen by the other groups of Germans as a marker of high culture, religion, or European history.

The German transnational businesspeople's definition of the City is also affected by the definitions given it by groups which they regard as outsiders.

In short, then, the City of London is an area which can be defined in varied and complex ways, according to the particular needs of the individual or group under consideration. However, this process of selection and definition does not take place simply within the ranks of German transnational businesspeople, and therefore as part of the definition of a solidary transnational culture. Rather, it is shaped and influenced by local and outside patterns of self-presentation and cultural construction, by literary and media tropes, and finally in relation to other transnational Germans, suggesting a broader, widely-connected transnational social entity, comprising many groups with diverse cultures.

## Loose Change: Recent Events in German Transnational Banking

German businesses in the City of London had, at the time of my study, been affected by several trends within their environment: the adoption of the Euro by Germany, the recent series of mergers on the part of German companies, and the so-called "e-commerce boom" (and, later, the so-called "dotcom bust" which followed). Again, the way in which they deal with these issues appears on one level to define a transnational capitalist class; however, the very nature of these issues entails a strong degree of local engagement, internal division and complex negotiation between groups, indicative of a more complex social formation.

### German Banks in London and Elsewhere

According to a 2000 survey by *The Banker*, there were, at the time of my fieldwork, 27 German banks and/or financial institutions with City branches or representative offices, the latter being a small office of two or three employees set up to keep an eye on the London market and engage in networking. (*The Banker* 2000: 43; see also Braun 1993; *The Economist* 1998d). Most banks started out with representative offices in the 1970s, and expanded to full branches in the mid-eighties. In the 1980s, some German banks joined with other European banks in coalition or joint investment banks, but recent years have seen an abandonment of this strategy in favour of independent branches. There are thus a sizeable minority of German companies in the City, with connections to Germany and the German financial system.

The German banking system consists, roughly speaking, of four different types of banks (described more fully in Anonymous 1995). First and most visible are the "Big Three," Deutsche Bank, Dresdner Bank and Commerzbank. All of these are old established universal banks—that is, banks with a global presence which provide a "universal range of financial products"—independent of the state but larger and less specialised than the *Privatbanken* (Chetham 1994: 73; von Stein 1998: 37-8). Recently, following the merger of Bayerische Vereinsbank and Bayerische Hypotheken- und Wechselbank, the resultant entity, HypoVereinsbank, is sufficiently large and universal to be considered with the Big Three (*Financial*

*Times* 1998b; *Frankfurter Allgemeine Zeitung* 2000). Secondly, there are the banks owned by the federal state (or in which the state is the majority shareholder), which include cooperative banks (*Genossenschaftsbanken*), savings banks (*Sparkasse*) and the Girobank. Like the Big Three, they tend to have small local branches backed by a Frankfurt-based head office; however, in their case, the branches are effectively independent entities (von Stein 1998: 37). Next there are the *Landesbanken*, banks associated with the various states of Germany, such as Hessische Landesbank (HeLaBa) or Westdeutsche Landesbank (WestLB) (Ibid., 37-8). Finally, there are the *Privatbanken*, merchant banks which tend to deal with trade and corporate customers (Ibid., 36). Most of the banks were founded between 1850 and 1890, with numbers peaking in the 1870s during German unification (see von Stein 1998; Eisenberg 1985; M. Klein 1997; Gall 1995: 1-17). Both the *Sparkassen* and the cooperatives started as independent small banks from 1800 on, but by the 1860s-70s had established central banks (Eisenberg 1985). Most German banks were officially closed down and reformed after WWII, although some, as noted above, had been shut down by the Nazi party upon achieving power (Klure 1985: 126-148, Holtfrereich 1995: 439-486). German banks thus have a distinctive history and structural system within global finance. We shall now look at three trends which had been affecting German banking at the time of fieldwork: the Euro adoption, the spate of mergers which followed the changing of the German laws regarding mergers and acquisitions, and the "e-commerce" boom.

## German Banks and the Euro

The first significant trend which we will look at is the adoption by Germany of the new European currency, the Euro, at the end of 1998 (with the physical currency coming into circulation in 2001). In the London context, this was a controversial subject: while the German banks were officially pro-Euro, the English tend to be hostile to the Euro, with the media frequently using it as a symbol of foreign, and often of German, attempts to impose upon the British way of life (Jones 1998). In fact, the British media often conflate the European Union with Germany, and consequently hostility towards the Euro, as towards all European Union development efforts, tends to be tinged with anti-German rhetoric (Ibid.). The City's position, in keeping with its role as a financial Utopia, tends not to be actively hostile to the Euro but it is divided over the question of whether or not its adoption by England—and hence the City—would be a good thing. The Euro was frequently described to me as "just another currency" by City people; however, a conference paper by David Lascelles of the Centre for the Study of Financial Innovation, presented during my fieldwork, argues that to keep the pound would better enable the City to maintain neutrality between the American and Continental European markets (2000). However, at the London branches studied here, people seemed to be less anti-Euro than others in the UK, due to the banks' official pro-Euro position; while personal views on the Euro tended to be variable, most people were united in viewing it as something to be accepted as part of professional life. In institutions linked with German transnational business, then, the symbolic value of the Euro, to say nothing of European Union development, is subtly different from that of the rest of the City.

## The Millennial Trend: Mergers and Acquisitions

Secondly, around the turn of the millennium there was a spate of mergers and attempted mergers in the German business world, with varying degrees of impact. The relaxing of German laws regarding mergers and acquisitions, followed by the successful mergers of Daimler-Benz and Chrysler, and, in banking, Bayerische Hypotheken- und Wechselbank and Bayerische Vereinsbank (*Financial Times* 1998a), prompted a wave of merger talks and restructuring throughout German business. However, there followed a stream of spectacular failures, most notably the Rover-BMW merger, which became a symbol of German and English inability to coexist, and which was frequently invoked by people from both ethnic groups when in a state of dissatisfaction with the other one (*Financial Times* 1998b). The attempted merger between Deutsche Bank and Dresdner Bank, which was announced as a move which would revolutionise German banking if it succeeded, and which failed with much publicity shortly thereafter, also caused many institutions to rethink their own merger plans (Major 2000). Finally, the Vodafone-Mannesmann merger (or, arguably, takeover), while ostensibly successful, created much bad feeling between the English and German business communities (Höpner and Jackson 2001). All these combined to create an atmosphere of discontinuity and faster-than-usual change among German banks in London, and to create symbolic focuses for Anglo-German conflict and cooperation.

## Banking and the Internet

The third major factor impacting on the banking world was the Internet revolution and, more specifically, the "e-commerce" boom. Over the two years of the study, banks and City institutions made increasing use of the Internet. Finally, in 2000 came the Internet banking explosion, with the establishment of Internet-only banks, and older banks setting up online wings, in the banking version of the so-called "Internet goldrush." As with the mergers, the "dotcom phenomenon" was viewed cynically by bank employees, but they continued to participate, citing the fact that it made it possible to reach international customers without needing a branch in that country. Not surprisingly, given their transnational connections, the City's German banks have found themselves increasingly preoccupied with IT-related issues.

## Analysis

While it may seem as if all of these trends have had an across-the-board impact on German banks in the City, this apparent uniformity of impact may have more to do with the ways in which the banks and their employees presented themselves than with actual events. For instance, the differences between the types of German banks were not particularly emphasised in the City, with few English people who are not specialists being able to distinguish between them; instead, they all are subsumed under a general "German" label. The promotional material for ZwoBank emphasises its focus on the *Mittelstand* in the German market, but its UK promotional material labels it as "a specialist in Germany for its international customers." The larger banks, furthermore, frequently tried to dissociate themselves from Germany and give themselves a more global image, chiefly by merging with British and American financial institutions. Through the strategic selection of different modes of self-presentation, the German banks give themselves the appearance of a united front.

Furthermore, the fact that the three abovementioned trends take on the significance which they do, and the ways in which these are discussed, also indicates strategic self-presentation. The association of industry with Germanness, mainly down to the importance it has to German nationalism (Seger 1997: 2), takes on a different significance in a country in which this is the norm than in one in which it is unusual; most banks may continue to focus on the *Mittelstand* in England, but generally only mention this when addressing German customers. However, it may also have to do with the fact that the English also conceive of German business primarily in terms of manufacturing, and that German manufacturing companies are the most visible German MNCs (Head 1992). The emphasis on symbols of manufacturing thus also shows a bias towards those symbols which are suited to a transnational environment and a British location.

Similarly, many German banks use symbols of Europe, such as European flags or Euro accounts, in the promotional materials which comprise a part of their self-presentation. While, as the discussion in Chapter 3 suggests, a pro-European stance can be a symbol of Germanness, many German interviewees described it as indicating their openness to new cultures; most, even those who were anti-Europe, spoke of it in terms of bringing cultures together and promoting mutual understanding. Many people spoke of European development initiatives, however, in interestingly superficial terms. Some described the benefits of the Euro and European passport to tourism, for instance, and others of the development of closer cultural ties between European countries, rather than of the political issues; the focus on the purely monetary aspects of the Euro is similarly a presentation of the concept seen as positive in the City. In the case of European initiatives, then, we also see a bias in the presentation of symbols towards those suited to the environment.

The e-commerce boom, similarly, was described in ways which highlight its globalising and communicative aspects. Banks generally presented their e-commerce wings as extensions of the banks (which the presence of Internet-only banks suggests need not necessarily be so), with an emphasis also on the flexibility of the concept and its links to traditional banking (manifested through the use of the logos and brand names of older banks, and of the same sorts of products and services). Again, the ways in which banks socially engage with each other and with the issues important with them shows a process of self-presentation which not only fits with their role as transnational business institutions, but with their current environment. Banks and bank employees are taking into account the diversity of the outside groups with which they must interact, and the internal diversity of

German transnational businesspeople as a group, and present themselves in ways which can accommodate this.

The way in which this process of strategic self-presentation took place points to diverse cultural elements within German transnational business, with different sorts of engagement with global and local cultures. The banks themselves, for instance, view presenting a global image as more important for the large banks than the smaller ones; similarly, the employees of different banks have different engagements with Germany and the globe, depending on the company's strategy and position. Furthermore, the issues affecting them tend to blend and intersect in interesting ways; the failed Rover-BMW merger at once refers to ambivalencies about Europeanisation on both sides, English xenophobia towards Germans, and the association of the manufacturing industries with discourses of Germanness. The diversity of elements within the German transnational banking world makes for much variation, and means that, even if the people and corporations within it are affected by the same issues, one cannot talk of a uniform German "business culture."

The diversity of strategic self-presentation can also be said to indicate the diversity of outside groups with which the banks must engage. For instance, in Germany, the adoption of the Euro sparked parties; the head office of one bank distributed packets of Euro-shaped sweets among the employees, and well into the autumn of 2000 one could buy Euro-commemorative souvenirs, including teddy bears, T-shirts and key chains, in most Frankfurt shops (see also *Spiegel* 1998b). That autumn, also, the city of Frankfurt sponsored a project in which schoolchildren and artists decorated four-foot-wide Euros, which were then displayed in the city centre and auctioned off for charity. In the City branches of German banks, by contrast, most employees said that there had just been a bit of extra work around the end of December 1998; there was no evidence of any particular celebrations or commemorative activities. Effectively, then, the ways in which the presentation of self was expressed and interpreted, were affected by the environment in which the expression was taking place.

There also appears to be a strong element of strategy in the banks' responses to the various issues at hand (cf. Schwarz 1989). Firstly, due to the considerable variation between German banks in terms of their economic niches, they all tend to follow different strategies. Within the City context, the larger banks tend to be competing with the larger transnational and global banks, where the smaller German banks seem to compete mainly against each other, and so the ways in which they present themselves are different. Similarly, the strategy one employs depends on the client; one senior manager, who had spent over ten years in the UK, said that he tended to emphasise the image of Germans as good businesspeople only when dealing with English clients. In general, then, banks present themselves according to strategies in response to outside trends.

As an example, consider the e-commerce boom. At the beginning of 2000, most people were talking publicly in terms of e-commerce as a symbol of the future and of a new global order, even if privately they expressed doubts. When the first major e-commerce failures occurred, in the middle of the year, it began to be spoken of more as a symbol of carelessness and poor business practice, of unrealistic beliefs in a global corporate utopia. This shifting of meanings in response to outside trends was, additionally, at least to some extent a conscious process. One UK-born senior manager, for instance, remarked in a formal interview that he felt that a particular programme which his bank was implementing was costly and not well-thought-of as a strategy by most of its managers. I asked him why they were implementing it, if this was the case. He responded that most other banks in the City were adopting similar programmes, and therefore they had to keep up or risk losing clients. The self-presentation of the German transnational businesspeople thus is done according to a strategy which takes into account local conditions and the actions of other groups, rather than simply occurring in response to internal and/or global trends, and this is consciously recognised by at least some of its members.

In sum, then, the City's German transnational businesspeople operate successfully in the social environment of the German bank branches and representative offices of the City of London. However, the ways in which they present themselves within this environment are made not as a solidary national or transnational group, but with reference to other groups of varying degrees of transnationalism. Furthermore, this process is subject to variation depending on the bank's position in the German and local market and with reference to wider trends in the financial world. Not only do the German transnational businesspeople and their banks represent themselves with reference to other things than simply the world of transnational capital or their country of origin, then, but they adjust their representations of Germanness in line with variations in outside circumstances, according to particular strategies.

## Analysis: Being German in Utopia

The German transnational businesspeople thus consistently appear, in the City of London, to project an image of unity which belies an actual diversity. The reason for this dichotomy lies not only in the shifting, fluid and complex nature of the City environment, but in the use of strategic self-presentation in the global financescape. We shall now look in greater detail at the role of self-presentation and culture in the City context.

### The Big Bang and Postmodernity

From 1986 onwards, and possibly since the oil shocks of 1973, the City has been in a state of perpetual flux, both in the financial sense of the "free fall" which the market has experienced since the end of the Bretton Woods agreement, and the social sense of the hire-and-fire, trend-following culture which has developed since then, finding its most recent manifestation in the recent spate of attempted mergers and joint ventures (Augar 2000; Fay 1988: 104-138). The City's present ethos, as has been said, embraces change and discontinuity; few City people stay more than a few years in the same job even if they continue to work for the same company, and City dress follows changes in fashion moreso than elsewhere, with the London

*Metro* (the free paper aimed at City commuters) devoting large sections to identifying the latest trends (for more on the use of newspapers in constructing City culture, see Owen 1999). Hence, perhaps, the lack of interest in the City's history on the part of its members, and their emphasis on the discontinuity of 1986 at the same time as their affirmation that London has always been global. The City is thus conceived of as an environment in constant flux, and paradoxically as always having been this way.

Furthermore, due to its engagement with globalisation, the City's ethos is best described as "postmodern," in Harvey's (1989) sense of being comprised of flux, fragmentation and discontinuity, all linked to technological change. City people often voice feelings that they are experiencing ever-more-rapid social changes around them, and tend to emphasise communications technology and travel, both in conversation and in daily activity (Leyshon and Thrift 1997; see also Augar 2000). This again fits with London's position as a global city; one of the reasons why so many financial companies choose to set up a branch in London is because of its position in the middle of the New York and Tokyo time zones, allowing people to operate in both markets, suggesting that time itself can be colonised (Douch n.d.: 57). It is possible, too, that the importance given to e-commerce and the way in which it was wholeheartedly embraced by the City was due to its fitting in with this ethos of change, global activity and discontinuity. The City is thus an example of a postmodern culture: globally engaged, in continuous flux, driven by changes in technology and transportation, and inhabiting, in a sense, a discontinuous, Utopian space—a place of people living, as one German auditor put it, "above the Earth."

Furthermore, the City contains diverse elements, all defining themselves through the possession of different interpretations for the same symbols. For an "old City" man, shopping at Harrods may be keeping up with tradition; for a "new City" man, it may be a way of demonstrating affluence; for a German expatriate, it may be a way of showing a *Weltoffen* appreciation for local specialities. The use of symbolic self-presentation thus provides a means of handling diversity and allowing for frequent changes within the City environment, in which no one group can exist without interaction with many if not all of the others, not to mention with groups outside the City.

*Self-Presentation and the City*

In such an environment, it should be not surprising that self-presentation through symbols takes on such importance. The City frequently underscores its position as *in* London but not *of* it through ceremonies such as the annual Lord Mayor's Show and signs such as the City police uniforms. There are also more subtle markers, such as the architecturally distinct mix of glass towers with old houses, which makes it possible to identify City areas in Canary Wharf and Knightsbridge. The nature of the City, in particular those traits which make it a "global" city, means that membership therein is more a matter of a symbolic code than anything else, and thus that the presentation of self takes on a great deal of importance, as it is through self-presentation that one marks out one's place—and thus, defines oneself—in the City environment.

The City's Germans, like the City itself, are, as we saw in Chapter 3, a discontinuous, fragmented and change-focused group, lacking a sense of connection with the earlier London German communities, and very much focused on the careers of individuals and temporary residence as a means of defining themselves. Like the City people, also, they present themselves as a group through such symbols as membership in particular organisations, sending their children to the same school, experience of expatriation and so forth. By defining their social structure through strategic self-presentation, the City's Germans remain a distinct group while still fitting in with their City surroundings, and can thus, as one German bank employee suggested, take the best of the German and the English worlds. The Germans thus inhabit two self-presentation-focused environments: the City and the German non-community.

The German transnational businesspeople, furthermore, like the City, include among themselves a diverse array of types of persons, professions, and working environments. Individuals may seem to form an undifferentiated transnational business culture when considered as a unit, but within this group one can see a number of differences with regard to length of (expected) stay in London, reasons for coming to London, areas of origin, professional specialty and so forth; additionally, these identifying factors vary over the course of an individual's working life. Like the City itself, then, the German transnational businesspeople comprise a number of different elements within the global financescape, and have different sorts of engagement with outside localities and global entities.

German companies in the City therefore employ symbols as a means of presenting themselves without reference to a common location or affiliations. German firms define themselves as a group with reference to their economic niche, position on Europe and marketing and client-finding strategies, and also by their long-termist hiring and business practices (see Stewart et al. 1994), and by their focus on the German or German-related markets. The employees of these firms have similar practices: the employees of one bank described their organisation as "just like any other merchant bank in the City"; the same employees, however, also noted that all their clients, German and non-German, had an interest in Germany. The self-presentation of their firms thus sets German transnational businesspeople off as a distinct group within the City, even as they form a part of it, indicating complex relations between cultural groups.

Due to the shifting, "Utopian" nature of the City, however, its Germans have of necessity to learn local meanings for particular symbols as well as their own. This process is visible in their interactions with English workmates; a new arrival generally stands out strikingly in terms of dress, manner and behaviour. One German who had lived in England for over ten years commented dryly that one could always identify visitors from Germany by their preference for clashing patterns and wildly contrasting colours, and another at one point remarked that the fact that Germans have smaller personal space and engage in more physical contact in daily interaction had caused one new arrival to appear overly forward with a colleague of the opposite sex. Within the space of three months they have usually altered all three to be more in tune with the local norm. Newcomers to the firm learn about where to go, what to eat, what to watch on television and where to shop from colleagues. Furthermore, while for the most part the governance of the City does not impact directly on them, they are affected on another level by its regulations and periodic displays of collective self-presentation (e.g. the Lord Mayor's Show) as well as by the English media. Finally, in the case of employees sent over from Germany by their firms, many have contact with relocation agencies, organisations which help them to get language lessons, rent houses, find the "right" schools for their children, arrange to move their families to England, and so forth, and through this learn the symbols and interpretations which are current in the City. The Germans thus learn local modes of self-presentation through various formal and informal channels, which they can put to strategic use in the City context.

Because of their engagement with multiple localities, also, the German transnational businesspeople have at the same time to deal with German modes of self-presentation. This is primarily, of course, because all the Germans in the study were socialised in a German context; in addition, all have greater or lesser continuing contact with the country. Short-term expatriates make frequent return visits; while longer-term residents may not return as frequently, there are few, if any, who lack an ongoing connection with Germany. The degree of contact also varies; someone who has not had much to do with Germany in the past may become more engaged with it when, for instance, she has children. Simply working at a German bank causes a degree of engagement with Germany. Many people, including some who were otherwise assimilated, read German newspapers and some magazines (although only a couple admitted to watching German television via satellite). The Germans thus both learn and maintain knowledge of particular ways of self-presentation in the German context through past and continued contact with Germany itself.

The flexibility of self-presentation, however, provides a means of handling this diversity of engagement, as actors present themselves within the City and global contexts using the same symbols of national culture, but distinguish themselves through the meanings they attach to them. The banks, for instance, present a united front to the outsider through their German names and focus on the German market; however, these same names and connections provide a means for people in the German business world to distinguish between them. Similarly, German transnational businesspeople share many of their symbols of self-presentation with the City as a whole, such as their emphasis on consumption, cosmopolitanism, business orientation and meritocracy; however, by virtue of their background and position, these all have different connotations for them. German newspapers, a symbol of Germanness for those who read them, form a symbol of global awareness when on a newsstand with French, Italian and American papers. Through the strategic use of self-presentation, German transnational businesspeople can remain a non-community, united and yet possessed of diverse elements at the same time.

This flexibility also comes into play in interactions with other German transnational groups, as with the students, refugees, and tourists. All can be said, and seem to be, German and cosmopolitan, and all use the same symbols when presenting themselves: all define Germanness through images of industry and Europe; all value "world-openness" and the ability to acculturate within other countries. However, a student's "world-openness" has a different sort of cultural capital than a businessman's, and "Europe" takes on a different meaning for an old refugee than for a young expatriate, even if the two are both, as one City thinktank member noted, influenced in their definition of it by images of WWII. Furthermore, all groups seem aware of the others' interpretations of the relevant symbols. Once again, it is the strategic use of flexible self-presentation which distinguishes these subgroups and yet allows movement between them.

*The City in Context*

Interactions in the global financescape appear to take place along similar lines. It cannot be denied, for instance, that the Germans do appear to form part of a global transnational capitalist class, as can be seen in their shared valuation of global consumption, cosmopolitanism, business orientation, financial engagement, meritocratic ethos, international education and the aesthetic view of history with other City professionals. Bank employees whom I interviewed, who had worked or were still working in New York, Hong Kong and Tokyo, also remarked upon common points between themselves and local employees in these cities on most of these points. Within this, however, they have a distinctive take on the meaning of these, shaped by their being German, the distinct corporate cultures of the institutions for which they work, and by their experiences of the City. Effectively, then, the City's Germans may seem to form part of an undifferentiated transnational culture in that they do hold common beliefs and present themselves in similar ways to others in the same profession. However, their particular interpretations of the symbols used in self-presentation set them off from other ethnic groups and professional elements within this wider social unit, meaning that they should perhaps not be considered simply as a transnational capitalist class, but as a series of groups linked together within a wider transnational social formation.

This internal diversity and external engagement among German transnational businesspeople is therefore made possible by flexible self-presentation. Because the meaning of a given symbol can vary with the circumstances, it allows the actor to vary his or her self-presentation accordingly; furthermore, it can allow for many different ways of being German, and define different groups within German transnational capitalism. It also allows them to engage with other groups, through adopting their meanings for the symbols which they have in common, or finding common ground for communication with them through these: while this can lead to misunderstandings (see Head [1992: 105-6, 112-113] on how English consumers read German automobile advertising), it can also be a means of positive self-presentation, as with the German bank employees who emphasise their bank's resemblance to local merchant banks in order to appear more locally oriented. Furthermore, individuals' self-presentations are not fixed; they continually learn new interpretations and ways of presenting themselves, and maintain an awareness of the changes in the received interpretations. Effectively, then, were it not for the flexibility of self-presentation and actors' abilities to learn and use other interpretations of symbols, they would be an undifferentiated elite global culture; as it is, however, they form a culture which learns and acts in response to other groups within and outside itself.

The flexibility of self-presentation, additionally, allows actors to switch between one set of meanings and another. For instance, when I asked a board member of the Bank of England whether he would describe it as an "English" institution, he first said that no, it was the bank of the United Kingdom, and then read some statistics to me from the personnel records, indicating that a sizeable percentage of the employees are non-English (see Kynaston 1995: 51-52). However, given the current emphasis on multiculturalism in England and the fact that England is the hegemonic voice within the United Kingdom (see Banks 1996: 159), not to mention the City's geographical location, the same symbols can cause the Bank to be English at the same time as it is being non-English; its service staff are clearly visible in the City due to their early eighteenth-century-style livery coats and top hats. Similarly, a bank can use its connection to Germany to symbolise either Germanness or cosmopolitanism in the UK context. What results is a complex engagement with multiple cultures and multiple forms of transnationalism, using the same symbols—but these exist in all the groups' repertoires, and consequently can be used to bridge the gap from one to the other. While the flexibility of self-presentation might at first seem to lead to homogeneity, in fact it encourages diversity, and facilitates a complex engagement which is at once local and global.

## The City's Germans: A Community or a Network?

The ways in which the Germans define themselves as a national group in the City, as elsewhere in London, also allow them to affiliate themselves with other groups as well, through their multivalent properties. Symbols representing Germanness, such as economic specialisation, a particular clientele, and a positive orientation towards Europe can also represent transnational business (see Head 1992). Furthermore, the historical German community, and other elements of the German diaspora, are defined using the same symbols as the German businesspeople (common residence, WWII, ethnic clubs and so forth), and yet the various groups view themselves as distinct from each other. The fact that the Germans are influenced by the self-presentation of other groups speaks of the use of self-presentation in the process of day-to-day interaction. In addition, the flexible properties of self-presentation explain the selective way in which the Germans can remain, as we saw in Chapter 3, a "non-community"—not a solidary unit but a flexibly connected population. Through strategic self-presentation, then, German transnational businesspeople can exist as a unit, as part of larger social units (e.g. the German diaspora) and can maintain diverse internal and external engagements.

Furthermore, the flexibility of self-presentation allows the Germans to interact with diverse groups in many settings simultaneously, as the interacting groups pick up on and react to each others' self-presentations in a process of mutual construction. The multivalent properties of symbols provide the common ground on which such interaction occurs, and allows a bank to operate in two contexts, Germany and the City, simultaneously: a bank may be a *Sparkasse* in Germany, but in the City it is just another German bank. The same process allows the City to be located "in" England but at the same time to be not actually "of" England. The engagement of both the German transnational businesspeople and the City with other groups and cultures of varying degrees of transnationalism is possible due to, and is carried out through, the strategic self-presentation of the groups involved.

German transnational businesspeople are therefore adept at switching back and forth between sets of symbols for self-presentation and the meanings assigned to them as part of their strategies in this symbol-focused, diverse environment (cf. Schwarz 1989: 41). The Germans in question have to operate in the same environments as the other groups mentioned. Consequently, they have to learn the meanings other groups attribute to the symbols they use in order to judge the impact of such means of self-presentation as advertising campaigns, self-presentation and market position. This also explains the importance of gossip, advertising and maintaining an Internet presence for achieving success in a transnational market through keeping abreast of the diverse interpretations of symbols. Furthermore, the manipulation of the symbols through which a company presents itself can to some extent allow it to adjust its image, even reconstruct itself totally. Many German banks attempt to appear "more global" by dropping the local tag from their name or disguising it, as in the case of WestLB and others; it is interesting, and rather telling, that the Big Three do not feel any need to do so. There is thus a strategic element to the self-presentation of actors in the City, as they attempt to define themselves as they feel best fits their situation.

In a complex, "Utopian" place such as the City, then, strategic self-presentation provides the means of constructing the environment, and thus it is essential for individual actors in the City to have a good grasp on modes of strategic self-presentation. Individuals and groups thus become expert at using the flexible meanings of symbols to present themselves as positively as possible to as many people as possible. It is this which allows the group to exist as a transnational social formation; symbolic self-presentation is therefore essential to their existence. As such, German transnational businesspeople are a varied and flexible, rather than homogenous and undifferentiated, social group.

The strategic use of self-presentation thus not only allows businesspeople to define the City as a social entity and its Germans to remain a distinct group within it, but allows the City to be global and the Germans to be a varied and diverse non-community linked to, but also removed from, the City. It seems that not only are the City and its German transnational businesspeople much more diverse and internally complex than traditional descriptions of national business cultures would suggest, but this complexity is in fact inherent in their nature as transnational social formations.

## Conclusion

An examination of the form, structure and history of City of London thus allows us to tentatively conclude that, while the German businesspeople who operate in it may appear to fit with the standard description of business cultures, both national and transnational, the shifting, financially-focused, globally engaged nature of both the City and the Germans themselves makes it difficult to claim either as an undifferentiated social formation. Similarly, the internal diversity of London's German population, the fact that its members act according to particular strategies which vary over the actor's life cycle, the different positions, cultures and strategies of the corporations they work for and the shifting, postmodern nature of the City, all combine to foster diversity and discontinuity rather than solidarity and unity. German transnational businesspeople thus appear to comprise a variety of modes of transnationalism and engagement with the financescape rather than be a single group with a uniform symbolic definition of Germanness. Through strategic self-presentation, German transnational businesspeople form part of an internally differentiated and externally engaged social formation, rather than a single, solidary class.

The Germans who work in London therefore, through their ways of portraying and experiencing the City, seem to present themselves as a unified elite business culture. However, their strategic use of self-presentation makes for a diversity of interpretation, suggesting that internal diversity and outside engagement, rather than homogeneity, is their defining property. While the City's Germans do in some ways appear to be a solidary unit, they are by no means a unified and united force, even in the financial Utopia of the City of London. We shall now consider whether this chapter's conclusions are supported by an examination of the transnational German and British employees of a specific German bank branch in the City.

Chapter 5

# Branch Mentality:
# Change and Self-Presentation in a
# German MNC

## Introduction

Much as the Germans in London appear in their personal lives and their interactions with the City's business community to be a solidary transnational group, yet on closer inspection appear to form a diffuse group, linked to many different cultures and incorporating a number of different subcultures within it, the same appears to hold true in their professional lives. As in the consideration of the City in Chapter 4, while a cursory examination of the structure and self-presentation of the London branch of a German bank might suggest that both it and its transnational German personnel are unified social formations, a closer inspection indicates a much more complex reality. In this chapter, I challenge the monocultural view of businesses by examining how a seemingly unified MNC branch in fact included at least four different subcultures, and how the failure to recognise this had a detrimental impact on the success of a restructuring programme aimed at bringing the branch into line with its Head Office.

As noted in Chapters 1 and 2, most of the literature on the cultures of the branches of MNCs tends to concentrate on whether the "home" culture (i.e. the culture of the MNC's country of origin) or "host" culture (i.e. the culture of the country in which the branch is situated) of the branches have the most influence on their cultural makeup (Mueller 1994). More recently, researchers have begun to take a more complex view, arguing that "country-specific patterns… interact with company-specific patterns to form varying blends" (Ibid., p. 40). Despite this, however, branches are still usually seen as having single cultures with little internal variation, and, although Kristensen and Zeitlin refer to company-wide internal power struggles (forthcoming), the agendas of individuals and groups within the company is also seldom considered. An examination of the way in which the employees of ZwoBank London describe the culture of their place of work, interact with each other and relate to the Head Office might well present an even more complex picture of culture in the global financial world, and suggest new insights into the way we view culture in MNCs and social behaviour in the global financescape.

## A Small World Here: ZwoBank as Seen by its Employees

Although an outsider coming into the London Branch of a German bank might see it as a unified institution whose members all define their national and business identities in much the same way, in fact, an examination of the ways in which they define themselves reveals a diversity of cultures within the same office. In this section, I will describe the culture (or cultures) of the bank which is the setting of the study, its London Branch and the different groups which can be found there, with a view to examining whether there is a single solidary culture or, instead, a system of diverse, ever-changing discourses with different sorts of links to each other and to the outside world.

### ZwoBank London

"ZwoBank" is a Frankfurt-based universal bank which, while it is one of the largest banks in Germany and maintains an above-average number of foreign branches, is still fairly limited in its international operations, a not-atypical state of affairs in German banking (see Ebster-Grosz and Pugh 1996). It has maintained a presence in London since the early 1970s, with a full branch being opened in the early 1980s. The longest-serving employee (a senior manager) had been with "ZwoBank London" for fifteen years at the time of the study, the shortest-serving (a trainee), three months, and the General Manager had been in his post for nearly ten years. The branch had about 160 employees, including trainee, temporary and service employees (the latter frequently being on contract from other organisations). Of these, about one-third were German, Swiss or Austrian, one-tenth were non-German foreign employees (mainly from former colonies of the United Kingdom) and the rest originated from the United Kingdom. Contrary to the usual pattern for German overseas bank branches, in which the German employees tend to be concentrated in the upper echelons, the Germans were fairly evenly distributed throughout the branch (Arthur D. Little Ltd. 1979: 73). This was partly due to the relatively large number of trainees, partly to a management initiative to place more UK employees in the top echelons of management, and partly to certain specialised functions within the branch's remit which required a knowledge of German, making the presence of a number of German-speaking front-line and junior-managerial employees necessary. Apart from its unusual ethnic distribution, then, the branch is more or less typical of the London branches of German banks.

When describing their workplace, employees tend to refer first to its economic activities. The focus of ZwoBank as a whole is on the German market; London Branch's main function is to administer its foreign investments (as opposed to supporting German clients in the UK—see Moore 1999). Employees also frequently referred to the branch's close-knit social structure (as defined in Bott 1957: 59-60). The branch boasted a subsidised onsite canteen and social activities prominently advertised in the branch newsletter, with group excursions once a month and branch-wide sports teams. Informal parties and pub nights were also regularly held, with news of these gatherings spreading by word of mouth. The branch was repeatedly described as a "very friendly office"; temporary employees and trainees were frequently encouraged to stay on after their initial contracts were finished. Occasionally, however, some were uncomfortable with this solidarity, one English middle-manager describing the branch as "like Sleepy Hollow," and a German who had been with the branch for over five years remarking with slight irony, "no one here is ever not happy." Employees felt less solidarity with the rest of the bank: interbranch exchanges and meetings occurred, but for the most part the branch seemed to be relatively isolated. To its employees, then, London Branch is "German-focused," "friendly," and "independent," in keeping with its role as the overseas representative of a German bank.

The branch occupied six floors of a brutalist building in the City, which two or three offices on each floor (the exceptions being the second and ground floors, which were taken up with meeting rooms, the canteen and the main reception area). All floors other than these also had a small kitchen with coffee machine, water cooler, fridge and bulletin board with announcements, adverts for charities, cartoons and flyers. The second and ground floors, as well as the third floor (which housed the HR department and senior managers' offices, and as such was the "backstage" area most likely to be seen by visitors to the branch), were decorated in a formal style, with thick pile carpets, rose-tinted walls, elegant rosewood-veneer contemporary furniture and pieces of modern art strategically placed about the corridors. Other floors (as well as the canteen area) were decorated in a more utilitarian fashion, with grey walls, industrial carpeting and fluorescent lighting; the furniture was more modern and functional, and the decorations, apart from a few potted plants, largely restricted to personal touches added by employees (for instance, posters, cartoons, calendars, and, in managers' offices, the occasional framed print or photograph). There was thus a sharp visual distinction between the "public" and "private" areas of the organisation.

All offices were open-plan, with managers' areas usually separated from the rest of the floor by glassed-in partitions, marking the social division between "managers" and "staff" (for clarity's sake, "employees" will refer to persons employed by the bank at all levels, and "staff" to those employees who are not managers). Beyond the managers' offices were small "islands" of desks, with employees with similar functions being grouped together in clusters of two to four. Desks were strongly associated with the people assigned to them: as one of the bank's maintenance men put it, "you need a desk. Even if you're never at your desk you need some place to pick up your mail." The fact that floor plans are continuously changing, with whole departments moving between rooms at a few days' notice, gives desks even more power as a means of self-presentation: the location of the person may shift, but their desk gives them a permanent presence in the office. This was further marked by the fact that a desk's occupant was expected to add items representative of their personality and interests: photographs and cartoons taped to the computer monitor, a stuffed toy or action figure perched on a corner, and so forth. The fact that all of these are easily transportable and yet instantly recognisable also contributes to the mix of permanency and flexibility seen throughout the branch. The office's geography is thus both stable and shifting, giving the impression of a culture at once static and in flux.

The official length of the working day is 9 AM to 5 PM, but this schedule was adhered to by very few. Most employees arrived by eight-thirty, and certain of the dealers were at work at seven in order to operate in the Japanese market. Most left between 5:15 and 6 PM, but on exceptional occasions people would work until eight or later. Additionally, in some departments, staying late had a quality of "machismo," as it were: one member of such a department half-seriously said that there was competition as to who stayed the latest. Lunch was usually half an hour long, taken between 11:30 and 1:00; sandwiches were also available for those who did not wish to leave their desks. Occasionally people would go "out to lunch" at a nearby restaurant; this was a special event, taking up to 1.5 hours and often ending with drinks at another establishment. These occasions, along with "meetings next door" (informal working sessions held in a nearby pub or cafe), tended to occur around the end of the week. This schedule seemed to be more or less typical for German bank branches in London.

*ZwoBank Head Office*

ZwoBank's Head Office, by contrast, consisted of a complex of modern buildings close to the centre of Frankfurt; the buildings were linked by a series of underground tunnels. At the time, it employed approximately two thousand people in total, with all employees belonging to particular departments generally being housed in the same area of the complex. The main building, containing the divisions most vital to the bank's functioning, had been completed in the late 1990s, with a grey marble-faced lobby sporting a rotating display of sculptures by modern German artists; visitors must announce themselves at a reception desk and wait in a designated area nearby to be picked up by an escort, usually followed by a trip through long underground tunnels or up high-speed elevators to some other part of the complex. Head Office is thus larger, newer-looking and more impersonal towards visitors than the branch.

Inside the main part of the building, the corridors were decorated in shades of grey, with art photographs at intervals. Each floor contained a small kitchen (none of which, as far as I could see, had bulletin boards), meeting rooms and offices. The offices themselves were sparsely decorated and painted in the same shades as the corridors, with two or three people sharing an office or two connected offices rather than the big open-plan rooms of London Branch. My impression was, however, that this was not as much of a deterrent to social interaction as might be thought, as people were frequently "out of the office," in quest of some colleague down the hall. The décor also tended more towards framed prints than pinned-up cartoons and calendars, and with fewer of the personal touches on the desks than was seen in London. One expatriate, Joachim (see below) described it by saying that "it's a lot of politics in the organisation, very bureaucratic. Here it is a small branch, no need to phone, you just go next door and talk to someone... in Head Office I would be one of many, but here I am just one."

Head Office is thus larger, more formal, possesses fewer demarcations between public and private areas, and maintains more obvious spatial divisions between employees than London Branch.

It was more difficult to tell whether, as many London employees asserted, employees in Head Office kept more rigorously to the traditional nine-to-five schedule than those in London: only one of my Frankfurt-based contacts, Michael, would see me outside of these hours, and he worked in a division which is said to keep an unusual schedule. In purely impressionistic terms, there were far fewer non-German employees at Head Office than there were non-English employees at London. While I could not obtain educational statistics on Head Office, I spoke with a number of people there who possessed postgraduate degrees, including doctorates, which was almost unheard-of in London. Head Office thus appears much larger, more monoethnic and more education-focused than London Branch; its employees are thus starting from a very different position than their London counterparts with regard to understanding the organisation.

Culturally, people at Head Office also tended to define themselves as "German," but in different ways to their colleagues at London Branch. Several spoke of its German focus and clientele: others, in terms of its relation to the German banking system as a whole. London, one said, may be a big branch, but the main reference point of the bank is Germany. Other than one (a HR manager), however, they did not speak of it having a "German" structure, but focused on its history and place in the German banking system, and of the distinguishing points of German law as it relates to banking and finance. Only two (again, both middle-managers with the HR department), furthermore, described the bank in terms of the reputed traits of German business culture such as bureaucracy, hierarchy, loyalty and long-termism (see Binney 1993; Lawrence 1980; Posen 1993). Michael, who was from a Front Office division, said that the bank as a whole is associated with Germany due to its links with *Mittelstand* companies, which are strongly tied up with discourses of Germanness (Hutton 1996: 266-267; *The Economist* 1995; Viehoff 1978: 11). As at London Branch, people at Head Office thus define the bank in terms of its relation to the German business world; however, their descriptions have a different emphasis.

In sum, then, ZwoBank appears to have a definite, unified corporate culture, based on its role as a German bank with overseas offices. There were, however, significant differences between London Branch and Head Office in terms of how they presented themselves as such, with London employees emphasising staff welfare programmes, English and German as the dominant languages, and the large number of German nationals among the staff, and Head Office emphasising their market specialities and target clientele. ZwoBank thus appears at first to be an undifferentiated business organisation, but the fact that even a cursory inspection reveals cultural differentiation within it strongly suggests that it is less solidary than it seems. We shall now consider the nature of social organisation at London Branch, and whether it does in fact consist of a solidary organisational culture, a mixed culture in which British and German business cultures are opposed, or something rather more complicated.

## Four into One: The Cohorts of ZwoBank London

Although conventional wisdom would suggest that ZwoBank London should either consist of a solidary Anglo-German culture, a transnational capitalist class dominating a local subaltern class, or two national cultures (possibly interacting to form a "third culture"), the reality was somewhat different. In terms of national culture, four social groups could be broadly discerned within London Branch, which were distinguished by use of language (which is the subject of the next chapter, and so will be only superficially dealt with here), favourite topics of discussion, sitting together at lunch and in meetings, and so forth. These categories, which I will outline below, can best be described as "semi-indigenous." That is to say, people at the branch definitely spoke in terms of it being divided between "English" and "German," and acted in ways which presupposed the existence of two further subdivisions of this, but in the final analysis these groups are an artificially simplified classification device used for the convenience of analysis. For the purposes of this chapter, however, we shall divide up the employees according to these categories. The term "cohorts" will be used to refer to these groupings, in order to avoid confusion with any other sort of social group which may be referred to in this chapter.

### Cohort One: German Expatriates

The first cohort was the *German expatriates*, which can be split into two further subgroups: specialists and trainees. The specialists, much like the elite labour migrants described by Beaverstock over a series of articles (1991, 1994, 1996a, b, c), had been brought over from Head Office to remedy a skill shortage or ease a department through a transition period, usually for between one and three years. All had at least a vocational-college education; most were in their thirties, had spent seven to nine years at Head Office, and, with one or two exceptions, had prior experience of living, studying and/or working in London. All had volunteered to be there, mainly to gain international experience and/or to "see the world." Trainees, similarly, were either from other branches of the bank or from an outside trainee programme, and had applied to spend time in London. All were or had recently been students in higher education, and were with London Branch for between three and eighteen months; most were from small German towns. They formed a close-knit social group, spending most of their free time together, and were the subject of gentle teasing by more long-established employees. As most were not directly involved in the restructuring of the bank, they do not figure heavily in this chapter. The expatriate employees thus seem to be a unified group, but are a relatively small part of the organisation.

In terms of their business practices, the expatriates tended more towards the German than the UK model of business. Most did make an effort to accommodate certain UK practices—one expatriate, for instance, made a point of speaking to UK visitors about the weather for approximately two minutes before getting down to business talk, in line with what most guides to UK business say is polite (e.g. Hickson and Pugh 1997)—but most of these were either superficial, as in the example given above, or to do with laws and regulations which they were unable to break. Although they were happy to adopt certain UK practices, such as flexible meeting times, they tended to focus more on bureaucracy and procedure than more UK-focused employees, and occasionally complained about certain aspects of flexible working: "I want to spend my free time at home, with my family, not working," said one expatriate. The expatriates thus formed a subculture within ZwoBank London which was distinct from other German groups in terms of its attitudes and practices.

## Case Study: Joachim

*Joachim is thirty-four, and had worked for ten years at a financial consultancy in Frankfurt before accepting a job in the Auditing division of ZwoBank; his previous job had involved frequent periods in London, New York and Singapore, and so he was considered a good prospect to go to ZwoBank London to implement the new, matrix-structured reporting system which was intended to bring ZwoBank London in line with the other branches. Colleagues generally described him as "friendly" and "social" but also as "very German" and "very correct and bureaucratic." Joachim has a wife, also working in the financial industry, who remained in Frankfurt, but he frequently visits her at the weekends—taking advantage of cheap London-to-Frankfurt flights—and she is hoping to arrange to take a job in London later in the year to be able to join him.*

## Cohort 2: Locally Hired Germans

The second cohort was the *locally hired Germans*. They were fairly diverse in terms of age, background and length of time at London Branch, but all were living in England permanently for one reason or other which was not business-related. They tended to be more oriented to UK than to German business practices and culture, and are seen by many UK employees as "more like Anglo-Saxons than the other Germans" (to quote one UK-born male senior staff member). Most have worked at other (frequently, though not always, German) financial institutions before coming to this bank, and tend to follow the City pattern of employment; all are fluently multilingual, and do not show any particular solidarity with each other or the expatriates. The Germans of London Branch are therefore not a united group, national or transnational, but an assortment of people with greater and lesser orientations to Germany and the UK.

In terms of business practices and subculture, the locally-hired Germans are harder to distinguish within the organisation than the expatriates. Nonetheless, they could be distinguished from other groups by their distinctive mix of German and UK business practices: while, for the most part, they tended to adhere to and embrace UK practices and business culture over German ones, they tend to slip easily back into German practices when necessary, albeit with a certain amount of complaint and criticism. Much as Germans in the rest of London form a kind of "invisible community," the local hires do form a kind of "invisible business culture" within the organisation, sometimes in line with and sometimes opposed to that of the expatriates.

## Case Study: Jutta

*Jutta came to the UK from Munich twenty years ago to be with her English fiancé (they later married, then divorced). Since arriving, she has had a variety of jobs in the City, mostly in German banks but including a stint with a well-known UK merchant bank. Currently, she is the manager of a team dedicated to selling and advising on a specialised financial service, SPIRE System, which consists largely of young German local hires, trainees and Germanophiles. She prefers to speak English to German, and makes jokes about the negative traits of Germans, such as poor dress sense, drunkenness and xenophobia; she seldom talks about Germany otherwise. She has two teenage children and an American partner.*

## Cohort Three: "Germanophiles"

The third cohort consisted of *"Germanophiles"*: non-German (normally British) staff members who felt a strong connection with Germany and its culture, and who spoke the language with relative fluency. This group showed a good deal of variation, including as it did people with German partners, ethnic Germans born elsewhere, and people who had been sent on employee exchanges to Head Office. Some had joined the bank due to their interest in Germany, while others had acquired their interest due to working at the bank. Many also form part of the pool of German-speaking skilled workers who circulated among the German banks of the City, along with German local hires and a scattering of Swiss and Austrians (see Wraight 1991). Most, though not all, tended to have university degrees, and to socialise mainly with each other and with German employees. Some British people were thus more oriented to Germany than others.

The business practices and culture of this cohort were at first glance broadly similar to those of the local hires, in that they tended to be a mix of UK and German practices with an emphasis on the UK. However, there was a subtle distinction in terms of orientation, in that the Germanophiles tended to be proud of their ability to adapt rapidly to German business practices, and to be openly critical of UK business culture, whereas the local hires tended to play down their connections with Germany and to express more positive feelings about Germany. Although this cohort does share a number of traits with that of the local hires, the Germanophiles definitely had a distinctive organisational subculture, rather than being consistently united with either the Germans or the other non-Germans in the organisation.

*Case Study: Brigit*

*Brigit was born and raised in Northern Ireland, where she studied German to A-level. While attending university in Birmingham—where she studied German literature—she took a year off to teach English in Dusseldorf, which she thoroughly enjoyed. After finishing university, she took a job with ZwoBank London in the SPIRE System product division, intending to stay only a short while, but has now been with the bank for five years and was recently made a junior manager. She has a partner but no children, and frequently expresses the ambition to go back to university and do postgraduate work once she and her partner are in a financial position to do so.*

*Cohort Four: "Anglophiles"*

The final cohort is the *"Anglophiles"*: UK-born, mostly English, employees with no particular connection to Germany or German banking beyond their having been hired by this particular corporation. This is not to say that they bear any particular antipathy towards Germany, but they were not as strongly oriented towards it as other groups. They tended to conform more to City norms and behaviour; few had university degrees, most having been educated on the job. They were, however, no less transnational than other groups, frequently travelling or having worked abroad, or having relatives and friends in other countries. Their business practices and culture tended to be firmly oriented towards the British norm, although this did not mean they were entirely uncritical of it. The bank branch under study thus contains a number of diverse groups, all of whom approach their workplace from different starting points, rather than simply dividing on grounds of nationality or global orientation.

*Case Study: Keith*

*Keith is fifty-two, and a senior manager with ZwoBank. He started work at a large English bank after leaving secondary school, and continued working there until he lost his job during the "Big Bang" of the 1980s and took up a managerial post at ZwoBank which he has held ever since. In the late 1970s, he spent two years as an expatriate in Hong Kong, and has travelled to most of the major financial centres of the world, as well as holidaying regularly in the USA, a country of which he is very fond. He is married; one of his children is travelling around Australia before starting at London Business School, and the other is working for a Dutch bank branch in Singapore.*

**Table 5.1 Summary of cohorts and cohort positions**

|               | Origin  | German orientation | UK orientation | Business practices | Head Office      |
|---------------|---------|--------------------|----------------|--------------------|------------------|
| **Expatriates**   | German  | strong             | weak           | German             | Pro              |
| **Local Hires**   | German  | medium             | strong         | German/UK          | Con              |
| **Germanophiles** | British | strong             | medium         | UK/German          | No preference    |
| **Anglophiles**   | British | weak               | strong         | UK                 | Con              |

*The Cohorts' Positions on ZwoBank*

The German expatriates described ZwoBank's culture in terms evoking a particular sense of Germanness. They emphasised its position in the German banking system, comparing its history and structure with those of other German banks. All spoke of the "Germanness" of the institution as a whole in terms of its focus and "business culture," by which they seemed to mean the sets of vaguely stereotypical "traits" attributed to businesses from particular national origins in business literature (e.g. Trompenaars and Hampden-Turner 1996, Hickson and Pugh 1997). However, when describing London Branch, they tended to focus on stereotypically "Anglo-Saxon" traits. Most also described the branch as being in tension between the Anglo-Saxon and German banking systems, the trainees adding to this the perplexity with which they viewed the English bureaucracy in general. One noted London Branch's small size relative to Head Office, and one brought up the paradox of London Branch being smaller than Head Office but "more global" because of its place in the City, and thus being at once superior and inferior to the Head Office. The bank was thus presented by the expatriates as German, with London as an aberrant segment.

All expatriates also emphasised what they saw as the multiculturalism of London Branch as a sign of cosmopolitanism (*Weltoffenheit*), one of them, a single man who had spent a year in London as a student ten years earlier, saying "So London, there is a small world here." It is significant that the branch is actually not very multicultural in British terms, in that there were relatively few non-White or non-European employees, and the European employees were divided mainly only between two ethnic groups, English and German. However, by the standards of Head Office, in which I did not see a single non-White bank employee and very few non-Germans, the branch was multicultural. Once again, also, very few expatriates particularly discussed UK culture, except with reference to the images of UK "business culture," taken more or less wholesale from interculturalist texts (see Schnyder 1989). Asked how they would define their *Heimat* (see Chapter 3), some expatriates gave fairly classic descriptions, referring directly to particular regions where they were born or where their family came from; others, however (generally those who were better-travelled), said either "the world," or "Europe."

The German expatriates thus described London Branch as "global," but the terms they used were ones associated with German culture.

Finally, a few described the branch in terms of a conflict between English and German "business cultures," as defined by popular business literature (see, among many others, Scheuermann 1997; Hickson and Pugh 1997; Trompenaars and Hampden-Turner 1996; Lynn 1997). While the employees generally believed that the traits attributed to each nationality were actually present, they tended to use the concept of "national business cultures" more as a marker of the division between "English" and "Germans" in the office; they did not anticipate inevitably finding "English" or "German" traits in their colleagues in actual practice. The ways in which German expatriates describe the bank and its London branch thus emphasise its Germanness in particular ways.

Locally hired Germans define the bank's culture in similar ways to the expatriates, but with significant differences in emphasis. While they too spoke of the bank in terms of its position in the German banking world, only one, Lise, a senior manager who was in regular contact with Head Office, referred to its history and structure. Others spoke about it in comparison to other German banks, at whose offices some of them had worked. They also described the bank in terms of its German focus and business culture. Jutta, for instance, noted that the average length of service for employees was quite long in comparison to similar banks in other European countries, and one middle-manager noting the relatively high degree of centralisation of the bank (see Stewart 1994: 81). While only Jutta's supervisor, a German senior manager in his mid-forties, spoke of the branch's multiculturalism as a distinguishing feature, most defined its business culture as "a mix" of English and German traits. All, however, emphasised the difference between English and German business cultures, and in virtually identical terms to those used by the expatriates. The local hires did, however, tend to speak in more general terms rather than applying lists of traits to the bank in question:

> **Jutta:** The real difference between English and German is how they react. Germans like to argue and the English never do. It's not that they won't disagree, it's that they'll disagree with you behind your back. Whereas German people will argue in meetings.

They also tended to express more ambivalence about the benefits of the bank's German focus than the expatriates. The same descriptions of the bank's culture were used by the local hires and the expatriates, but with slightly different glosses.

The concept of *Heimat* was more complicated for the local hires than the expatriates. Some, interestingly, said that they had no sense of *Heimatsgefuhl* (feeling of *Heimat*) for any particular place, German or otherwise. Jutta said that she thought of England as her *Heimat* when she was in Germany and Germany as her *Heimat* when she was in England. A female P.A. in her late twenties, Greta, identified as a "cosmopolitan" (she used the English word) which she seemed to define in the Hannerzian sense of being open to all cultures but also a bit removed from them (1990: 238). Those who did claim a *Heimat* tended to name a city to which they had moved rather than their birthplace, suggesting that they defined their positions relative to Germany with a degree of detachment, and thus had more of a stake in emphasising the mixing rather than the tension between groups in the branch (compare Borneman and Peck 1995: 76). East Germans usually claimed the Western region where they settled after coming over from the East as their *Heimat*, rather than their birthplace. A few—generally older employees, and usually managers—claimed London or England as *Heimat*, and one, slightly younger than average, named Europe. The locally hired Germans thus defined *Heimat* in a more complex way to the expatriates, and, while they used much the same terms to define the bank's culture, interpreted it in a subtly different way.

The Germanophiles, like the expatriates, also focused upon the bank's place in the German banking world. However, the Germanophiles defined it in terms of its smallness and insularity rather than its structure and history; it was through them that I learned about the presence of the labour pool of German-speaking skilled workers. Many were more emphatic about the bank's Germanness than were their German colleagues. Brigit said that the bank was not so much "global," as a German organisation pretending to be global through maintaining overseas branches whose focus was nonetheless German. Like other cohorts, they spoke in terms of German and Anglo-Saxon "business cultures," and described these in virtually identical terms to the others, referring to Germans' reported emphasis on bureaucracy and focus on the long-term customer relationship over the quick deal (see Carr et al. 1994: 210, The Bank Relationship Consultancy 1997). Unlike the native Germans, however, they focused on such minutiae as German dress styles, body language, and attitude to the working day, as witness this remark by Tom, a male staff member in his forties, who had participated in an exchange to Frankfurt a few years earlier:

> It strikes me that the Germans... don't work as hard as we do. You see them and they're always having a laugh. It's like the Americans.... They never work late, they've always got their free time— they get the job done, but they work smart not hard. I was in a meeting in Frankfurt and at 7:30 these guys just walked out, said they couldn't stay past 7:30. End of story.

The Germanophiles thus had similar definitions of Germanness to both groups of Germans, but interpreted these definitions in different ways to them.

The Germanophiles tended to express the bank's cosmopolitanism differently to the Germans, however, seeing it as stemming from the bank's German connection. They distinguished themselves by a willingness to talk about Germany with other Germanophiles and with Germans (although not so much with the Anglophiles). Interestingly, where the locally-hired Germans tended to distance themselves from Germany through loss or transformation of *Heimat*, Germanophiles achieved the opposite through constructing "ersatz *Heimats*," claiming *Heimat*-like affiliations with the part of Germany where they once lived, or with their partner or parent's *Heimat*. The German language, similarly, is for them both a symbol of personal status as a Germanophile, and of the bank itself. Once again, the Germanophiles define the bank and London Branch in the same terms as German colleagues, but with different interpretations.

Anglophiles also had more or less the same descriptions of German and ZwoBank culture as their colleagues, but again, with different interpretations. The structure of German banking did not feature strongly in their descriptions; however, its "business culture" was once again said to be very significant. Once again, this was explained in the same terms drawn from popular business literature, without reference to other forms of "culture." Keith argued during several formal interviews that there was a fundamental conflict between the Anglo-Saxon and the German business cultures of the branch, the former being, in his opinion, conflict-oriented, the latter being consensus-oriented. He also repeatedly stressed the hierarchical nature of German business as compared to what he saw as the egalitarian UK one. Other Anglophiles of all ages and backgrounds spoke in terms of textbook images of German bureaucracy—one junior manager, Steve, complaining "if your head's on fire in this organisation, you can't put it out with a bucket of water without the proper forms"—sense of humour, and so forth, recalling such works as Lane (1989) and Lawrence (1980). As with the expatriates, the ethnic mixing of the branch was a defining marker of its cosmopolitanism for Anglophiles, but the Anglophiles focused more on the relatively high percentage of English managers than did the expatriates. The Anglophiles' use of descriptions of the culture of both the bank and the branch thus superficially resembled that of the other cohorts, but was aimed largely at defining differences between Englishness and Germanness.

The Anglophiles, like the expatriates, also tended to focus on the Englishness of the branch. When preparing for the annual interbranch football tournament, younger English staff members suggested making UK-style football-fan gear for the London Branch cheering section. Afterwards I was informed by those who had attended (mainly young and single employees, with one or two older and/or attached ones who were either skilled footballers or were among the branch's "party animals") that London "lost the game but won the partying," evoking images of rowdy UK football supporters. The trainees, similarly, were often said by older Anglophiles to have spent too much time in higher education and not enough learning the ways of the world, reflecting a common Southern English working-class view about the value of education vis-à-vis experience. All Anglophiles seem to take for granted the presence of diverse ethnic minorities more than do the Germans. In sum, then, the Anglophiles define the bank and its London branch in much the same ways as the other groups, but the meanings and interpretations which they associate with these are different.

*Analysis*

It thus seems that all the cohorts at the branch do define the bank's culture in similar ways. However, the interpretations of it vary from organisational subculture to organisational subculture. All, for instance, spoke of the branch as having a combination of German and English "business cultures," and did this using virtually the same trait-focused model of "culture" in all cases. Despite this, whether these "cultures" were described as mixed, harmonised or in conflict varied from group to group, in accordance with its position in the branch. While all acknowledged the German business system as a distinguishing feature of the bank as a whole, the significance of this varied depending on whether the speaker was from a group regarded as "close to" or "distant from," Germany and/or Head Office. Multiculturalism and was also said to be a key part of the branch's "culture," but where the Anglophiles construed this as "taking a global perspective," other groups tended to refer to it in terms of ethnic mixing. The definition of "multiculturalism" varied considerably. Finally, as seen above, definitions of *Heimat* varied strongly from group to group. Again, then, people at London Branch define the institution's culture in similar terms, but with different interpretations, suggesting not a matter of solidary cultures belonging to particular groups, but diverse interpretations of symbols and forms of self-presentation interacting in a dynamic process.

The key to the differences in interpretation appears to hinge on the position which each cohort occupies relative to the others in the branch, and on their strategic activities relative to each other within the institution. During formal interviews, I was aware not only that my interviewees were making their statements with reference to their own agendas vis-à-vis the HR department (which I believe also affected what was said to me in less formal contexts), but that, in volunteering, they were acting for reasons relating to their personal interests and strategies. In addition, the expatriates' representations of themselves and the bank shifted gradually over the course of the study, as they picked up on and adopted local discourses of culture. This suggests a strategy for adaptation to, and cooperation in, different settings, much as Beaverstock (1996a: 468) describes expatriation as not only the transfer of knowledge, but as the embedding of labour in a local context, and the development of networked social relations. The definition of the bank's culture thus does not only vary from cohort to cohort, but according to the cohort's position and agenda within the group as a whole, meaning that the use of culture has a strong element of strategy to it.

Finally, it is worth noting that these strategies are developed and implemented with reference to other cohorts and their positions in the branch. A German who describes London Branch as more "deal-focused" than Head Office, to take but one example, is adopting a symbol used by the Germanophiles and the Anglophiles to define UK business culture (see Peppercorn and Skoulding 1987). It is also significant that all four groups, despite their different origins, had very much the same definition of "business culture" and what it entailed (see Wright 1994: 1-5). Thus, no cohort is operating in a vacuum, but all are learning from, and acting in response to, other groups within and outside the bank and its London branch, hence the differences in their interpretations.

As was the case for the German expatriates considered in Chapter 4, then, London Branch thus seems to present a unified front as a German bank branch in the City of London. Within this apparent unity, however, one may discern at least four different cohorts, all of which describe their national culture and that of their workplace in similar ways, but which distinguish themselves through different interpretations of these cultures. The diversity of interpretation, furthermore, hinges upon the fact that each cohort has a different position with regard to the rest of the bank, and acts strategically with reference to the actions of other groups. Therefore, the MNC seems to be unified, but in fact incorporates a number of diverse groups, who may or may not be in accord with each other, suggesting again that culture in MNCs is not so much a matter of solidary or bounded groups possessing particular traits, but of fluid and dynamic ways of representing oneself being used in a dynamic process of expressing different allegiances within a wider transnational society.

## Matrix Revolutions: The Restructuring of a German Bank

At the time of the study, the bank had embarked upon a restructuring initiative, which it had almost completed by the time I left in June. The first involved the matrix integration of the bank, to be followed later by a merger with a second bank (which will not be discussed here for confidentiality reasons). This event was not only disruptive to the bank's established culture, but, within London Branch, immediately set the stage for a conflict between the British branch which did not wish to change, and the German Head Office imposing changes upon it. An examination of how the different cohorts reacted to this programme reveals not only their different positions within the branch, but also how their definitions of culture relate to their particular strategies for action. By looking closely at how the different cohorts reacted to the restructuring initiative, we can see whether they do in fact form two solidary national cultures, or one national and one transnational culture, or whether, instead, they react to a crisis in different ways, along the lines of the social orientations described above.

### Background to the Matrix Integration

From its establishment until July 1999, London Branch had effectively operated autonomously from the rest of the bank; the heads of individual departments reported to the General Manager, who mediated between the branch and the Head Office, and who was as such the only employee in regular contact with superiors in Frankfurt. Under the matrix integration, however, individual department heads now reported directly to individual departmental superiors in Frankfurt, in what was referred to as a "matrix integration structure"; rather than viewing themselves as members of a local business within a financially-focused global city, then, London employees now have to consider themselves as a local segment of a German-focused, but global, business group. My own position within the bank was related to this initiative, as I had been brought in about six months into the process with instructions to assess the impact of the restructuring on Anglo-German relations in the branch. The new initiative thus entailed a number of changes in the social organisation of the bank for its employees, particularly with regard to the relationships of local and global cultures.

The main result of the changes was that many employees were brought into closer daily contact with Head Office, and that there was an increased presence of visitors and expatriates from Frankfurt at the London branch. At Head Office, those involved with the restructuring expressed the hope that the initiative would bring the foreign branches more into line with the domestic group, some saying that they felt that the increased contact would allow Head Office to learn from the branches and vice versa. By contrast, London employees expressed a sense of uncertainty regarding the outcome; many spoke of practical problems of adjusting London Branch to the Head Office system, and an atmosphere of suspicion prevailed. The result of the initiative was thus to cause the branch's employees to engage in strategic activities in order to establish themselves within the renewed institution to their best advantage. It remains to be seen, however, whether these strategic activities took place along the cohort lines described above, along lines of national culture, or with one group operating according to local, and the other to global, interests.

This tension was also visible in a two-day meeting of HR managers from all non-German branches of ZwoBank and the Head Office in order to discuss the form that the structure and culture of the reorganised bank should take. Much of the meeting seemed to involve defining ideals which they felt the restructured organisation should hold, which were expressed in very general terms such as "fairness," "success driven" and "responsive and flexible" rather than with reference to the specific (and possibly contested) symbols of national culture which employees expressed outside of such meetings. This suggests that, by sticking to neutral terms, participants were avoiding potentially controversial subjects. Despite this, however, a kind of counter-discourse of culture existed under the surface: when the meeting was unable to achieve all its stated goals before the end of the session, the Germans wanted to stop and make do with what they had done, while the English and American employees wanted to schedule another meeting in order to complete all their goals. A marked ambivalence was also visible, with attendees tending to sit with their fellow branch- or office-members rather than to mingle. While there was more mixing during the coffee breaks, conversation was mainly on neutral topics such as work and travel, significantly, avoiding the contested questions of national culture in favour of "cosmopolitan" images of the transnational business lifestyle. When the new system was discussed, it was mainly through jokes, suggesting both a certain tension and the tacit redrawing of social boundaries to fit the new organisation (see A. Cohen 1985: 31). The meeting thus suggested that part of the strategic activity which took place around the bank was an active redefinition of the culture of the organisation, with particular regard to its relationship to German and British national cultures. In a situation in which visible lines are drawn between national cultures, then, it is open to debate what impact this will have on the tacit diversity of the culture of London Branch.

*Reactions of the Cohorts*

The different cohorts, significantly, all reacted to the restructuring in different ways, which reflected their different positions relative to Head Office and to each other. The German expatriates, to begin with, described themselves as forming a bridge between Head Office and London Branch, as all had been sent from Head Office to ease key departments into the transition. Most of them described the initiative in terms of London's former independence, and its being brought into line with the rest of Head Office. They said that Head Office had, and still has, very little to do with London and consequently has difficulty understanding the culture (by which, as above, they seemed to mean the mixed Anglo-Saxon/German "business culture" which they attributed to London Branch). Some, generally those in functions, also spoke of the tension caused by the fact that they had taken jobs which local employees had wanted. They noted that the reporting structure brought in by the initiative is not new for them as it is to other London employees, and one even questioned the applicability of Head Office's structure to the much smaller branch. The expatriates thus described themselves as mediators between the global Head Office and the local London Branch, in line with the way in which they define themselves elsewhere.

The expatriates, furthermore, described the initiative very much in terms of tension between German and British business cultures. Joachim said that the main issue was that in Head Office "you get people who've never been outside Germany... who have difficulty understanding certain things which are going on over here." He noted that in his experience Germans, if they say they will call at 9:00 AM, will call at that time and be upset when nobody is there to talk with them, and do not like working on their lunch hour. The English, he explained, expect delays because of their legendarily bad transportation system, and have less of a problem with a flexible schedule, working through lunch if necessary. Furthermore, the expatriates tended to broaden their focus to speak of the differences between the educational systems, social systems, and career paths of UK and German bank employees (although, significantly, they did not refer to these as "culture"), rather than simply focusing on the business aspects of culture. For instance, the length of time which the expatriates had spent working at a single bank was considered unusual among British people of the same age. The expatriate employees thus not only portrayed themselves as bridging the segments of the bank to develop a global organisation, in line with their position as a German group with a global orientation and a positive view towards Head Office, but also adapted extant descriptions of the branch's culture, regarding its Anglo-German cultural influences, to support this self-presentation.

The locally hired Germans also defined their position vis-à-vis the restructuring as a transnational, culture-bridging role, but in a different way to the expatriates, presenting themselves as both German and of the City rather than as external mediators. Many described their role in the branch as that of interpreters between German and English, linguistically and culturally; they often expressed frustration with both Anglophiles and recent expatriates, due to their lack of familiarity with the customs of other group. Jutta had been asked to head up a project "mediating UK and German business culture" within the restructuring. Most, interestingly, did not speak of the restructuring so much in terms of the globalisation of the bank as in terms of its Europeanisation, which has more positive connotations for Germans. This seems to be particularly true for Germans living abroad, as an identification as "European" allows them to present themselves both as German and cosmopolitan. Many, also, seemed to feel that their origins might cause people to assume them to be partial to Head Office; all members of this cohort often began sentences with "While I'm German, I disapprove...." The locally hired Germans thus expressed their role in the matrix integration using the same terms as the expatriates, but with different interpretations of their role in accordance with their different position in the branch. They presented the situation not so much in terms of general tensions between Anglo-German business cultures as in terms of local conflicts, and emphasised that their ethnic origins did not necessarily make them partial to Head Office. Rather than all the Germans in the branch presenting a united cultural front, then, there are strong differences between the reactions of the recent expatriates and the local hires, suggesting that culture does not follow along national lines within ZwoBank London.

The Germanophiles also, like the Germans, described themselves as a transnational elite mediating between Germany and the City, but once again the interpretations which they gave these were slightly different. Like the locally hired Germans, they expressed frustration with what they perceived to be the other two groups' local orientation, and were in fact more critical of the Anglophiles than were both groups of Germans. Germanophiles who had participated in company programmes which allowed them to spend time in Head Office and "learn the culture" often criticised Anglophiles for not taking advantage of such programmes. Interestingly, by this they seemed to mean the wider culture of Germany rather than only its "business culture." Like the Germans, the Germanophiles spoke in terms of clashes of national business cultures within the restructuring. However, they implied that this was less an inevitable conflict, and more a matter of individuals failing to understand; significantly, by doing so, they can acknowledge their own connection to German culture despite their being technically outsiders to it. Not only does culture not follow national lines, then, there also does not seem to be a firm division between the transnational capitalist class and local subaltern classes.

The Germanophiles, like the other groups, tended to emphasise the Germanness of Head Office. One middle manager, Toby (who shortly thereafter accepted a job at another bank), prior to making a comment critical of his Frankfurt opposite number, asked me "have you any German blood?" implying, like the local hires, that German ethnic origin implied approval of Head Office. Many also described the initiative as an aggressive action on the part of Head Office, saying that it imposed a new set of rules, nomenclature and structure on the branch without consulting those directly affected. Again, then, the Germanophiles defined the issues involved in the initiative in similar ways to the German employees, but with an angle on the affair which emphasised the responsibility of individuals rather than the effect of external "cultures," again bolstering their own claim to Germanness and the possibility of national lines to be crossed.

Finally, the Anglophiles, like the three other cohorts, describe themselves as a transnational elite bridging the gap between cultures. However, in this case they do this by separating the German and the transnational, presenting the City as globally oriented and Head Office's focus as overly local. Most spoke in terms of "English" and "German" business cultures, but as the imposition of one upon the other rather than as conflict between them, as witness this statement from an interview with Keith:

> What we've got here is a structure which derived from Head Office—in a branch. Which is in my judgement organised as if it were part of the Head Office. You've got a bunch of people in a different country, with a different character and background, and a different sort of—a different *understanding* of the way business functions.

The Anglophiles thus defined the initiative and their position with regard to it in similar terms to the other groups, but their interpretations of the relationship between "business cultures" is quite different to that of the others, portraying the situation in terms of hostile takeovers rather than misunderstandings and bridges. There thus does not appear to be a single "German" and a single "British" way of reacting to the restructuring; furthermore, all groups appear to take transnational *and* local issues into account in their reactions to it.

*Analysis: Considering the Positions*

The branch which appears to be unified on one level, therefore, in fact incorporates several different subgroups, each with a slightly different position with regard to Head Office and the matrix integration. Significantly, these neither follow on national lines, nor on lines defining a transnational/local power relationship. The

**Table 5.2 Differences in cohorts' descriptions of the restructuring**

|  | Cohort role is: | Restructuring is: | Restructured bank is: | Head Office is: |
|---|---|---|---|---|
| **Expatriates** | Bridging gap | Globalisation | Global | Benign |
| **Local Hires** | Interpreting | European-isation | European | Ignorant |
| **Germanophiles** | Facilitating intercultural understanding | Cultural merger | Anglo-German | Failing to understand |
| **Anglophiles** | Defending London | Takeover | German | Hostile |

expatriates spoke in terms of broad differences between national business cultures and the need to bridge the gap between Head Office and London Branch; the local hires focused instead on the day-to-day problems of individuals adjusting to a new system, distancing themselves from Head Office as they did so. The Germanophiles, by contrast, focus on the globalisation-related aspects of the situation, presenting the problem less as one of national cultures and more of lack of "cosmopolitan attitudes." Finally, the Anglophiles present the situation almost as one of cultural imperialism on the part of Head Office. Although one might, broadly speaking, argue that all the issues stem from the fact that a German Head Office was brought into closer contact with its UK branch, in practice each of the cohorts has slightly different issues within this process, which divided the branch internally.

The result of this was the expression of a good deal of inter-cohort suspicion—as each suspected the other of either being partisan to or resistant to Head Office, depending on their feelings towards it—which made for less easy acceptance of the matrix integration, and unnecessary friction between colleagues and departments, as various individuals were suspected or, occasionally, accused, rightly or wrongly, of adopting a position which was unpopular with another group. These differences thus indicate that culture within ZwoBank cannot simply be put down to a dynamic between national cultures, or between one local and one transnational culture, but to more complex interactions between diverse groups with different connections to national and global cultures.

The differences in interpretation also reflect different strategic agendas within the matrix integration. While there is a common concept of German business culture, for instance, the cohorts with more of an interest in staying close to Head Office tend to have a more positive interpretation of the matrix integration than those with more London-focused interests. Similarly, those cohorts which are betwixt and between the English and German business cultures—the Germanophiles and the locally hired Germans—are safeguarding their positions by downplaying the possibility of interpreting the conflicts as the result of a simple English/German opposition. Although these different agendas could not be said to totally disrupt the restructuring, they did lead to increased tension and lack of communication. Several of the expatriates commented that the local hires and Anglophiles were not willing to talk freely around them, and interviewees from all cohorts generally evinced a lack of sympathy for the issues of other cohorts when these were raised in interviews. Many of my informal interviews, for instance, were initiated by a staff member approaching me during a break and telling me an anecdote about their frustration in working with some colleague from another cohort, ranging from mild (a Germanophile laughing over an Anglophile's inability to speak German) to severe (an Anglophile expressing the fear that they would be "promoted sideways" in favour of an expatriate). The cohorts were thus divided along the lines of their interests in the organisation, again indicating that these are definite subgroups with different relationships to Germany, the UK and the global financescape rather than ad-hoc, temporary social groupings.

Furthermore, all of these positions on the restructuring are not formulated in isolation, but with reference to each other's strategies. The presence of other interpretations affects the process of defining culture: people show their allegiances to different groups by accepting or rejecting different interpretations in different contexts (Strecker 1988). A junior manager might, for instance, talk about the globalising potential of the matrix integration in a meeting with her supervisors but to an anthropologist describe it as an exercise in orienting the branch towards Germany. Finally, people were also aware of the flexibility of the definitions of culture in other cases cases: during a difficult point in the integration, for instance, two or three interviewees brought up the conflict-fraught Rover-BMW merger, which consequently became a tacit symbol for the incompatibility of English and German managers to get along. People thus are aware of other groups' definitions of national and ZwoBank "cultures," and operate strategically with regard to these. The cohorts thus also do not act as bounded cultures, but relate to each other and to outside groups, again indicating the weaknesses of theories predicated on the interactions of solidary cultures.

This strategic activity, furthermore, is inevitable in the case of a corporate restructuring (see Cody 1990). For the changes to be accepted, bank employees must be able to shift from one structure, and therefore corporate culture, to another. This is achieved by defining both cultures in similar terms, but reinterpreting them in light of the changes, and this in turn takes place through the conflicts and tensions between groups as they struggle for dominance in the new organisation. Given that change is such a large part of banking culture, furthermore, and the emphasis placed on flexibility in popular works on business (e.g. Heller 1995, Hussey 1995, Falham 1999), this sort of cultural game-playing is an inevitable part of business life; as the different groups within the bank adjust their interpretations in line with the situation, so the bank's collective strategy is developed. Furthermore, the fact that culture is a complex and flexible concept means that new definitions can come to the fore and old ones can be accepted by various actors. The diversity of interpretation is therefore not only inherent in a globalising business setting, but is necessary for the corporation and its employees to exist in the perpetually changing culture of global finance. Conflicts during cross-cultural business activities, such as mergers and matrix integration schemes, are thus not a matter of a simple clash between national and/or corporate cultures, but complex negotiations between a variety of groups within the organisation.

The sense of hostility and occasional intergroup conflict which London Branch experienced as a part of the matrix integration therefore did not stem particularly from the irreconcilability of Head Office practices with the London business environment, as both offices had been mediating the two systems for decades. Rather, these problems stemmed from the unacknowledged fact that there were at least four different interest groups within London Branch, each with a different position relative to Head Office and to the other groups, and a different aim with regard to its objectives in the restructuring of the bank. It thus seems that to define problems within cross-border business activities in terms of national business cultures—or even of class conflict between local and transnational social strata—is not only inaccurate, but might even exacerbate social tensions within the organisation Furthermore, the fact that this diversity of cultures existed within a single corporation suggests that, in fact, the notion of a diverse transnational capitalist society, incorporating different groups within itself, may not only be viable but a useful theoretical model for considering global businesses. We shall now consider how this diversity of cultures affected London Branch's relationship with Head Office.

### View from the Forty-Ninth Floor: Head Office-London Branch Relations

The relationship between London Branch and its Head Office (whose cultures are contrasted in Section 1, above) is, again, not quite as the literature might suggest. Once again, we see a case in which the employees of the bank all define the corporation's culture in terms of the same traits, but distinguish themselves within the bank as a whole through having different interpretations and valuations of these. However, although employees of Head Office were willing to accept the idea of London Branch having a different culture to their own, their failure to acknowledge the level of diversity within the organisation, preferring to describe it instead in terms of divisions between British and German national business cultures, caused problems with the acceptance of the matrix integration programme.

*Case Study: Lars*

*Lars is a Human Resource Manager in his late thirties. Born and raised in the Frankfurt area, he joined ZwoBank as a trainee while he was still at university, and has continued to work there ever since finishing his degree, apart from taking time out to do a doctorate in his late twenties. Although his job involves acting as liaison to all of ZwoBank's foreign branches, he has never actually worked abroad for a long period. He speaks fluent English but regrets that he gets little chance to practice it. He is married with one child, and lives in a suburb of Frankfurt.*

*Head Office, the Global and the Local*

Head Office's main strategy appeared to be a drive towards being seen as "global" in the eyes of its customers and competitors. As Michael put it, "globalisation is a very good word at the moment." Consequently, many emphasised what they saw as the globalising aspects of the matrix integration. One HR senior manager, Anne-Marie, attributed its implementation to the increasingly global focus of the German companies who were the bank's main clients, meaning that ZwoBank would also have to become globally integrated in order to serve them (this was somewhat counterintuitive, as the overall trend in the restructuring was towards increased centralisation). People at Head Office thus, due to their aspirations to be seen as "global," play up the globalising aspects of their own activities.

By contrast, the branches were said to be strongly oriented to their particular national cultures: Michael also spoke disparagingly of "regional princes" who run branches according to their personal agendas (see Prahalad and Doz 1987: 267). Head Office was said to take a global, and branches a local, perspective; one HR manager from Head Office described the London Branch as important to the banking system simply because a lot of German businesses operate in the UK, rather than due to its location in a "global city" with connections all over the world. Another said that local influence was what distinguished the branches from Head Office. The branches are thus described at Head Office as single units, taking a local perspective, and the diverse groups within them are not acknowledged.

The matrix integration, similarly, was described in terms of incorporating solidary units of "foreign culture" into the "German culture" of Head Office. Most people at Head Office spoke of the need to "integrate the overseas branches into the system," on the grounds that they were isolated from the culture of Head Office. The expatriates were, furthermore, expected to replace "local" practices with ones compatible to Head Office's. One HR manager said that the aim of expatriation—and in particular the increase in expatriate numbers during the matrix integration—was to instil better knowledge of Head Office practices in the branches (see Edstrom and Galbraith 1977), but there was never any discussion of the possibility of the two systems coexisting. Finally, other possible influences on the branch's culture (establishment mode, for instance) were never acknowledged. The matrix integration was thus discussed, not only in ways which assumed the branches to be monocultural, but which assumed that the branches must be either dominated by the local or the bank's home culture.

Consequently, London Branch's difficulties in adjusting to the new practices brought about by the matrix integration were discussed at Head Office in terms of branches, dominated by their host-country cultures, resisting the imposition of the home-country culture. Anne-Marie, after saying that the impression she got of the reaction to the matrix integration was that the employees of the branches felt that Head Office was imposing its corporate culture on everyone else in the bank, she added that the branches described this as acting like "typical Germans—they all say typical Germans." This is a curious impression as, in London Branch, this interpretation applied only to the Anglophiles. She then remarked that the restructuring was "good for Head Office because it helped us to realise that we are not a German, we are an international bank" and for the branches, it "helps them realise they are not just lone banks but part of a big family" (again, statements which do not take into account the German orientation of the expatriates and local hires). Head Office managers thus described the branches in ways which assumed that the problems of integration came from the resistance of the branch as a whole to outside cultural imposition rather than recognising the internal diversity of the branches.

All people at Head Office, furthermore, spoke of the value of cosmopolitanism, in the sense of *Weltoffenheit*, but with strong associations with one particular culture over others (see Vertovec 1996b; Appiah 1998). Michael defined the "typical cosmopolitan" as being like Tara Palmer-Tomkinson: wealthy, with a superficial knowledge of many cultures but at home in none. Lars, similarly, said "It is good to know where my perspective lies as a German, but not to say as a German [that] only German is right" (this interview was being conducted in English, at his request). Again, these are images of cosmopolitanism which, although they are similar to those used in London, differ in that they are made with an eye on the globalising aspects of the initiative, and their need to establish the bank as a "global" institution with the branches as "local" outposts. The Head Office employees with whom I spoke thus had particular takes on cosmopolitanism in their definition of the bank's culture, which relate to their strategies for success in the Frankfurt business environment and the global financial world, and their positions vis-à-vis the branches.

In addition, people in Head Office spoke of expatriation in terms relating to the globalising aims of the bank in general and the matrix integration in particular. Lars said that the aims of expatriation—and in particular the recent increase in expatriate numbers following the matrix integration—were to instil better knowledge of Head Office in the branches and vice-versa (see Beaverstock 1991: 1134, 1996a: 468). However, of the HR department employees with whom I spoke, only one had direct personal experience of expatriation. Outside of the HR office, and in particular that section of it with specific responsibility for contact with foreign branches, moreover, few in Head Office seemed to have much contact with, or even be aware of, current and/or former expatriates (see Beaverstock 1996a: 459). Lars casually remarked that many returnees came back disoriented, subsequently becoming upset to discover that the skills which they had learned in foreign branches were not considered useful in their "home" departments, and disappointed that their international experience was not, as they had hoped, a "fast track" to promotion (see Hamada 1992: 153, Beaverstock 1994: 327, 1996b: 430 for similar experiences among expatriates of other nationalities), before changing the subject. In Head Office, then, expatriation was described in terms of its "globalising" strategy, but again this was done in such a way as to define the branches as solidary units of "local" knowledge, rather than diverse, "globalising" entities in their own right, and without acknowledging their internal diversity.

## London Branch's View of Head Office

The result of this failure to acknowledge and incorporate the diversity of the branches caused an unnecessary amount of friction with the London Branch. Relations with Head Office were not unpleasant, or in any way atypical for any German foreign bank branch with which I have had contact (or indeed, according to William Kelly [2001], for foreign bank branches of other nationalities). However, London employees said that there was little contact between the two sections of the bank. Some employees continued, even after the restructuring, to speak of Head Office as if it were a separate entity. Several employees, from all categories, likened the matrix integration to a merger with, or a takeover by, another bank. Many, particularly Anglophiles and German local hires, said that "they don't understand how we do things out here." Many participants both commented on, and employed with varying degrees of consciousness, the practice of using Head Office as a "scapegoat" to blame for the branch's troubles; while my experience of other German banks suggests that this was not atypical behaviour, it varied in intensity with the state of the matrix integration. Any interest in the branches on the part of Head Office was described as suspicious. Tom, a former exchange-programme participant, described some colleagues as having a certain hostility towards it, born of indifference:

> **Tom**: I mean, some people don't even want to GO there. I'm not, well, you look at that and you say I'm not going to force people but you should at least GO, and see what they say in Head Office...er...

> **Interviewer**: So you know what it's like?

> **Tom**: Yeah! Yeah... I'm used to it... it doesn't just happen. You have to make it happen.

London Branch employees thus often described Head Office as an outside force which attempted to exercise control over them without understanding their position, a situation at least partly developed by Head Office's monocultural view of culture within the bank.

In fact, contact with Head Office occurred more often than was acknowledged. A small number of employees were "commuters," travelling back and forth between London and Frankfurt every week or two weeks. Most employees visited Head Office at some point, if only on a two-day business trip. Managers from certain departments would send people on three to six month exchanges to Frankfurt. All the expatriates, and some of the "local hires" who had come over as expatriates and stayed, maintained contact with former colleagues in Frankfurt, and Joachim was not the only one to make frequent return trips on their own initiative. Head Office was thus portrayed as aloof and disconnected, in a way which obscured the large number of connections between it and its branches; nonetheless, the connections are maintained on other levels.

Furthermore, London Branch employees distanced themselves from Head Office by defining themselves as "global," and their Head Office as "local." Head Office was described as German-focused, and without much interest in the international market, employing Head Office's own self-description but interpreting the images of Germanness as denoting parochiality rather than a global focus. Certain of the phrases used to describe Head Office—such as "bureaucratic," "slow," and "hierarchical"—were also associated with stereotypes of German business culture. Most contrasted London's "hybridisation" with Head Office's "German monoculture": one of Keith's senior management colleagues, who was in charge of the restructuring efforts at London Branch, spoke of a non-German at Head Office who, after twenty years at the same firm, was still called "*der Ausländer*" (the foreigner) by colleagues. Rather than viewing this as a central core of the bank, it was compared unfavourably with London Branch's self-perception as possessing a mix of UK and German business cultures. By doing so, they are setting themselves up as global and cosmopolitan according to City standards, which emphasises multiethnic offices and cultural mixing, rather than Head Office's vision of a German bank with offices in every port. In order to retain its autonomy in face of the matrix integration, London Branch therefore presents Head Office as monocultural, much as Head Office presents London Branch as monocultural in order to justify their actions towards it during the integration.

*Relations Between the Offices*

Despite this, the strategies of each office are in fact devised in relation to each other. London's position, as a small offshoot maintaining a presence in a global city, both looks to and contrasts itself to Frankfurt. Similarly, Head Office is the hub of the business, and as such emphasises an ideal of uniformity throughout the bank. In London Branch, the differences between internal cohorts is partly reflected in how close their interpretations are to Head Office's, and the various cohorts maintain an awareness of Head Office's interpretations of culture in their definition of the bank and of their position within it. This suggests that these interpretations are, while not necessarily adopted, at any rate employed as a means of defining oneself and one's allegiances in branch politics. The flexibility of the concept of culture means that the branch and the Head Office are linked and divided on different levels, a situation which is continuously changing, and which is reflected in the relations between the different groups' interpretations of the culture of the bank.

The problems with the matrix integration, therefore, had less to do with a "monocultural" branch in conflict with a "global" head office, or vice versa, but with the fact that both were operating according to the view of business culture defined above in which branches and head offices each have distinct and solidary cultures, the former local, the latter global. Head Office's failure to recognise the diversity of cultures, and their different orientation to local and global, both alienated the branch's employees and made the process of integration harder; London Branch's failure to acknowledge Head Office as "global," albeit in a different way to themselves, meant that they were unable to recognise that they are part of the same organisation, with common goals and interests. Failure on the part of both groups to recognise cultural diversity within the organisation thus meant greater difficulty in furthering the matrix integration programme, and later the merger.

This is further affected by the ways in which the Head Office chooses to manage its overseas subsidiaries. The impact which the way in which the headquarters choose to manage its branches has on the subsidiary companies been recognised since Bartlett and Ghoshal's study of different styles (1992), from more hands-on to more hands-off; Norderhaven and Harzing (2003) discuss how these styles change over time according to the pressures on the company. Up until recently, as noted, Head Office took a fairly distant perspective on the branches, which would have encouraged Head Office personnel to view the branches as something different, separate and therefore not to recognise particular diversity within them. This would have been exacerbated by the fact that much of the management literature on business culture with which the managers were familiar, such as Hofstede (1980) and Trompenaars (1993) treats "business cultures" as unified entities, rather than, as more recent works do, considering it as something more fluid (Bloom et al. 2003; Moore 2003). Because the corporation was making the transition from a more distant to a more close-knit mode of subsidiary management, then, the Head Office failed to recognise the diversity within the branches and its impact on the way in which they did business.

Although it might seem like an obstacle to progress in the case of ZwoBank's matrix integration programme, this cultural diversity and complexity is in fact integral to the operation of the bank. For instance, as per the discussion of City banks in Chapter 4, London Branch, in order to operate in the City, needs to adopt some of the local definitions of cosmopolitanism (for instance the focus on "business cultures" and the valuation of hybridisation), but in order to communicate with Head Office must also define itself in terms of its links to Germany. Head Office likewise must be able to maintain connections with the foreign branches at the same time as it focuses on the German market. The different elements within London Branch, also, mean that a single organisation can accommodate multiple perspectives, and prioritise each in turn as the circumstances demand. In order to run a multinational corporation, diverse elements need to be incorporated in a way which also permits cooperation on some level. The diversity of cultures thus comes into play in the interaction between branch and head office, and is part of the strategic operation of the bank in the diverse environments in which it finds itself; it is not a pathological aberration to be avoided, but a necessary part of interaction in the global sphere.

While Head Office and London Branch define themselves, each other and the bank in much the same terms, therefore, the different interpretations which various groups give these terms mean that in fact, the seemingly unified group incorporates within itself a variety of different cultures. The result is a sort of connected independence, which allows each unit to operate in its own context and yet to maintain a connection with each other, which changes as the strategies of each element in the group change in response to their outside environments. Consequently, the organisation is not so much a case of a "global" Head Office culture in conflict with "local" branch office cultures, but of different cultures, with different orientations to the local and the global, attempting to further their own strategies within an organisation which encompasses a number of diverse groups; the failure to recognise this causes friction and conflict within the MNC. We shall now consider how this situation came about, and consider why this sort of cultural flexibility may have emerged in the global business context.

## Analysis: Banking on Culture

Although traditional representations of MNCs suggest that they are defined by interactions between a "globalising" Head Office culture and various "local" branch cultures, our examination of the ZwoBank case suggests that in fact, banks consist of a diverse variety of groups which interact with the aim of furthering their particular agendas within a loosely defined, networked transnational society. We shall now examine the reasons behind this situation, and the role which it plays in the image-focused transnational business environment as well as in the negotiation of branch-Head Office relations in MNCs.

### *Self-Presentation and ZwoBank*

The importance of self-presentation in global business is visible from the moment one walks into any part of ZwoBank, from the décor to the employees' continual emphasis on the impression which clients and competitors receive. One of the more senior trainees stopped by my office one day to complain about a situation in which, a meeting room being unavailable, he had been forced to leave a group of clients in a free area while he arranged for another. He exclaimed angrily that they would therefore not think well of the bank: "What sort of image does that project to clients, to *customers*, to these people if we put them in a room where they are staring at our *garderobe* [coat closet]?" Business letters are written to a particular formula, without which, I was both reliably informed and personally discovered, they will not be read. The bank's logo appears on stationary, e-mails, websites, publications, and, at Head Office, on Post-It notes, pencils and the maps of Frankfurt given to overseas visitors. As the evidence from the City as a whole suggested, strategic self-presentation is a major part of the operation of transnational businesses such as ZwoBank.

Self-presentation is also a key factor in differentiating subgroups within the branch (to say nothing of the bank as a whole), and defining their relationship to each other. The decor of particular offices reflects the ethos of the department: Information Technology, for instance, which is generally said (including by its own members) to be a young and fairly offbeat department, has posters of popular comedians Mike Myers and Sacha Baron Cohen ("Ali G") on the walls; Auditing, spoken of with ambivalence by most of the rest of the branch, had several faintly insubordinate cartoons. The bank's Germanness is subtly expressed: while there is nothing in the branch's public spaces to suggest a German connection (the decor being neutral and the artwork from international sources), the machines, computers and telephones which kept the system running were all manufactured by German companies (a situation which my experience suggests is not atypical for German bank branches in London). Within London Branch and the bank as a whole, then, groups and individuals habitually rely on strategic self-presentation to communicate their status, orientations and allegiances to various global and local groups on a day-to-day basis.

Furthermore, it is clear that expressing affiliations to "global" and "local" cultures is not simply used to define an organisation or group, but in complex ways which continually change as the group's environment changes. The Germanophiles, for instance, define themselves in much the same way as actual German transnational businesspeople, and it is culturally difficult to distinguish between them and the local hires. In some cases, furthermore, the boundaries between the categories are hard to discern— some members of the Germanophile group are ethnic Germans, some are married to Germans, and all are engaged with Germany, which suggests that it might not be totally out of line to define them in some ways as *part* of the "German transnational capitalist class," particularly as Sklair counts local managers in MNCs as part of the TCC, regardless of whether they are actively engaged in globalising activity (1995: 72). Furthermore, among German transnational businesspeople themselves, the categories are flexible. Not only are there actually *two* different sorts of German transnational businesspeople, the expatriates and the local hires, but an expatriate can, if s/he remains in London for long enough, become a "local hire" and, although admittedly I heard of no cases of this happening, a local employee could equally become an expatriate. In the setting of a bank, the strategy and self-definition of the German transnational businesspeople is thus influenced by people who are both affiliated with it and with other groups, such as the City, the English transnational businesspeople, and the wider global financial community, calling into question the notion of definite "corporate cultures," "branch cultures," "transnational cultures" and "national business cultures."

The Anglophiles, furthermore, while they may be engaged with the City, are also engaged with Germany by virtue of the work they do and because of the fact that the German business system provides, for them, a classic "Other" against which they define their particular "Self." At the same time, the two groups have to work together: the Anglophiles' perspective on the organisation is thus likely to inform that of the other cohorts. The German transnational businesspeople were quite definitely aware of the Anglophiles' views, as witness expatriates' concerns about "offending the English" due to ignorance of local customs. The Anglophiles, furthermore, also provide expatriates with many of their interpretations of the City. The German transnational businesspeople, like all employees in London Branch, thus are acting according to particular strategies which are developed through mutual influence on and from other groups within the bank; the strategic nature of interaction in the City means that the German transnational businesspeople cannot operate as an isolated group, but must make connections with, and draw boundaries against, other groups both local and transnational.

Finally, the German transnational businesspeople at ZwoBank are also, as with Germans in the City as a whole, affected by external groups and their definitions of local and global culture, from consultants brought in to assist with the matrix integration, to outside contracting firms which supply the catering staff, language teachers and so forth, to pub and cafe staff. This influences the ways in which they define the office, and the interpretations which they give to its culture. ZwoBank's German transnational businesspeople, just by virtue of being in the branch, are in contact with other outside groups of varying degrees of Germanness and types of engagement with Germany. In short, while the bank is a cultural unit on one level, at another, it incorporates diversity, through different uses and interpretations of its culture. This diversity reflects a variety of influences on German transnational businesspeople, and the way they alter their strategic self-presentation in accordance with these influences in turn shapes the way in which they perceive and define the concepts of "global" and "local" culture.

## Heimat and the MNC

It might, at this juncture, be worth considering again the issue of *Heimat*, following on from the discussion in Chapter 3. Most Germans in London had quite diverse notions of where, and what, *Heimat* was. Some said that they did not have one. Of those who admitted to having a *Heimat*, answers ranged from classic references to specific regions of Germany (Borneman and Peck 1995: 272, 76; Weigelt 1983: 19), to simply stating "*Deutschland*" or "Europe" even when asked to elaborate. Others gave more complicated definitions along the lines of Borneman and Peck's transnational journalist, who maintained a sense of *Heimat* by reformulating it to include German overseas institutions (1995: 76), or of that given by an interviewee who did not work at this bank, a German who had married an Englishman, who stated that while her *Heimat* is Germany, for her children, *Heimat* is London, and that she knows other women in her position who "adopt" London as *Heimat* upon arrival. As noted, Germanophiles would even develop ersatz *Heimats*. Rather than as a simple image of "homeland" or marker of "German culture," *Heimat* was defined in diverse ways by German transnational businesspeople, which revealed complex negotiations between a variety of global and local positions.

This trend is even more surprising in that it goes against the standard literature on *Heimat* described elsewhere in this book (e.g. Greverus 1978, Applegate 1990). While many interviewees said that they considered England "home," or, as one put it, his "*zu Hause*" (an expression roughly denoting a place where one "feels at home"), this does not necessarily mean that England was their *Heimat*, as the words are not entirely equivalent. Similarly, while it is possible that some interviewees may have been less vague about the location of their *Heimat* if they had been speaking to a German interviewer, the fact that some explicitly said that they had no *Heimat* is remarkable, particularly given the place which *Heimat* is said to occupy in German consciousness (see Applegate 1990). This diversity of ways of defining *Heimat*, in which varying degrees of global and local orientation are negotiated by individuals according to their particular circumstances, goes against the classic formulation of the expression.

However, more recent studies of *Heimat* have suggested that, in transnational situations, the concept may be quite flexible, as in the case of Goltz' Argentinean Germans (1998) or Borneman and Peck's Jewish "sojourners" (1995). The varied definitions—even rejections—of *Heimat* by my interviewees suggests that they are adapting the concept to fit the English/City of London context, particularly as strong, classical associations of *Heimat* with a particular region or town might make it harder for individuals to show a connection with the UK local culture (Borneman and Peck 1995: 184). The variety of answers also suggests that there are many different strategies for self-presentation being deployed in the same social context. It seems, then, that German transnational businesspeople adjust the concept of *Heimat* to their situation, whether by losing it altogether, transferring it to other locations—or even, in the case of those who cited Europe as *Heimat*, concepts—or by reformulating it in terms of multiple *Heimats*. There are thus diverse ways of constructing a *Heimat* in a transnational situation, and the way in which it was constructed—and the degree to which it is oriented towards the global and/or the local—depended on the history and strategy of the actor in question.

The presence of multiple forms of *Heimat* thus suggests many ways of defining national and global cultures among my interviewees, and of relating the global to the local. Even if some interviewees were tailoring their responses to my questions, this still implies a flexible concept of *Heimat*: if an interviewee is defining their *Heimat* in different ways to interviewers and others, then the individual is changing his/her self-presentation to give him/herself the cultural affiliation which s/he feels will be most useful in that situation. The various constructions of *Heimat* thus show how images of Germanness are used to strategically define different groups and positions within the transnational business world, rather than to outline a nationality-based monoculture, and consequently to allow people to associate themselves with local and global culture to varying degrees in different circumstances.

*Cohorts and Social Relations: The Need for Diversity*

Furthermore, at times of stress—such as the restructuring of ZwoBank—the different elements within the bank's German transnational businesspeople become points in a continuum, along which the MNC's culture is challenged and reinterpreted to fit its changing circumstances. For instance, the polarization of the London branch along ethnic lines suggested a rethinking of what it is to be German, and what this means within the branch, in a matrix integration system. It is interesting also to note that the local hires did not seem to have a particular solidarity with the expatriates even though both were German transnational businesspeople; in fact, the two groups tended to set themselves off from each other, for instance through their choice of language. The expatriates were brought together as a group through shared experience and common language, but also because they were assumed by the others in the branch to be a unit. The conflicts within the organisation thus became the site of cultural discourse, as the introduction of a new system causes the MNC and its diverse subgroups to redefine their strategic positions in the global financial world.

Similar things can also be seen in the negotiations between Head Office and London Branch as to what their relative positions should be after the matrix integration. For example, within London Branch, the different cohorts were a least partly defined according to lines of proximity to Head Office; the expatriates' portrayals of the bank and of good business practice appear more in line with the views in Head Office than those in London Branch. Germans in general were assumed to be sympathetic to Head Office, meaning that locally hired Germans, whose sympathies were more strongly aligned with London branch, often felt obliged to define themselves explicitly in opposition to Head Office. The different cohorts thus expressed their positions relative to Head Office through strategic self-presentation in terms of Germanness, Englishness and cosmopolitanism.

At the height of the restructuring, furthermore, the branch employees interpreted the inevitable tension with Head Office in terms of ethno-national incompatibility. As noted above, both the branch and the Head Office described each other in terms of their local and global associations, with frustrated London employees accusing Head Office of being "too German" and Head Office accusing London of being "not global enough." Within this framework, however, we can see that both groups were using discourses of cosmopolitanism to further their own position, with each using a slightly different meaning of the word, but both also using it as a means of, as Bloch would have it, restricting the discourse such that the other group cannot contradict their position without being deemed overly parochial and not interested enough in global matters. Although they may seem to interpret the difficulties with the matrix integration in terms of national cultures, the fact that each have different positions on what this entails means that the restructuring is not so much a matter of a local culture being absorbed into a global culture (as Head Office would have it), or a global culture being overwhelmed by a local one (according to many at London Branch), as a competition between different cultural groups with different positions relative to the global and the local, interacting in a wider social sphere.

Whether anyone at ZwoBank realised it or not, the different positions of the cohorts came into play in terms of negotiating the new structure of the organisation. The local hires and the two cohorts of UK-born employees frequently made use of the expatriates' closer cultural position to Head Office by employing them as unofficial "mediators," having them negotiate with Head Office colleagues on their own behalf, thereby allowing them a voice in the negotiations while still maintaining their position of aloofness. For their part, the UK-focused cohorts were able to interpret the changes taking place in the organisation to clients, and the local hires and Germanophiles were able to explain the culture and practices of Head Office to, and negotiate on behalf of, the Anglophiles. The different cohorts thus played roles in negotiating the final form of the restructured organisation, through their various connections to different local and global cultures, suggesting that culture is a matter of dynamic negotiation rather than of static traits.

As a result, despite the initial conflicts and friction, the restructuring was able to be successful. By the time the study was completed, people were well established in the new structure, and new interpretations of the organisation's culture were becoming the norm. The different cohorts were developing new discourses by which to describe the organisation's culture, as well as new counter-discourses in the form of jokes and complaints about the new practices. The expatriates, for instance, were defining their role as mediators in terms of being the representatives of London to Head Office; many Germanophiles were capitalising on their greater knowledge of German culture to consolidate or further their positions within the organisation. The use of self-presentation within the restructuring thus not only highlights the diversity among German transnational businesspeople, but also the fact that, as I suggested was the case for the City of London, diversity and flexible self-presentation are essential to allow individuals and groups to adapt to a changing system, and to negotiate the form of the newly restructured organisation into one which is more or less agreeable to all parties.

This diversity also comes into play in interactions with other bank branches in London. While nobody talks directly about the competition, the progress of other restructurings taking place at the time affected how people at other bank branches felt about what was going on in their own offices; the matrix integration was itself a response to then-recent events in German banking. Furthermore, most employees of all nationalities had worked for other banks, both German and non-German. The bank also required cultural engagement with other banks in order to compete with them in the City environment, and to define themselves relative to their fellow organisations. Consequently, confirming the findings of the previous chapter regarding the use of self-presentation in the City, the diversity and complexity of culture within the banks permits these organisations to maintain varying degrees of closeness to each other, according to their changing strategies in the London and global markets.

The globally engaged nature of the financial market also affects the bank as it struggles to be, in its employees', clients' and competitors' eyes, both German and global. In order to call a bank "German," there has to exist a category of "non-German"; furthermore, to define a bank as "global" is to define that which is not global. In order to present themselves as a "global" firm, then, they have to know how to present themselves as German, and at the same time to present themselves as globally oriented. In order for the bank to be German but not isolated as such, its employees turn to the culture concept to bridge the gap and allow it to be simultaneously German and global. Furthermore, different groups within the bank have different definitions of German and corporate culture, but these nonetheless are all subsumed on another level within the self-definition of the whole organisation. The actions and cultures of German transnational businesspeople are formed and developed through strategic interaction with other groups; therefore, as per the earlier discussion of the City, they cannot be considered in isolation, without reference to others in the global financial world.

ZwoBank, furthermore, like other City companies, requires all of these different engagements with diverse groups as it continually adapts to the changing business environment. Whatever its employees may say, neither the bank nor its branches are, or ever have been, islands. Head Office, London Branch, other branches and outside banks both German and non-German all influence each other's strategies and self-presentation, even if this may be more obvious at some times than at others. By the same token, the different groups within the bank are not isolated from each other, having to interact through the makeup of the branches and the nature of its structure. The bank effectively needs a way to be diverse and unified at once, which is provided by the flexibility of the concept of culture. For the bank to operate as a unit, its culture must be defined so as to allow for internal and external diversity, but without preventing interaction between different cultural groups. The internal diversity of German transnational capitalism, and the flexibility of culture, is thus integral to German transnational businesspeople' interaction with other groups.

Finally, this cultural engagement allows them to compete in the wider financial sphere described in Chapter 4. Within the global financial world, the bank needs to carve out a niche and present a united front, but it also needs to be flexible, respond to other groups, and blend in with these if necessary, in the cases of merging, restructuring and periods of greater and lesser expansion. MNCs appear to alternate between centrifugal and centripetal periods, depending on politics and economic currents in the world as a whole (compare Behrman 1970; Bergsten et al. 1978; Prahalad and Doz 1987 and Bartlett and Ghoshal 1992). A continuous strategy is thus impossible; instead we see a continual dynamic between unity and diversity, achieved through changes in self-presentation. The flexibility of the concept of culture thus allows for a dynamic between flexibility and stability, unity and diversity, which is necessary to the bank's operations in the global sphere, but which mean that neither the bank nor its the German transnational businesspeople can be considered as a single unit.

While the bank may appear on one level to be a single cultural unit, and on another to be a simple case of a "global" Head Office negotiating with "local" branches, a closer examination reveals the different strategies of the diverse groups within it and outside influences upon it, as well as their varying degrees of engagement with each other, confirming the pattern noted in Chapters 3 and 4. This diversity is not only inherent within the bank's structure and composition, it is necessary for its interactions in the global business environment.


## Conclusion

An analysis of how the definitions of German and corporate culture are strategically used by the various types of employees of a German bank branch in London thus suggests that, as we discussed in the two previous chapters, it cannot be considered in terms of single, solidary cultures, whether the divisions are national or between local and transnational "classes." Rather, any study—or successful restructuring programme—must take into account the bank's internal diversity, and the strategic discourses going on between the bank, the groups within it, and other groups both local and engaged with global finances, and the place of all of these within the global financescape. Furthermore, it seems once again as if this diversity is not only natural within the transnational business environment, but is actually necessary to survival within it, as, in the ZwoBank case, it enabled the negotiation of an organisational culture which was more or less satisfactory to both branch and Head Office. It is also crucial to negotiating the positions of various cultures relative to the local and the global, and how these are defined and constructed in a business context. We shall now consider how this strategy is played out in the use of communications and language in ZwoBank, with a view to examining whether the media through which these cultural negotiations take place within and outside the organisation support this kind of complex, flexible diversity.

## Chapter 6

# "Mobile Phone Wars": Language and Communication in the MNC

### Introduction

A key point regarding the interaction and self-presentation which we have discussed in the past three chapters is that none of it would be possible without language or, due to the transnational context, communications technology. While most of the extant theories regarding the use of language in multicultural and transnational business environments suggests a pattern in which a group of local and/or subaltern employees are dominated by a, possibly transnational, elite elite, this hypothesis is incapable of fully explaining the complex uses of communication which we have seen so far. A closer examination of material from ZwoBank with regard to employees' choice of language, jargon, jokes and uses of communications technology, suggests that language is in fact part of a strategic discourse between diverse groups within the organisation, which does not so much define bounded groups as diverse relationships with other local and global communities in a wider social environment.

In this chapter, I will expand upon the discussion of culture in ZwoBank begun in Chapter 5 by narrowing the focus to consider the medium through which it takes place, language and communication technologies. I propose that they are not, as both those researchers prioritizing national and those prioritising global cultures have argued, tools by which one group dominates another, but that they are the site of conflict, negotiation and discourse between cultures, incorporating global and local elements. I will finally develop the argument outwards to discuss whether communications technologies are really a tool of globalisation, or whether they also have a strong role in defining organizational cultures and national business cultures as well, and if so, how the two are reconciled. I will conclude by briefly examining how communications relates to the transnational capitalist society hypothesis.

As they are applied to transnational communities, business or otherwise, studies of communication often draw from linguistic works which focus upon the uses of language as an agent of domination and of resistance in situations in which one group is oppressed by another (e.g. Lakoff [1979]). Roberts et al.'s 1994 study of immigrant labour is typical of the way in which theories of language and power have been adopted into the study of transnational workplaces, discussing how language and "officialese" are used by UK managers to control and dominate the–largely immigrant–workers. In studies of migrants and developing/developed World relations, transnational communication technology is also portrayed either as an agent of Western dominance (Drainville 1998: 41) and/or a means by which transnational actors can organise themselves worldwide against oppressive local governments (Zachary 2000: 21; Cesari 1999). Most studies of linguistics in transnational culture thus argue that language is a site of contestation between groups in a borderless world. Following the logic of these studies, it must also be the case that, in the business world, language is the locus of conflict between a coterie of globalising expatriates and their local employees. It thus remains to be seen whether this will prove to be true in the ZwoBank case, or whether the situation seen in Chapter 5 in terms of the restructuring and the relationship between London Branch and Head Office also extends to linguistic issues.

### Speak English: "Global" and "Local" Languages

In the present period of globalisation, English is generally agreed to be the lingua-franca of the transnational business world, or, as some commentators put it, the "global language of business" (W. Klein 1998; Crystal 1997). This was visible, not only in ZwoBank itself, but in other transnational business environments which its employees frequented. I multiethnic settings such as the educational institute which supplied the banks' trainees, for instance, English was used as a lingua franca. In Frankfurt Airport, the signs were in English as well as German and there were a large number of English-speaking attendants. English-speaking was also treated as a marker of cosmopolitanism by my interviewees, and as such accorded high status among transnational businesspeople, German and otherwise. I will here explore a variety of scenarios which illustrate how English and German are used relative to each other in ZwoBank-related business settings, with a view to considering how the two linguistic/cultural groups related to each other in the bank.

*Scenario A: Head Office*

It might be instructive, first of all, to consider the relation of German to English in ZwoBank Frankfurt. In Head Office, despite the fact that English was the "official language" of the bank, German was the most frequently-used language: while no statistics were available on the linguistic competency of employees, anecdotal evidence suggested strongly that relatively few employees spoke English fluently. The consensus at London Branch was that Head Office, as Keith put it, "suffered from lack of English." Head Office is therefore an environment in which German is theoretically the dominant language.

Even though it may be seldom used, however, English is still rated more highly than German as a business language by Head Office employees. Lars described for me how his entire department in Frankfurt had used the announcement of the restructuring initiative as "an excuse to sign up for English lessons." Most of my contacts at Head Office initially agreed to interviews at least partly to improve their language or practice on a "genuine" native English speaker. Most of the trainees at London Branch cited wanting to improve their English as a key reason for requesting to work in London. For the expatriates, speaking English was a symbol of *"Weltoffenheit."* A telling incident also occurred at the meeting of HR managers from all branches mentioned earlier (at which, significantly, English was used as the lingua-franca): when two Head Office delegates briefly conferred in German, and an American exclaimed "Speak English!" in a faintly exasperated tone, the Germans complied without surprise, comment or evidence of hurt feelings. The rationale behind declaring English the official language of the bank was that it would facilitate its development into a truly global organisation. The most visible received linguistic discourse at Head Office is therefore that English is a more global, cosmopolitan and prestigious language than German.

This attitude also seems to hold true in the rest of Frankfurt as well. German as used in business and the media possesses a large number of English loanwords; a *Spiegel* article describes how English is used in advertising in Germany for no reason other than to seem "cool" (1998a). According to an article in *The Economist* (1998a) a number of German banks, even those without a sizeable global presence, have made English their official language in order to appear more cosmopolitan. The available evidence thus suggests that, even in Frankfurt business circles, English is the dominant language.

German, following this pattern, is defined as a local and therefore low-prestige language in a business context, even a German one. On my first visit to the Head Office, the employee who showed me around, Maria, expressed her surprise that I spoke German (as had most of the expatriates in London). I replied with, "Why not? You speak English." Her reply was "Yes, but you're English [sic—I am Canadian]—you don't have to learn it." She, like most Head Office employees, had not worked outside of Germany. Subsequently, many HR managers remarked to me that German skills are not much of an asset in global business, only for dealing with the specialised German financial market. Consequently, the learning and speaking of English acquires a strong symbolic value for Germans, and in particular for those involved in transnational business. Even in a German setting, then, English is seen as a global language, and German a local one.

However, in its dealings with its overseas branches, Head Office would subtly assert the dominance of German over English. Internal memos had German letterhead or instructions (confidentiality envelopes, for instance, read *"Streng Vertraulich"*), making German, in this context, the language of international dealing. On occasion they would actually be written in German, which usually led to a flurry in London Branch offices as an employee capable of translating was located, and again defines German as the global, and English the local, language. The bank's newsletter, produced in Frankfurt and distributed throughout the group, was printed in German; recently it had added an English supplement sent—significantly—to all the international branches, but the greatest prominence was given to German. A number of Head Office employees who were less than fluent in English would gratefully lapse into German if the opportunity presented itself, despite making valiant efforts to communicate in the other language. In Head

Office, then, whether English is the more global and German the more local language, and which dominates the other, depends on the context, suggesting that there is more at issue here than simply one national or transnational culture dominating another.

### Scenario B: London Branch

In London Branch, similarly, English appeared to be the dominant language, and German was treated as a language which was esoteric and restricted to one or two particular national contexts. Most people around the office were curious as to how I had learned German, and when they learned that I had German relatives, assumed that this was the reason. One locally-hired German manager, who was in fact in a relationship with a non-German, stated to me that he could not see anyone being interested in studying German if they did not have German family by "blood" or marriage. Even though the branch had several English-language employees who were fluent in German, this was still seen as unusual (even, interestingly, by the Germanophile employees). English would thus appear to have more of a "global" status than German in London Branch as well as in the Head Office.

Language use, furthermore, seemed to play into the unspoken divisions between cohorts in the office. Multilingualism was a strong symbol of the branch for the expatriates, all of whom cited wanting to improve their English as a key reason for volunteering to come to London. However, one distinguishing mark of the expatriates was the fact that they spoke German more often than any of the other groups. Local hires distinguished themselves from expatriates by refusing to speak German, or doing so only in specific contexts, such as with recently-arrived trainees. Most English Germanophiles seemed to be less open about their linguistic abilities than were bilinguals from other countries, suggesting that their skill was a distinguishing marker which placed them in a liminal position with regard to the Germans and the English. Language is also used to mark off the Anglophiles. While some took advantage of a programme of German language lessons offered through the HR department following the announcement of the bank's matrix integration, this was said to be a commitment "above and beyond the call of duty." While most spoke about language courses in positive terms, they also said that such skills were less important than the "practical" aspects of business. There were often hints, in such conversations, of linguistic xenophobia, the English seemingly using the discourse of cosmopolitanism to excuse an isolationist reluctance to learn another language on the grounds that it is "local." The German language is another symbol representing the bank for all cohorts, but where the expatriates and Germanophiles express this by speaking German, local hires do so by avoiding speaking it (or by asking to "practice their English"), and Anglophiles by either learning or refusing to learn it. Which language is thus the more global, and the more highly valued, varies from cohort to cohort.

This was also the case with the use of language in group conversations. As the use of German was generally acknowledged to be restrictive and exclusive of people who do not speak it, it was mainly used in cases in which the group was German or a mixture of Germans and Germanophiles, and most often by trainees and recently-arrived expatriates. This also held true for conversations in the office or at the coffee machine: while these were conducted in either English or German in all-German or German/Germanophile offices, they were conducted in English in all other cases. Significantly, German was only spoken in the workplace when German-speakers (of whatever nationality) were working together, and would cease if an English-speaker joined them. German employees, particularly expatriates, usually seemed more relaxed when working with English-speakers whom they knew to speak German than with monolingual coworkers, even if they communicated with these people mainly or only in English. It thus seems that English is the dominant language, defining a firm boundary line between two groups of different nationalities, and between more global and more local employees.

This proposition is, however, challenged by the official uses of German within the branch. The branch management formally encouraged employees to take language lessons; most of the top rank of UK-native managers consequently had at least passable German, although they never, to the best of my knowledge, admitted to this outside of formal interview settings. Despite the assertion of many English employees that they need not learn German as "they (i.e. the Germans) all speak English," many were conversant with popular books on "Business German" (for instance Hartley and Robins [1996] or Nicholson and Hill [1992])—that is to say, books outlining useful phrases of German for English-speakers, to use on the telephone, in letters and so forth, either as a courtesy or in case one should find oneself speaking with someone whose English is not very good. Although this was never said directly, learning German did have prestige value for some of the English, as it marked the learner off as someone committed to the company or with cosmopolitan leanings. One Anglophile spoke with irony of the fact that during the matrix integration, English was declared the official language of the bank, but that the end result had been that more people went out and learned German in order to communicate better with colleagues at Head Office. In London Branch, there is a lot of unspoken pressure for the use of German in top management policy, suggesting that German may be the dominant language in this context. German can, therefore, sometimes be the more global language.

In addition, English could also symbolise a person's local connections rather than their global leanings. Most UK-born English speakers took their monolinguality as a marker of ethnic affiliation rather than of cosmopolitanism, proudly announcing that as English people, they spoke no other languages (other English speakers at ZwoBank had fewer issues with this: Canadians and South Africans are used to state-sponsored bilingualism, and most of the Antipodeans and Americans whom I encountered in the City were similarly at home in multilingual environments). In more relaxed contexts, such as the canteen, Germans frequently fell into a playful "German English," using English verbs according to German rules (two young German local hires, debating whether or not to order an apple crumble for dessert: "Are you crumbling?" "Yes, I'm crumbling"); this was done mainly by fully-bilingual individuals—local hires or longtime expatriates—who were aware of the proper English grammatical rules and were deliberately breaking them in play to suggest a parochial Germanness (see Rampton 1995 for similar behaviour among Asian schoolchildren in England). The use of English thus could indicate local connections for both English and German-speakers, calling into question the global-local identification of English and German at the same time as it affirms it on another level.

It is also worth considering the numerous cases of Anglo-German linguistic "crossing" in ZwoBank London (Rampton 1995). At meetings with Head Office personnel, Anglophile employees tried to learn phrases of German off their counterparts as a conversational gambit at the breaks. In London Branch, the use of German courtesy phrases such as *"Damen ersten"* (ladies first) and *"Tchüss"* (goodbye) had acquired common currency among the (exclusively Anglophile and generally working-class) support staff, mainly as greetings and interjections. As noted, the only people to actually conduct all-German conversations were trainees or expatriates new to London. In phone conversations, bilingual speakers of all national origins would alternate between English and German depending on who the phone call was from and what it was about. The use of German by English employees thus was framed either as a courtesy to international visitors or a cosmopolitan interest in and knowledge of other cultures, making German the more global language in these contexts.

This linguistic crossing suggests that language use has less to do with intercultural conflict and more to do with strategic self-presentation. For one thing, the Anglo-German divide is not a simple one: the inclusion of non-native speakers of German in the speech community suggests a continuum rather than a boundary. There were also occasions on which one German would address another in English in telephone conversations, usually on matters pertaining to an English client. When Anglophiles used German, it mainly took the form of short greeting phrases, and thus seemed mainly to indicate identification with their corporation or division; furthermore, these phrases seemed to be mainly used by older English men, who distinguished themselves within the branch by a form of gentle teasing of employees in other groups. Even with each other, German employees generally spoke a mix of German and English, or *"deutschlish"*; none of my interviews were conducted strictly in one or the other language, even when the decision was taken at the outset to speak only one. The bank's SPIRE System programme (mentioned in Chapter 5) was in fact given its name by its designers, who were German, but even the English employees pronounced its name, without a trace of irony, in the German way. Linguistic mixing was thus more common in London than the use of one language as a lingua-franca, and was not so much a way of indicating a boundary as a means of expressing different social allegiances in different contexts.

The choice of language also appeared to be more a matter of strategic self-presentation than of excluding others. Several German interviewees, mainly local hires, expressed no preference for one or the other language when asked at the beginning of interviews; while many did choose English as a "default language," they would also switch to German when, as one put it, "things get technical." Also, the "monolingual" English often knew several stock German phrases for telephone conversations, even if the conversation was conducted in English after the initial formalities were concluded; on at least one occasion an Anglophile (of the abovementioned older male cohort) jokingly treated a Germanophile in the same way, employing stock German phrases before getting down to business. When I first spoke German to Greta, who had been in the UK for about ten years, she did not register this until five minutes into the conversation. When I expressed surprise at this, she assured me that after a while in the office, one did not notice switches in language. After two months, I discovered that I did stop registering such changes consciously. Language thus seemed mainly to be a means of continually defining and redefining the nature and composition of social groups, rather than only a site of contestation between two such entities.

It is also worth considering the after-work context. German was more often used in private contexts, and therefore also to mark these; at the pub after work, German-speakers were more inclined to speak German, and much less concerned about excluding English-speakers from the conversation. One interviewee, furthermore, was impersonal and businesslike when dealing with me until he encountered me speaking German to another colleague at the pub, at which point he became effusively friendly. German's "local" status could thus be used in some contexts to indicate a private conversation, rather than to dominate other groups.

Similarly, German could also be used in "public" contexts, such as the canteen, to delineate a private subject. "Mad Cow Disease" (BSE), for instance, was never referred to by its English name by Germans in such areas; as German indicates a private context, this places the phrase firmly in the "inside-joke" sphere, and also ensures that Anglophone colleagues are unlikely to realise that a delicate subject is being discussed. Once, during a conversation between myself, a local hire from the former East Germany and a Germanophile colleague from another department, the conversation was conducted in English apart from when discussing the fall of the Berlin Wall, at which point the East German suddenly began speaking German, and then reverted to English when the subject changed. Similarly, Germans discussing business matters in the canteen would speak in German, partly in order to communicate better, but also partly to indicate a wish to be left alone. On some occasions German was used to actively conceal the topic of discussion from an Anglophone (a strategy which occasionally backfired on the users). German is thus again used in ways which suggest different sorts of strategies within the office, not simply always as a form of domination and/or resistance.

*Analysis*

The use of language is not so much a tool of domination and resistance in the organisation as it is a way of performing multiple functions on different levels. It is, for instance, possible to argue that the mixing of language is paradoxically "German": Wiesand's *Kunst Ohne Grenzen* has a three-quarter page quotation entirely in English, with no translation given (1987: 133). This, however, suggests that the definitions of particular local identities (in this case, German) are bound up with the definition of a particular global identity. A *Der Spiegel* article (1998a) also suggests that the ungrammatical English used in advertisements may be leading to a new, standard form of *"deutschlish."* Language was thus not so much a means of defining one social group against another, as a means of negotiating a series of interconnected social groups through self-presentation.

Furthermore, language could be used to elide distinctions between groups, both on a conceptual level in the Head Office and on a personal level in London. The grammatical play of the "crumbling" incident metamorphosed into a reinterpretation of what it means to work in banking, as the linguistic joking gave way to mock-negotiations of the price of dessert complete with bidding and taxation. On one occasion, I heard the phrase "it doesn't matter, they all speak English," normally used by English people to explain why they had not learned German, from a young German local hire taking a new job with a Dutch bank in reference to why he was not going to learn Dutch. This not only altered the group divisions from English/German to German/non-German, but defines all English-speakers, regardless of mother tongue, as part of the same group. Language schools teach a particular sort of English known as "business English" (as opposed to colloquial or conversational English), suggesting that it is not English per se which is the global language, but English with a business focus. In one interview with a London manager, I remarked that I was surprised at the lack of English skills at Head Office, as English was said to be the international language of business. The response was "not in Germany it isn't.... International business is a very different thing," making it ambiguous whether German is international or local, or indeed whether there exist different ways of being "international." Language does not therefore relate, as Engelmann suggests, directly to Germanness, but is a means of redefining Germanness as the expression of belonging to a particular social formation not incompatible with, and even capable of combining with, other groups in a wider social context (1991: 58).

Leaving aside its role as a means of communication, then, language is not simply a form of national identification or a site of conflict between a dominant and a subordinate group, but a means of self-presentation whose complexity and flexibility allows for the negotiation of various positions along a continuum between global and local. Rather than defining a boundary between two national groups, or allowing a transnational elite to dominate a local subaltern group, then, language use reflects a diversity of ways of being a transnational businessperson, suggesting not so much a case of global and local groups in conflict as of diverse sorts of conflict and consensus in a situation incorporating varying degrees and kinds of global and local engagement in the global financescape.

## The Language of Business: Meetings and Jargon

Another seeming site of power relations is the use of jargon. Certain buzzwords and phrases seem to be universal throughout the business world; terms like "Joint Venture" "Human Resource Management," "Success driven" and so forth are peppered throughout the conversations of businesspeople of all nationalities. These have become pervasive to the point which "Business German" and "Business English" are taught almost as separate dialects of their respective languages. One might thus almost see business jargon as more of a "global language of business" than English. Here, we will consider the use of jargon in meetings, with regard to how it reflects power relations between groups in London Branch and what it can tell us about culture in the global financescape.

*Scenario A: The Meeting*

Meetings are protracted, even ritualised, communicative acts which normally follow a specific pattern which varies little from corporation to corporation, or country to country (Boden 1994: 80ff). There would be a brief period in which the participants assembled, accompanied by joking and conversation; people generally sat in groups, frequently with others from their department, although senior managers tended to sit closer to the front, and trainees to form their own group towards the back. This was followed by two to five presentations, either by senior managers, managers assigned to lead a particular project, specialists within the bank and/or the occasional external expert. While the length and content vary according to the topic and group, most formal meetings included PowerPoint slides, illustrated with cartoons drawn from the PowerPoint software, which were almost inevitably followed by a joke about the cartoons' incomprehensibility. The tone of each meeting was generally as positive as possible, even if the purpose of the meeting was to discuss or deliver bad news. Question periods inevitably followed; these also had a pattern, with the general rule being the more formal the meeting, the more senior the questioners and the more serious the questions asked. In most cases, the senior managers (both German and non-German) tended to ask the first questions and to be the most outspoken. Meetings thus form a cross-cultural secular ritual in the transnational business world.

In these meetings, business "jargon," buzzwords and phrases are often used as a form of restricted code. In the HR managers' meeting mentioned above, people of all nationalities continually came up with the same catchphrases: flat structure, high integrity, success driven, performance criteria. Throughout the meeting it was assumed that everybody would know and understand these; on one occasion, when I asked the meaning of a particular phrase, the person to whom I was speaking was quite taken aback. Jargon, more than English alone, is the "global language" of business.

The ritualised nature of this vocabulary, furthermore, has the effect of controlling the discourse. Jargon resembles Bernstein (1971)'s concept of restricted code, that is to say, high-context, jargon-heavy language, which draws a barrier between the users and the outside world, limiting the discourse to a particular group of people. It also recalls Bloch's monograph (cited in Chapter 1) on the way in which ritualised, symbol-heavy speech restricts the listeners' possible responses to the speaker's words, thus quelling potential dissent before it begins (1974: 58-71). In the case of meetings, the use of language would thus suggest the reinforcement of a hegemonic, hierarchical ideology throughout the business world, in which some groups, with the ability to employ a "global" discourse, dominate more "local" groups.

Despite this, much is made in popular works aimed at transnational businesspeople of alleged differences in the way in which people from different national cultures hold meetings (e.g. Hickson and Pugh 1997, Trompenaars and Hampden-Turner 1996). British people are said to insist on personal chatter before the meeting and Germans to begin straight away and conduct proceedings in an impersonal style (Scheuermann 1997: 20). It seemed to be expected that my report would cover the differences in meeting styles of different nationalities. Some of these differences seemed to be more perceived than real; I was on more than one occasion the recipient of discourses on English rudeness (contrary to the stereotype of them as overpolite) or German disorganisation, from members of the opposite group. Some of these "cultural differences" in fact appear to be self-fulfilling prophecies. One recent expatriate made an almost fanatical point of engaging in small talk for two or three minutes at the onset of any meeting held in English, which this person did not do in German, suggesting that this trait owed more to having read books on English "meeting style" than anything else. Nonetheless, by asserting the existence, and acceptability, of alternative discourses, they provide a counter-discourse to the restricted code. Consequently, the meeting can be an exercise in self-presentation, in which various individuals express varying degrees of connection with global and local social groups.

Meetings are thus simultaneously seen as universal and controlling in form, and yet on another level as encompassing diverse styles and bringing different groups together. While some writers have debated the extent to which "national business styles" exist as such (e.g. Millar 1979), the fact remains that they were a significant way in which my interviewees presented themselves. Whether the meeting is a global or a local act, or indeed whether it is a point of unity or of division among businesspeople, depends largely on the context. Once again, the language used in meetings is a force for dominance on one level, but this is only one of a variety of strategic uses, some of which also referred to other discourses than those of power and national culture. In line with what was seen during the restructuring initiative, then, meetings thus were less about defining dominant and subaltern groups, and more about negotiating social relations through defining culture.

### Scenario B: The Office

We shall now look at the small, informal meetings which took place when two or three people came together within an office to discuss their work. As with the more formal meetings, jargon seemed at first to form a restricted discourse. Employees incorporated phrases of jargon into their daily speech totally without irony or apparent realisation that these are anything other than normal language, thereby unconsciously restricting their own discourses. This is not to say that there are no forms of resistance; a common style of joking in banks is to repeat some phrase of jargon in an ironic tone or the wrong context. For instance, upon my remarking that my computer was having problems to Keith in the canteen, he remarked "Oh no— your computer is *facing challenges*," the last drawled broadly with a grin and a wink, and alluding to the fact that, in business jargon, problems are referred to by euphemistic phrases. However, this form of resistance also affirms the use of restricted discourse as a necessary part of business, and setting off businesspeople from other actors. Jargon would thus seem to be a site setting off the global from the local aspects of business, and restricting local discourses.

The language in which the jargon is spoken confirms this hypothesis. Even in cross-cultural settings, jargon is generally English: much of the jargon in "business German" is also in English. When I asked a Germanophile for the German equivalent of the phrase "corporate culture," she responded that there was none, and that Germans used the English phrase; looking in a dictionary, she found that there was a German word, *Wirtschaftskultur*, but added that even in Frankfurt, the English term was used, albeit with German plurals and verb structures. For that matter, when running a keyword search for books on corporate culture at the Deutsche Bibliothek in Frankfurt, the search term "*Wirtschaftskultur*" produced only half as many results as the search terms "Corporate Culture." Most of the books whose titles included the phrase "Corporate Culture" were, in fact, written in German (e.g. Lippert (ed.) 1997). The fact that English is, symbolically at least, the "global language" of business, and that much of the international business jargon is in English regardless of the native language of the speaker, suggests that jargon fits in with the discourse of English as global language, acting to exclude and dominate local languages.

The same jargon, however, also incorporates local expressions. German is frequently used in cases where there is no English equivalent (as when discussing *Heimat*, or on one occasion when a formal interview degenerated into a discussion of the exact semantic difference between cosmopolitanism and *Weltoffenheit*), or when a German does not know a particular English word. German technical terms and section designations are also frequently used by all cohorts, due to the fact that the branch's structure was developed by Head Office in response to German market forces. Anglophiles on the German language course would also use German expressions in order to practice them. English also had its regional expressions which have global currency, as it were, thrust upon them: the nickname "Footsie" for the *Financial Times* Stock Exchange Index, for instance, started as a piece of City slang, but has become universal as the FTSE index is quoted all over the world. Local terms are thus not always in opposition to global terms, but display a variety of local and global language uses, which are subject to constant negotiation.

Furthermore, knowledge of British or German jargon words can be taken as much as a marker of global as of local orientation. For a British person to know the meaning of a German technical term, for instance, marks them as someone with inside knowledge of Germany, in the same way as the speaking of German does. The learning of such technical terms from colleagues also provides a bridge between groups at the same time as it marks them off as separate. As the knowledge of English of most Germans in ZwoBank includes a lot of technical phrases, jargon again provides a shared connection with the English; many Germans also picked up a certain amount of London jargon and used it to show a cosmopolitan understanding of local systems. It is thus difficult to say whether the use of English and German jargon is a challenge, a reinterpretation or a site of continual redefinition.

*Analysis*

On the face of it, the use of jargon in ZwoBank appears to support the idea that global business involves the domination of local subalterns by global elites. German technical terms could become common throughout the bank if their adoption is encouraged by Head Office; there was one department which was always referred to by a German name even in the UK, as the impetus for its establishment, and therefore its name, came from Germany. However, who is dominating whom is hard to ascertain: the continued use of English as a global lingua-franca means that phrases which would otherwise be local jargon are adopted into other languages. Acronyms and jargon used in one branch could speedily become general throughout the whole group, and the power of Head Office similarly ensured the spread of what would normally be fairly obscure German terms. Jargon, as much as linguistic crossing, appears to be a way of negotiating between different ways of belonging to different social groups, with different relationships to the global and local, within a wider society.

The use of jargon also reflects the importance of self-presentation in business. The reason for the prevalence of jargon is often not so much its utility, as the fact that it is expected of the user. The currency of jargon thus stems from social conventions of self-presentation in the business world; however, its explicit use as a form of self-presentation rather than of "meaningful" communication (as defined by my interviewees) puts it in a symbolic category, and thus defines it as something which can be used to link, rather than to divide, groups in the global financescape and the localities with which it connects.

Jargon also plays into the negotiation of diversity within the organisation. The fact that language can be used to define different allegiances at different levels allows the cohorts to define themselves as distinct groups while still broadly remaining within particular national cultures: Germanophiles defining themselves as "more German," for instance, by learning German terms, or expatriates displaying their knowledge of "British business culture" in order to present themselves as globe-trotting cosmopolitans (and, at the same time, express a connection to the UK). As discussed in Chapter 5, also, the situation in ZwoBank was such that Londoners frequently presented the restructuring as a dominant Head Office oppressing a recalcitrant local branch, but the complex use of language within the organisation allows Londoners to negotiate strategically with elements of Head Office while at the same time maintaining their position as a righteous, oppressed minority. Jargon was thus employed in ZwoBank as part of the strategic negotiations between various groups within it.

In short, then, the use of jargon in ZwoBank at first seems to define a global culture with German roots dominating a local English workforce. However, when one considers the self-presentational aspects of using particular terms, and that these words and phrases can be used to present oneself in a variety of ways according to particular strategies, it seems that the use of language in fact links German transnational businesspeople with other groups. Language use by and around German transnational businesspeople thus both separates them from, and connects them with, diverse groups and localities, in different contexts and on different levels.

## Jokes *Sans Frontières*: Humour and Strategic Self-Presentation

Humour is another form of communication in which complex social manoeuvring is hidden under a simple exterior. The jokes which will be considered here are those which took place in the London Branch office, during informal meetings and casual social interaction; gossip and joking between participants, ranging from mild to salacious or taboo humour depending on how well the participants knew each other, often seemed to be as essential as was the actual work. Jokes, albeit of a somewhat milder sort, were also used in more formal meetings in order to break the ice; here, however, their use was restricted to the presenter (although occasionally mild to biting sarcasm would be used by the more senior questioners). Humorous images of national affiliation and globalisation would thus be expressed in the same forum as the more serious, "official" ones, and also in a milieu in which power relations are also expressed. Significantly, much of the joking revolved around the supposed "character traits" of English and German "business cultures"; others revolved around transportation and communications equipment, transnational issues such as the Euro conversion, and about relations between branch and Head Office. We shall thus consider here two of the main genres of jokes, both of which link into power relations in the office: work-related and ethnic humour.

### Category A: Work-related Humour

In the office, transportation and communications equipment formed a continuous topic of discussion, and additionally a source of humour. Jokes of this sort often occurred as a result of the failure of one such piece of equipment. As a multinational corporation cannot operate without these, joking about them both relieved tension resulting from the accident and asserted the importance of such items of technology in representing the office's culture and "business culture" in general (Goffman 1961: 122-124); no magazine aimed at businesspeople goes for long without running a piece on the vagaries of trains, planes and computers (e.g. Naughton 1999). Consequently, joking about travel and technology reinforced the importance of transnational and global practices to business, as both are dependent on international communications and transportation technologies. They also, as a result, confirmed the place of the Germans as a transnational elite, as the German expatriates are the employees most closely linked with such items of equipment through their role as bridging the gap between Head Office and London Branch. Jokes about office equipment and means of transportation thus seem to reinforce power relations and interethnic boundaries in the office.

However, such jokes also provided means of expressing diverse allegiances at once. For instance, symbols relating to transportation could be used to denote Germanness, as punctuality is regarded by many, Germans and non-

Germans, as a German obsession (Lawrence 1980: 147). Since many expatriates made frequent use of the cheap Stansted-Frankfurt daily flights, it could also be associated with one cohort at the expense of others. Alternatively, joking about the fitting of the Euro key to the office's computers, which evokes associations of banking and international finance, also connected with discourses of the currency as associated with both Germany and Europe. Joking about communications and transport technology, then, was not so much a means of expressing or defusing power relations between global and local as it was of forming connections between them.

Jokes were thus a way of presenting particular groups in complex ways, and at the same time expressing areas of tension within the organisation. Staff from the dealing room, for instance, came in for a lot of teasing related to their reputation as "cowboys," rich and risk-taking but none too intelligent; this did not, however, simply reflect the tension regarding the prestige afforded the dealing room at the expense of other departments, but also reflected the fact that the dealers are the source of much of the humour in the branch, and are considered to be "good sports" willing to laugh at a joke on themselves. Similarly, an English maintenance man, asked how he had got rid of a mouse spotted in one of the kitchens, joked "I raised its rent"; this does not only express ambivalence about the high rents in the City, but also sends up the euphemistic nature of business jargon and portrays ZwoBank itself (through the image of the mouse) as helpless in the face of the fluctuating City real estate market. Joking thus seems to be more complex than simply reflecting tensions or defining intergroup relations.

This multivalent quality is also reflected in the two most popular cartoons in the City, *Dilbert* and *Alex*, both of which revolve around white-collar individuals employed by an information technology firm and a bank respectively, and which frequently appear on slides shown in meetings, office doors and the sides of computers. *Dilbert*, on the face of it, is a site of elite-subaltern protest, as it derives its humour from playfully exposing inefficient management practice and incomprehensible workplace jargon (see www.dilbert.com for examples); it is a common half-joking aphorism in business that the level of employee dissatisfaction in an office can be measured by the number of *Dilbert* cartoons in the leisure areas. However, much of its popularity stems from the way in which the cartoons creator, Scott Adams, a businessman in his own right, taps into the concerns of people on all levels of the multinational corporation. His parodies of business literature (e.g. *The Joy of Work* [1998]; *The Dilbert Principle* [1996]) are marketed by a press which specialises in actual management-development works, again blending antiestablishment humour with an establishment presentational form. *Dilbert* cartoons are also as likely to crop up in a managers PowerPoint presentation as on a staff member's cubicle. *Dilbert* thus simultaneously expresses protestation against and affirmation of the social mores of business in diverse ways.

*Alex* is equally complex, but in the opposite way. On the face of it, the cartoon is very much a reflection and vindication of the City establishment, revolving around a successful London businessman scoring points off the uncomprehending world around him. However, the cartoon is at the same time a sendup of money- and self-presentation-focused City attitudes (a typical cartoon depicts a businessman who was the subject of a documentary raging at the filmmakers, not for portraying his marital and social indiscretions, but for showing him recommending a stock which subsequently proved to be a bad choice [Fig. 6.1]). Furthermore, it is enjoyed by different groups on different levels: non-City people treat it as a send-up of City mores, City people treat it as an inside joke, line staff treat it as an example of the difference between managers and staff. Both cartoons are therefore used not only to defuse tensions and define images of particular groups, but to reinterpret, connect and define relationships between groups in a playful way.

*Category B: Ethnic Humour*

Nationality-related humour largely seemed to revolve around the tensions of a multicultural workplace in which one ethnic group appears to dominate. One common joke, for instance, involved someone responding to a question in a foreign accent or using a foreign idiom, as when Greta announced in a loud voice that she was going down the street for a *sarnie* (English slang for sandwich). One might also say something similar about the following casual exchange between two older male Anglophiles, upon hearing a nearby group speaking German:

**A:** There's too many Germans in the bank.

**B:** If it isn't Germans, it's people talking German.

Both of these appear to express Anglo-German conflict within the workplace, or possibly to be exposing a site of tension in a "safe" way through joking (see Strecker 1988: 110; Goffman 1961: 122-124) However, while both examples seem to express hostile power relations between English and German, they also call into question the whole notion of Germanness. In the first instance, the *sarnie* joke was

**Figure 6.1** *Alex* **(Peattie and Taylor, 29 July 1999)** (reprinted with permission)

subsequently taken up by an American in the same office who overheard the exchange, redefining the putative group boundary from German/English to non-English/English. The second instance, also, redefines the butt of the joke not as Germans, but as people speaking German, which, in ZwoBank, would include at least some native English-speakers. Furthermore, the joke is made with the unspoken knowledge that the speaking of German has a different meaning for other groups. Ethnic jokes are thus also a form of combination and boundary-crossing as much as they are a form of conflict and renegotiation, suggesting not so much divided groups as of different ways of being "local" and "global within a broader social remit.

There is also, however, the case of "wartime" jokes. This is a type of British humour which relates either to Nazism and WWII, or to the Anglo-American "wartime" genre of films, television programmes and popular novels (such as *Colditz, Secret Army* and *The Great Escape*), which present fictionalised accounts of WWII, often with stereotypically-rendered German villains (Beevor 1999, *Spiegel* 1998d; see Davies 2000 for an example of this genre's use in a British workplace). In the joking sessions in offices, in which employees make fun of each others' personal traits, portrayals of German managers and staff members can draw on "wartime" film clichés and images, albeit seldom in the presence of the subject of the joke. Again, the most obvious explanation is that joking is a form of resistance by English employees, or a form of contestation over power in the workplace.

In ZwoBank, Nazis were seldom referred to in even humorous interactions between English and Germans, but people were not unaware of them, nor necessarily averse to using these images. To cite one of the less offensive examples, when a client turned out to have the same name as a character in a popular British "wartime" comedy, *Dad's Army*, catchphrases from it were bandied about, and imitations of "wartime" stock film characters periodically surfaced during joking sessions. The sports-focused nature of the City also meant that whenever there was a Europe-wide football championship, chants and songs relating to the 1966 England victory over Germany, which often referred to WWII as well (one chant, for instance, began with the words "*Zwei World Wars and Ein World Cup...*") could be heard in the offices. Such images also crop up in "respectable" City newspapers, albeit often in a jocular way, as when a headline in the business section of the London *Metro* read "Germany Poised for Blitz on C&W" (examples can be found in *The Economist* 1998b, c; Hughes 1994; *The Metro* 2000). Even in bank branches in which there is a good relationship between English and German employees, then, jokes relating to WWII and Nazis can be heard, confirming the above hypothesis.

While the Germans with whom I spoke did not openly discuss these jokes, it was plain that they were not unaware of them. When I asked both expatriates and local hires whether they had encountered any preconceived notions about Germans in the UK, most took me to mean prejudices (*Vorurteile*), even though I used the more neutral phrase "preconceptions" (*vorgefaßte Meinungen*). One of the two who said that they had never encountered such stereotypes later said that she had misinterpreted the question. Furthermore, all Germans who had been in the UK for more than a year admitted, in private, to having encountered stereotyping of this sort, albeit normally outside the workplace. Even in non-hostile situations, then, people are aware of negative, anti-German humour.

Significantly, though, this humour was only used in particular contexts. Jokes about WWII only occurred in mixed or English-only groups, never in one-on-one Anglo-German interactions. Furthermore, the people who initiated this sort of joking were usually young English men, and therefore the humour has connections to British "lad culture," which incorporates frequent stylised displays of xenophobia which do not necessarily denote feelings of prejudice on the part of the speaker. The jokes were also used in different ways in each context; in mixed groups, they were never explicitly linked to Germanness or used in reference to German colleagues. In English-only contexts, with the rules being slightly more relaxed, such jokes were often made and linked to colleagues, with the thrill of addressing a taboo subject. When I unthinkingly made a facetious reference to Nazis in the presence of Tom, a Germanophile, while setting up for an interview, he coldly said "We don't say things like that around here"; in the same office, however, I would hear open discussions of "wartime" films in less formal English-only contexts, even some involving Germanophiles. Finally, the same "wartime" images also had a connection to a well-known episode of the popular British comedy *Fawlty Towers*, in which the protagonist Basil Fawlty, played by John Cleese, assaults German guests at his hotel with a ludicrously over-the-top impression of Adolf Hitler; as the incident is clearly played to show Fawlty as an insane xenophobe and his guests as decent, well-meaning people, the use of "wartime" images can also be taken in some contexts as ironic references to *British* insularity. The German-as-Nazi image thus crops up in City humour in a conflict-based way; however, its use in restricted areas, and the potential for irony, suggests that there is strategy involved in its use, and it is not just simply a question of conflict and consensus.

The Germans were also not above derogatory ethnic humour against the British, for instance, referring to Mad Cow Disease, in such a way as to imply either that a colleague has it, or that the British in general are incapable of coping with a crisis. Stereotypical images of the British as effete socialites or as antediluvian union leaders would also emerge in all-German conversations. As with the "wartime" jokes, furthermore, these were not only in monoethnic contexts, but were generally made in German, so as to further ensure that the humour remains private (although, again, the British are not unaware of the genre). Ethnic humour is thus not simply the private revenge of an oppressed group, but a means of building ethnic solidarity for both linguistic groups in the organisation.

One can even go further and say that humour actually crosses and effaces the distinctions between groups. For instance, while much humour revolved around stereotypes of Germans as efficient and work-obsessed, and a few, on the subject of whether a German could "become English," arguably related to *Blut*, none revolved around German foods, *Boden*, or other symbols of Germanness which my German interviewees cited as important, other than those that also tied into images of Europe and of the corporation in question. Even the arguably *Blut*-related jokes focused around issues of belonging in the office and in Europe, via the ongoing debate on citizenship criteria (see Janoski and Glennie 1995; Darnstädt et al. 1999). Also, such jokes seemed to build group solidarity as bank employees as much they seemed to define separate conceptions of German and English, as they could also be taken to reduce cultural differences to the level of eccentric traits. The Nazi-joke genre is more problematic; however, the fact that such jokes were avoided in mixed contexts but deployed in English-only ones suggest that they are used to build solidarity on different levels. An English person can build solidarity with German colleagues by not making the jokes in their presence, but with British colleagues by making them in private contexts; the Germans, for their part, return the favour by limiting their Mad Cow Disease jokes to particular settings. Tom's ostentatious concern about the political implications of "wartime" humour might thus have been intended to emphasise to me, an outsider to the organisation, that he wanted to be seen as sympathetic to the Germans within it. Ethnic jokes can thus build solidarity at the same time as they divide groups.

Joking thus allowed for considerable flexibility in defining and redefining groups, much as Czarniawska's civil-service interviewees were able to redefine their image of their recently-privatized governmental institution through jokes and stories (1997: 108ff.). Because jokes connect groups at the same time as expressing tensions, then, humour thus provided a means of self-definition, not as simple opposed groups, but as a series of different ways of operating within globalisation.

*Analysis*

On the face of it, humour in the office seemed mainly to be a means of breaking tension in a high-stress job, in a manner that recalled Goffman's observations on surgeons (1961: 50, 122-124) and Law's on commercial researchers (1994: 120). This was borne out by the observation that dealing rooms, where people are constantly making split-second decisions, had a more raucous atmosphere than other bank divisions. Most of this humour, as noted, revolved around points of conflict between groups in the office. Joking thus could be seen as a way of expressing and dealing with intergroup tensions in an office with a hierarchy based on ethnic origin and degree of globalisation.

Joking could, however, as Czarniawska notes, also be seen as a means of negotiating power relations within the organisation (1997: 137). The fact that many jokes focused on Head Office suggests that this is the case here; the joking about Germans also could equally be seen as negotiating staff-manager relations, as they were mainly made by English staff members about German managers. Some jokes worked to bring Head Office into the domestic realm, for instance when one locally-hired German department manager jokingly "spoke" for Head Office using the "Royal We," traditionally a UK monarchical form of speech. Joking thus can be a site of negotiating intergroup relations, not only—or even primarily—of dealing with workplace tensions. In the cases of joking, therefore, language and linguistic symbols are not used so much to define groups as to relate in different ways to the global and the local, causing the global to be locally interpreted and the local to become global.

Furthermore, the flexibility of self-presentation was also used as an escape mechanism to change the subject smoothly when the humour was approaching dangerous areas. A series of jokes about a "wartime" film could thus segue into a series about the reputed business efficiency of Germans, into the other personal traits of the individual who was the butt of the joke, or into the setup of the company. One rather clever sequence involved switching, through the metaphor of "takeover as war," from joking about "wartime" images to joking about the merger of two banks, one German, which had recently been in the business news (see Burrus 1997: 210 on warfare metaphors in business). Frequently, when the jokes began to approach too-sensitive areas, it was a common occurrence for participants to change the subject of the joke to a less sensitive topic, or to "turn the laugh onto" the joker by accusing him/her in jest of having something to hide him/herself (during which the abovementioned episode of *Fawlty Towers* was frequently invoked). Furthermore, the joking sessions which referred to Nazis did not refer to real WWII history so much as to images drawn from "wartime" films or television programmes; other groups, most notably Americans, were also made fun of in ways which referred to "wartime" film images of their ethnic group. Within ZwoBank, the image of Germans could be transformed from a negative into a positive one, thus saving face for participants in a possibly contentious conversation. The jokes are thus not exclusively about defining power relations, but are primarily about negotiations between groups in the organisation.

In the case of Germans in business, then, it seems that positive and negative images blend into each other in deliberate and nonconscious ways. For instance, Warner and Campbell's jocular description of German business style as *"Technik über Alles"* may evoke English fears of German "takeovers" (1993: 101). However, the same quality is used in the workplace to avoid, and even to actively pre-empt, the image of the German as Nazi from emerging in jokes, by deliberately situating the image of German-as-Nazi in a fictional context. In humour, then, the underlying meanings of a given discourse can change with startling rapidity.

The case of jokes in the workplace thus again gives us a pattern of a seemingly simple discourse with more complex operations going on underneath its surface. Joking appears to be a way of alleviating tensions, defining groups within the workplace and conveying messages about business practices to one's superiors or inferiors. However, which of these functions dominated depended on the context, and the nature of the jokes meant that they could also be used to blend roles with each other, and even to switch between topics and categories of discussion. This could be used in strategic ways, to actively control discourses within the office; however, who controlled the discourse depended on the situation. Like jargon and language crossing, then, humour defines a multiply-linked, multilayered series of interactions rather than defining solidary groups.

Joking in the office, therefore, does not so much form a site of conflict between groups as a complex site of renegotiation and affirmation on different levels. This, once again, can form the basis for strategising, both playful and more serious, in the financial sphere. This in turn suggests that relations in the business world are not so much a case of global versus local as of multiple forms of globalisation and localisation, linked through diverse forms of symbolic expression. We shall now consider whether the same holds true for the media of communication.

## What Colour is Your Mobile? Communication and Information Technology

Excerpt from my fieldnotes from the summer of 2000:

> Rick [my flatmate, an IT specialist for a non-German multinational bank] gets a call at 10 PM—something's wrong with the network at [his bank]. Even though he has a friend visiting for the evening, he proceeds to spend the next few hours, as far as I can tell, ringing up the rest of the staff, people who might be affected (Treasury mainly), etc., to tell them. He's going in early tomorrow to answer phones. Says a whole lot of equipment's down and they can't see how.

This incident illustrates, more than anything else, the importance of information technology to the modern multinational corporation. As with other means of communication, information technology appears to define a case of a global elite dominating local subalterns, but in fact may be the medium of more complex social processes.

The significance of information technology to business, which began to rise following the "Big Bang" of 1986, has increased almost exponentially of recent years (Castells 1996). In the first year of my study, Information Technology departments tended to be out-of-the-way and limited for the most part to assistance and maintenance functions, and employees had the use only of a basic Intranet; in the second year, the IT department of ZwoBank London expanded over the course of six months from a single office to two offices and a training room, and the employees not only had limited web and Internet access (the degree appeared to vary with rank and function within the company), but the canteen was supplied with computers for personal use on the lunch hour. In any given office, it was physically impossible for an employee not to be near one or more pieces of telecommunications equipment at any given time: one of the first lessons a new employee learns is how to operate the phone system, making technology as much a symbol as a tool of the profession. Within the past few years, mobile phones have gone from being a scarce, expensive resource, the privilege of the jet-setting transnational manager, to being relatively cheap and common. Communications technology is thus, as the incident with Rick indicates, an essential part of the banking world.

Secondly, however, the anecdote indicates the uses of IT as a source of power in the workplace. The fact that communications technology allows a bank to operate 24 hours a day, seven days a week, means that Rick had to interrupt a social engagement to cater to his employers' needs; he habitually kept quite irregular hours, and frequently went into work on weekends, something only rarely done in the City. Banks are now not tied to any particular place or time, but locate and hire wherever they feel is most cost-effective; all City banks have employees who effectively operate on New York or Tokyo time, and certain banks have recently excited controversy by outsourcing their UK call centres to India. Through communications technology, banks increasingly have a presence in employees' "leisure" hours.

This is also the case with the banks' clients. According to an article in *The Economist*, one German bank has closed its New York office physically, but retained a section of employees who live in Frankfurt but operate on New York time; as they have arranged for calls to their New York number to be routed to Frankfurt, many of their customers are not even aware of the switch (1998a: 6). Most banks had websites which they used as platforms for self-presentation; in addition, most were, as noted in Chapter 4, setting up "internet banking" wings, which would allow clients to make transactions at any time, from anywhere in the world (Gordon 2000). Communications technology thus appears to be a site through which banks can obtain increased control over their clients' lives as well as their employees'.

Furthermore, communications technology does appear to play into the national divisions in the workplace. The meeting rooms of the London branch of another German bank, which was the subject of my earlier research (Moore 1999), were each labelled with the name of a major German city, and the presence of videoconferencing equipment suggests that these rooms could "become Germany" on occasion, thereby symbolically locating the branch in another country to that in which it physically existed. In both this bank and ZwoBank, "Internal Only" memos were circulated from the Frankfurt to the London office, suggesting that London was "internal" to Frankfurt and symbolically locating the branch in Germany. Communications technology in the office thus seemed to play into the divisions already discussed, by allowing the German Head Office to define London as internal to itself.

This also held true for ZwoBank's online activities. When discussing plans to develop an Internet wing of ZwoBank with Keith, I asked him if it would still be a German bank in that case. He replied yes. "How can a bank be German and online?" I asked. "Have the website in German," he replied. I countered that most German banks also have their websites in English. "Yes," he replied, "but not a lot, you notice." Despite the much-repeated claim that the Internet is beyond nationality, the use of suffixes indicating a German origin (.de) is common among German transnational banks. The most notable exception is Deutsche Bank (www.db.com), which has recently been repositioning itself as a global bank with American, German and British components, and which uses the universalising .com suffix instead. Again, it seems that the way in which the allegedly globalising, division-erasing Internet is used by German banks continues to give the German part of the workforce the upper hand.

There is also the case of the Vodafone-Mannesmann takeover of late 1999. Both were mobile phone companies which were competing for international, rather than local markets; theoretically, the nationality of the companies should make little difference to the conduct of, and observers' reactions to, the venture. In fact, however, the takeover was described in the presses of both nations as a "war" between two companies, one "English" and one "German"; Germans often referred to it facetiously as the "*Handykrieg*," or "mobile phone war" (see Larsen et al. 2000; Dohmen and Kerbusk 1999; *Spiegel* 1999). The tensions were further exacerbated by a local matter-the fact that the German takeover laws had at the time only recently been relaxed, and that this was the source of much concern from local German businesspeople-leading to both companies taking out advertisements in the German national press openly denouncing each other (Höpner and Jackson 2001: 37-38). Again, business between international companies was formatted in terms of national conflict over communication, and was subject to local as well as global influences.

However, once again, the question of who is dominating, and who is resisting, whom is more complex than it seems. It is telling that "global" suffixes, such as .com, .org and .net, carry greater prestige than "geographical" ones; by using the .de suffix, the banks may assert German domination over the group, but at the expense of the cosmopolitan cachet of .com. Furthermore, English is still the most common language of the Internet, and most German banks (including ZwoBank) have an English version of their website as well—significantly, English is prioritised over the native languages of other countries with large media-literate populations and an interest in transnational finance. The Internet may be a site of conflict between a dominant and a subaltern group, but which one is which depends on the context.

In ZwoBank London, also, communications technology was used in a way which indicated national divisions, but not always in a way which implied conflict. Initially, I noticed that when I called individuals at London Branch, where English speakers generally answered the phone with "Good morning, [bank or person's name]," Germans would answer it either with their own names or with the bank's name, which sounded more or less the same in English and German. When thus addressed, I felt obliged to respond in German, even if the conversation subsequently switched to English; persons unfamiliar with German practice, however, undoubtedly did not feel so obliged. The presence or absence of the initial greeting was thus a means by which those who recognised the style could indicate familiarity with it—and which, significantly, left them the option *not* to do so—but did not exclude those who did not recognise it (see Strecker 1988: 110; Schegloff 1972). This also suggests that the strategic presentation of self does not just operate on the level of rational choice, but can also form a more general "cultural competence" for operating in a particular environment (Ahrens 1996b: 15-16). The use of English and German thus defined a flexible strategy rather than a rigid dividing line.

The result of this is that new communications technologies are neither a force for conflict or of homogenisation, but above and beyond both of these. It is, on the one hand, indisputable that such technology is on some level a globalising force, as it does enable simultaneous communication across the globe in real time (Castells 1996: 461). However, the suffixes of websites suggest that the Internet is not such a globalising force as is often claimed, but in fact is a complicated mix of globalising and localising tendencies. Recent studies of the much-vaunted developed/developing World divide with regard to access to and use of Internet technology also indicate that it is much more of a grey area than first thought (see Miller and Slater 2000). Information technology may, as some critics note, not be as "globalising" as it first appears, but it does appear to be, following Held et al. (1999), transforming social relations between groups in their cross-border activities; again, communications technology does not foster a simple ethnic and/or power divide, but allows for negotiation between different groups and facilitates the flexible presentation of self.

Communications technology is thus neither a globalising nor a localising force, but one encouraging dynamic interaction on a variety of levels. Many business expatriates, according to a recent article, keep in touch with "home" through the Internet; while only some of my interviewees used the Internet for this purpose, all used some form of information technology to keep up-to-date with events in Germany, for instance satellite television (Peraino 1998). However, the context in which they used these resources was a British one, and all used non-German Internet service providers. Most of my interviewees noted that telecommunications do not replace face-to-face communication, but supplement it (see Boden 1994: 209). The overwhelming majority of IT staff in the ZwoBank were young and English-speaking, but non-English and/or non-White, again suggesting social division on one level and mixing on another. Rick came from a Northern English working-class background, a type of person not often seen rising to prominence in the City outside of IT, and reported that, as well as being similarly multiethnic, his department contained a number of openly gay men, who are also seldom found in the hypermasculine culture of banking. Communications technology, like language itself, thus operates on multiple levels simultaneously, being at once a site of conflict and of collaboration.

In short, then, electronic communications media are neither a site of global homogenising nor of elite-subaltern conflict, but instead generate multiple, connected examples of each. Global communications activities could not function without local users and telecommunications managers; however, each actor in this field employs them in a different way. Communications technology thus does not, as some claim, divide groups and is neither global nor local, producing instead a set of linked "globalities" and "localities," meaning that the groups which use them are also multiply linked, displaying a variety of connections to different local and global groups within their social activities.

**Analysis: Talking Business**

It thus seems evident that to consider language and communications media as sites of global-local, elite-subaltern conflict in business—as, for instance, do Willis (1977), Roberts et. al. (1992) and Czarniawska (1997)—is to oversimplify the situation of the transnational workplace and of the German transnational businesspeople. The examples which we have seen so far—language choice, jargon, humour and information technology—all suggest that language use involves negotiation and flexible adaptation rather than straightforward confrontation, not so much defining bounded groups with a particular culture as allowing different groups to negotiate with each other in the global financescape. Furthermore, they suggest that these groups engage in flexible social interactions with other groups on both global and local levels consecutively and simultaneously, defining a kind of broader social form in which they are all engaged, rather than simply a random collection of isolated cultures.

The received view in ZwoBank was that communications activities draw straightforward if flexible boundary lines: German v. English, local v. global and so forth. However, on another level it is harder to say which has the more power and which is the more "global." English may be viewed as the global language of business, but this image is challenged in various ways even as it is accepted. I have been in situations in which the number of native English-speakers at a lunch table outnumbered the number of native German-speakers, and yet German was the language of choice; several Germanophiles became so, paradoxically, through teaching English in Germany. Language was also used by the various cohorts to differentiate themselves and to define each other, as well as in the negotiations with Head Office, rather than simply as a way of marking off two particular groups. Furthermore, the very fact that it is the Germans, not the English, in ZwoBank who are the transnational elite calls the theory into question; not only is the allegedly "dominant" language in fact that of the subaltern group in this case, but both languages are relentlessly mixed within the workplace. The use of language in the office therefore linked the local with the global, calling into question the concepts of local and global. Language is thus not so much a site of challenge as a site in which challenges, along with many other forms of strategising behaviour, take place, and through which intergroup links as well as boundaries may be constructed.

Furthermore, the use of language suggested not so much bounded groups as a series of continually shifting positions along a continuum between the global financescape, other global landscapes, and various other locations, again in line with the uses of culture noted in Chapters 4 and 5. English and German interviewees felt that the English used more courtesy phrases, such as "sorry" or "may I help you?" and indirect phrasing, such as "we suggest..." where Germans were more direct (K. Mann 1993: 7; see also Aitken 1973: 66-67; Ahrens 1996a). An interviewee at the London branch of the bank in the pilot study told me that its German managers should be addressed as "Herr" and with the formal "*Sie*" form of "you" (as opposed to the informal "*du*"), which is more of a German trait, English managers preferring the use of first names (Ahrens 1996b: 25). However, there was, in practice, no sharp dividing line as to how each "style" was used: all employees below a certain rank called the general managers by title and surname (although I was, significantly, informed that this was also typical of Germans at all levels), but all, whatever their status or nationality, used courtesy phrases; anyone not doing so, whatever their nationality, was often accused of being "German." Also, most of my German interviewees—particularly expatriates—said that they preferred the less formal "English" style of speech. Both of these suggest, firstly, that the "German style" does not set off Germans from the rest of the workforce, and secondly, that the designation "English" can relate to a business or corporate, as well as an ethnic, social group. Thus, supposedly "national" languages, instead of defining different and opposing groups, in fact refer to a series of ways of belonging to groups which vary from actor to actor and situation to situation, and which may or may not relate to Germany and England in various ways. There are thus not two national groups here, but a variety of different ways of relating to, and defining, different groups in a wider transnational social context.

Language thus becomes not only a site of power and conflict, but also (and perhaps more importantly) a means of playing with such concepts as national and corporate culture, challenging them on one level while linking and reinterpreting them on others. The fact that German and English can each be used to express slightly different concepts—for instance, the existence of formal and informal terms for "you" in German but not in English—further complicates their use; the relationship between colleagues and department heads could be constructed in several different ways, depending on the language being spoken (Brown and Gilman 1972). The uses of languages are thus complex, referencing multiple positions within globalisation at the same time. German transnational businesspeople, by extension, cannot therefore be defined as a single group opposing a single local group, but as occupying a series of positions within the wider concepts of Germanness, Britishness and global affiliation. Again, while national culture is important there appears to be a higher level, encompassing the interactions of diverse national cultures, at work here.

Similar complexities are visible in the concept, not merely the use, of language and communication in the City as a whole. Much as Leach (1976: 10) notes that modes of communication can be nonverbal as well as verbal, the means of communication itself becomes a way of communicating at the same time: in the case of mobiles, computers and so forth, not only is the medium the message, but, as these devices in and of themselves convey information about their user's origins, role and social status, it is both medium and message at once. Scholtz's (1987) observations on the symbolic value of computerised information, and how the choice and use of a computer system is an act of self-presentation in and of itself, are particularly relevant here. In German transnational business circles, then, language and the media through which it is communicated are thus much more complex than a simple site of conflict or boundary-building, suggesting that its users are less a clearly-defined group, or even set of groups, than occupiers of a series of different and intersecting relationships which change over time: global-local, elite-subaltern, English-German and so forth. Once again, and in line with the findings of Chapters 4 and 5, culture in the City is less a series of definite traits as a site of ongoing social negotiation within a transnational social formation including a variety of national and transnational cultures.

Outside the City, the situation is similar. Organisations set up to promote German business abroad, such as the Anglo-German Foundation or the Goethe Institut, also use English as their default language, and yet are considered no less "German" for that. Indeed, the use of English could be seen as symbolising the "German" trait of adaptability to one's clients' wishes. English itself is not necessarily symbolic of England—or even America—in a business context; at least one language school gives lessons in "Foreigner friendly English" to native English-speakers, instructing them on how to be understood when dealing with people whose first language is different to theirs. One relocation specialist (a professional who helps expatriates to settle in the UK), said in an interview on the structure and function of her company, "Our consultants are all multilingual but you rarely find any [client] who doesn't speak good English," a sentence which operates on multiple levels, simultaneously suggesting the dominance of English, underlining the importance of local knowledge, and expressing the social value both of bilingualism and of having "good English" in a business context. All of these are more important for their use in self-presentation than what they actually are. The use of language in the institutions which support German transnational businesspeople, like those discussed in Chapter 3, is thus not so much a site of conflict as of strategic negotiation of one's place in a constantly-changing transnational social environment.

This complexity means that language can also be used as a site of strategic self-presentation. While the Anglophiles, as noted above, take pride in their monolingualism, many do take language courses, and express no sense that there is a contradiction between this and their assertion that to be English is to be monolingual. Contrary to what one might expect, the learners included as many members of subaltern groups (maintenance staff, for instance) as elites. Their stated reasons for learning German were varied: it could be a career-furthering move, or an attempt to increase employability prospects, or due to personal interest. Some interviewees professed to being motivated by the incentive of taking an hour off work a week. However, individuals' motivations often combined and/or linked with each other, and the image which they presented by learning German was consequently variable. Language thus, rather than defining and dividing groups, in fact refers to different ways of operating within globalisation, and allows these to be shifted over the course of a conversation, again suggesting not so much a transnational capitalist class as different positions within a wider framework incorporating global and local aspects.

Communication is thus a key facilitator of strategic self-presentation in a transnational business environment, enabling actors to construct and reconstruct the positions which they occupy within the global financescape. Goffman speaks of the uses of language as forms of strategic self-presentation, as in the abovementioned case of joking to defuse conflict (1961: 124) or the use of different forms of language in public and private situations (1970: 95). Willis (1977) describes the multiple uses of restricted linguistic codes or "jargon" both as a practical shorthand within the workplace and a form of self-definition; Mars (1982: 178) describes the use of language and humour by staff members trying to get around restrictive management. Boden (1994), similarly, describes "talk" as a medium for negotiating the structure of the organisation; here too, however, one might note that it also negotiates other sorts of relationships at the same time. The complexity of language thus enables its use for strategic interaction.

Consequently, in the case of linguistics as in the case of the City and of ZwoBank as a whole, it is best not to see the situation as being a case of a German transnational capitalist class versus local or noncapitalist classes, but of diverse actors of varying degrees of transnationalism jockeying for position through linguistic signifiers which both express symbols and are symbols themselves. In transnational business settings, the situation is not so much like that described by Mars (1982) or Roberts et. al. (1992), in which language is a site of intergroup conflict, but more like Gerd Baumann's concept of language as a means of developing 'trans-community' orientation (1996: 3); of continually defining and interpreting culture and community—and the relations between communities—on multiple levels. Baumann's "Southallis" are neither resisting, nor are they a single unified community; Baumann describes how the different groups of Southall residents, white, Asian, black and of various religions, sometimes act as a unit, sometimes as several units, and sometimes both at once. In the banks, as in the "traditional" urban society, then, language seems to be less a means of affirming or resisting power relations between particular groups than of negotiating and redefining them in a wider social context.

Much as, in the multilingual environment of a German bank branch in the City, one learns to switch linguistic codes without registering it, people switch discourses, expressing Germanness and cosmopolitanism in different ways through the same means as the context changes. The fact that language can both be a form of self-presentation and also a means of expressing these makes for even more complex avenues through which strategies can be developed, and through which multiple globalisations, and multiple forms of being a transnational businessperson, can be defined according to diverse strategies. Language thus does not define particular ethnic groups, nor power relations between transnational capitalist elites and local subalterns, but different groups interacting in a broad, transnational, and business-focused social environment.

## Conclusion

The various uses of communications technology and language in self-presentation, and the ways in which this is used to negotiate between groups of varying degrees of global engagement, therefore rules against a simple scenario of an elite group versus subaltern local and/or noncapitalist groups, defined by nationality and connection to the global. Rather, it suggests that language in transnational business settings enables the strategic construction of a wider social environment, which contains multiple modes of existence which are sometimes in concert, and sometimes in conflict, with each other.

After looking at German transnational businesspeople as a social group, as a particular expatriate subculture within the City of London, as MNC employees and as users of language and transnational communications, a pattern has emerged which confirms the initial hypothesis that culture in MNCs is not a matter of individuals and groups defining themselves through allegiance to national or transnational cultures, which relate to particular groups, influencing a particular corporation. Instead, we have seen dynamic negotiation between different groups within and outside of the MNC, through strategic self-presentation, to define a constantly-changing social dynamic in the global financescape. We shall now consider the ramifications of the case of German businesspeople in the City of

London for the wider social and theoretical context, and whether they give us any insight into the form and nature that the transnational capitalist society might take.

# Chapter 7

# Global Culture Revisited:
# The Transnational Capitalist Society

## Introduction

The case of German transnational businesspeople in and around the City of London, taking into account their networking activities, their roles in the City, their activities as MNC employees ant their uses of communications media, thus confirms our initial hypothesis that culture in transnational businesses is a more complex and dynamic concept than most of the literature on the subject would suggest, and that the changes within it are driven at least in part by the self-presentation of individuals and groups. Building upon this, I would propose that the individuals concerned do not form a single "culture," affiliated with a particular national or transnational social entity, but that they are a part, or several parts, of an emerging "transnational capitalist society," incorporating more national and more global business cultures in a complex, ever-changing system of linked relationships.

In this chapter, I will first re-introduce Sklair's concept of the "transnational capitalist class" in light of its utility as a theoretical perspective for considering the situation of people and groups in the financescape (as discussed in Chapter 2), and debate how well it fits the evidence presented in the ethnographic chapters. I will then develop the alternative scenario briefly presented in Chapter 1: that these German transnational businesspeople are in fact part of a wider Transnational Capitalist Society, involving many groups of different degrees of transnationalism, which are linked in various ways. Using this theory, I will then investigate how the strategic use of self-presentation in such a context can form the basis for actors to negotiate between the global and the local. Finally, I will consider how my findings extend and develop, and cast new light upon, the case studies discussed elsewhere in the volume, and speculate on the practical impact of this on branch/head office relations, cross-border restructuring and mergers and acquisitions.

## The Transnational Capitalist Complex: National and Global Culture Revised

In order to consider the nature of social organisation in transnational business, we shall first return to the work of Leslie Sklair, and his depiction of the "transnational capitalist class" (TCC) model of culture in transnational social spaces, due to the fact that, as noted in Chapter 2, it can provide a more useful starting point for considering culture in a transnational business setting than the more monocultural theories (1995, 1998a, b, 2001). While Sklair's description can be broadly said to fit the cases described here, it can also be found wanting in certain significant aspects. In this section, we shall discuss the ways in which the German transnational businesspeople described over the past four chapters do in fact fit Sklair's model, and in which ways it must be modified in light of the evidence.

In terms of the debate outlined in Chapter 2 on the nature of culture in transnational business, the German businesspeople described here do seem to fit Sklair's definition of a TCC rather than simply being members of one or more national and/or organisational cultures. Sklair identifies the transnational capitalist class as consisting of four groups (2001: 17): 1) MNC executives; 2) globalising state bureaucrats; 3) globalising professionals and 4) merchants and media. In this monograph, we can identify groups which broadly fit these descriptions: the German expatriates, local hires, Germanophiles and Anglophiles of ZwoBank; the Embassy, school and networking institution staff; the various financial and IT specialists; and, finally, the advertisers and service providers of the City of London. According to Sklair's basic definition, then, the people whom I have considered over the past six chapters are in fact a German transnational capitalist class.

The Germans also appear to fit the social profile outlined by Sklair for members of the TCC. According to Sklair, a TCC is defined by, firstly, the fact that the economic interests of its members are increasingly globally linked; secondly, that it seeks to exert economic control over the workplace; thirdly, that its members take an outward-focused global, rather than an inward-focused local, perspective; and fourthly, that they share similar lifestyles (2001: 17). In his earlier book, *The Sociology of the Global System*, Sklair also defines the TCC as "[t]hose people who see their interests... and/or the interests of their countries of citizenship, as best served by an identification with the interests of the capitalist global system, in particular the interests of the transnational corporations [sic]" (Sklair 1995: 8). Again, as seen in Chapters 3 and 4, these traits do broadly fit my interviewees moreso than definitions based on national, or even third, cultures. My interviewees showed solidarity with individuals elsewhere in the globe in similar professions to theirs; the day after the World Trade Centre bombings, people in the City held a minute of silence in memory of colleagues in New York. The Germans' economic interests were linked with global finance both in their day-to-day work and through the restructuring of the bank from a locally-focused pyramid into, in theory at least, a global network; they also tended to value outward-focused cosmopolitanism and regarded world travel a sign of social prestige; and they tended to live in the same areas as well as having similar consumption patterns and life-cycles. Sklair's criteria do therefore fit the German and non-German transnational bankers discussed in this book better than more monocultural hypotheses.

If we consider the specific activities of the Germans, however, the TCC definition appears to be less appropriate. While the interests of the group's members are indeed globally linked, for instance, this connection takes different forms and strengths depending on the individual and their subgroup or cohort; as noted in Chapter 4, the relationship to the global of a German man married to an Englishwoman and having lived in England for ten years is quite different to that of a young German woman doing a six-month trainee stint in the hope of doing another in New York next year. While it is also broadly true to say that they "identify" with the global system, it does not seem to be a conscious identification, or even a total one, but more a sort of *habitus* into which they drift as a result of their transnational activities. It is also debatable how deep this sense of identification actually goes; it appears to be more accurate to say that they identify with and oppose it depending on what they feel is best for them under the circumstances. Sklair's own remarks on philanthropy strongly suggest that people can work for MNCs and yet still oppose MNC-caused phenomena such as environmental degradation (2001: Chapters 6 and 7). Although the TCC hypothesis is generally applicable to all my interviewees, then it is less useful with regard to specific cases.

This is also true of the suggestion that transnational business elites share similar lifestyles. While this was true in the broad sense, there were notable variations among bank employees in terms of how they lived, depending on age, marital status, gender, nationality, expatriate status and stage in the employee life cycle, and, broadly speaking, their "cohort." Although Sklair acknowledges variation in the TCC (as it consists, according to him, of executives, media people and bureaucrats), he appears to assume that these groups think more or less alike. As noted in Chapter 3, the different sections of the German TCC in London vary considerably in terms of their outlook on the world; while they may all live in Richmond and send their children to the DSL, the Embassy staff ("globalising state bureaucrats") have different attitudes, goals and experiences of England to the businesspeople ("TNC [sic] executives/globalising professionals"). Sklair's model, however, classifies the likes of Rupert Murdoch in the same category as a German-speaking junior manager who visits Frankfurt once a month, or a maintenance man who does not deal with international finance, but has been around the world several times during his holidays. It is also not entirely true to say that transnational businesspeople take a largely outward-focused rather than an inward-focused perspective, as the people with whom I spoke tended to take both, sometimes even at the same time. It is thus debatable how similar the lifestyles and attitudes of the TCC are; we therefore need a model which takes the complexity and diversity which the notion of a "transnational capitalist elite" entails into account.

Finally, there is the question of whether or not the TCC exert economic control over the workplace. While it may be possible to argue that this is true in some cases, most people did not seem to have much in the way of control over their own daily work activities, let alone the global market. All of my interviewees were subject to economic controls at one level or other: they may be an elite in financial and social terms, but how much influence they have over the marketplace as a whole is debatable. Finally, Sklair's list of traits could equally describe other sorts of transnational business cultures, including such low-level entrepreneurs and working-class migrants as Portes' Dominicans or Bauman and Gillespie's Southallis (1996; 1998). Sklair's definition thus appears to attribute too much agency to the German transnational businesspeople, and is painted in terms too broad to capture the diversity of transnational business activity. It might therefore be worth thinking of them less as a powerful group in their own right, and more as a system of groups negotiating and attempting to influence the society in which they find themselves.

It might also be worth looking at Sklair's most recent propositions regarding the ideals and aims of the TCC to consider how well they fit the earlier evidence. (2001: 5-6). The first is that "A transnational capitalist class based on the transnational corporation [sic] is emerging that is more or less in control of the processes of globalisation." In fact, as with the issue of control over the marketplace, it is very debatable how much agency my interviewees actually had with regard to the processes of globalisation; most if not all of them seemed rather to be acting on behalf of their superiors and Head Offices. It is also, for that matter, debatable how much control their superiors and Head Offices had over these processes; even at the top level, my interviewees seemed more influenced by the processes of globalisation than in control of them. Rather than being directed by a particular class, globalising activities appear to be the result of many actions and reactions by other actors, not all of them elite. The processes of globalisation do not seem to be in the control of any single group, but to be constructed through the activities of many, suggesting a diverse society rather than an isolated class.

Sklair's second and third propositions, that "the TCC is beginning to act as a transnational dominant class in some spheres," and that "the globalisation of the capitalist system reproduces itself through the profit-driven culture-ideology of consumerism" are also only applicable here in the broadest sense (2001: 5-6). The areas in which the German and/or British businesspeople acted as a dominant class seemed to be context-dependent: within the companies which I studied, it would be difficult to say that an expatriate "dominated" a local employee, as the local employee might well outrank, and certainly has more local knowledge than, the expatriate. Similarly, the transnational businesspeople did not reproduce their culture *only* through consumerist means; there were other ways of transmitting the culture across generations and cultures, as witness their use of the DSL, Goethe Institut and other non-business institutions. While Sklair does not provide an inaccurate image of the position and reproduction of transnational capitalist class, he does not consider the sheer range of activities which these terms cover, or whether the "class," as it were, is all there is.

Sklair's final point, that "the transnational capitalist class is working consciously to resolve... The simultaneous creation of increasing poverty and increasing wealth within and between communities... and... the unsustainability of the system (the ecological crisis)," is also open to question at the moment. While transnational businesspeople do engage in philanthropic activities (Sklair 2001: Chapter 6), the ecological crisis has been off most corporations' agendas since the end of the Clinton administration; most, also, seem to be more concerned about sustaining than resolving the simultaneous creation of increasing poverty and wealth. Interestingly, however, there existed a good deal more interest in the environment and in corporate philanthropy five years earlier (Renton 1998); this suggests that the traits defining the "transnational capitalist class" are in fact not static, but change and develop over time. Courtney and Thompson's oral history of the City of London suggests that the degree and nature of transnational engagement, capitalist focus and so forth of a given interviewee depends on the time period, the individual's experiences and many other factors (1996). Similarly, Augar (2000) and Lewis' (1989) respective personal accounts show that the degree and nature of their engagement with globalisation changed over their careers, as does the follow-up work which I have done with participants in the present study. Sklair's definition thus does not cover the dynamic nature of the transnational business world as experienced by my interviewees and other qualitative studies of business, in which groups interact with each other and change their views and positions over time.

The reason for this apparent unity at one level, but differentiation at another, within the purported TCC, has to do with the presentation of self. We have already discussed, in Chapters 4, 5 and 6, the fact that businesspeople attempt to present themselves according to what they perceive as the best advantage according to the strategy which they are employing (A. Cohen 1985; Goffman 1956). Following the anthropological works considered in Chapter 1, furthermore, one can say that the flexible nature of the symbols used in this process allow actors to change allegiances from one group to another (Strecker 1988; Sperber 1974; Bloch 1974). It is therefore possible for these individuals to define multiple group memberships and present multiple selves, as it were, simultaneously and consecutively. As we have seen, transnational businesspeople actively make use of this flexible property of self-presentation to retain links to multiple groups, to express unity at one level and division at another, or to reinterpret potentially damaging information in a more positive light. We appear to have here a series of positive-feedback systems, with symbols being deployed, interpreted and employed by many actors in communication with each other (see Burns 1992: 272). The use of flexible strategic self-presentation therefore enables the actors to appear to be a cohesive unit, while on other levels having complex and changing links both within and outside the group, forming a wider pattern of social interaction than simply membership in single national cultures (see Sperber 1974: Chapter 4).

While one should not totally dismiss the idea of the emergence of a globally-focused transnational business elite, then, it seems that, in order to properly consider the situation faced by global businesspeople, one must abandon the notion of a unified, solidary transnational capitalist elite existing in opposition to other, non-transnational and non-capitalist groups in favour of something more complex and self-presentation-focused. However, one cannot abandon the concept of a group of people who are transnational and engaged with capitalism, nor the fact that many such people are closely associated with MNCs, nor that they do appear to form some sort of social grouping. We must therefore find some way of expanding Sklair's theory to take this level of cultural diversity into account.

**Flexible Cultures: The Transnational Capitalist Society Defined**

One way of addressing this issue might be to consider German transnational businesspeople not as a simple transnational capitalist class on their own but as part, or even several parts, of a transnational capitalist society (TCS), developed and maintained through social interaction and self-presentation. This formulation would allow us to acknowledge the more viable aspects of Sklair's theory while at the same time taking into account the more complex picture which we have built up over the past few chapters. We shall thus here define a transnational capitalist society and argue, with examples from earlier in this book, that this model fits the situation described here better than the TCC concept does.

*Definition of the Transnational Capitalist Society*

The transnational capitalist society is a globe-wide social unit which comprises all forms of transnational capitalism, from tourism to migrant labour to transnational business, and the business-focused aspects of other types of transnational activity, such as Internet use and refugee networks. It also includes the links between different transnational capitalist social formations. We shall here define the TCS theory, and how it differs from the TCC theory and theories based on national culture.

      The notion of a transnational capitalist society is one which develops from the four theories discussed at the beginning of the book: the "third culture" theory, Sklair's TCC, Tomlinson's "complex connectivity" (1999a), Goffman's theory of strategic self-presentation, and Appadurai's concept of the unevenly-engaged global financescape (1990), as well as relating to Glenn Morgan's recent work applying the concept of the "transnational community" to the business world (2001), and Doz et al.'s concept of the "metanational corporation" (2001), producing the idea of *a globe-spanning, transnational but locally-engaged, social formation which does not comprise a single, solidary group, but a variety of different groups with complex social connections between them*. This formulation therefore has the benefit of acknowledging the distinctiveness of different transnational business groups and of different forms of transnational business activity, while at the same time recognising the connections, both weak and strong, between such groups and activities, rather than, as Sklair does, arguing for a single, solidary "class" detached from other groups. The TCS formulation also takes into account the fact that some transnational businesspeople have links to other sorts of globalising groups and/or activities, such as diasporas (R. Cohen 1997), displaced groups (van Hear 1998), and small-scale transnational businesspeople (Portes 1998). The TCS is thus a globe-spanning social formation which includes, not only the businesspeople whom we have encountered, but many other sorts of transnational business groups and activities as well, and the social connections between them, and therefore takes greater account of complexity than the TCC theory does.

The TCS also differs from the TCC in that it, following from Tomlinson's argument that globalisation is a form of "complex connectivity" between local sites and global entities (1999a: 149, 195), involves local components. These are included only inasmuch as they are connected to each other and to global social groups. The TCS formulation thus acknowledges the fact that all transnational business activities include local components, which therefore participate on some level in transnational business. Castells, for instance, talks about the irony of the fact that with increased globalisation, more people are moving into cities, when one would expect that the communications revolution would mean that more people would move into the country and work from home (2000). This, he proposes, is because of the concentration of skills: as social networking becomes more important, so companies realise that face-to-face contacts increasingly carry more weight than those made electronically. While the focus of the TCS is transnational, it also includes connections to particular locations in so far as they relate to global activities (see Fig. 7.1).

The TCS formulation consequently allows us to take into account the sheer variety of forms of transnational capitalism, and the fact that groups within it simultaneously remain distinct and yet have, sometimes quite strong, links to one

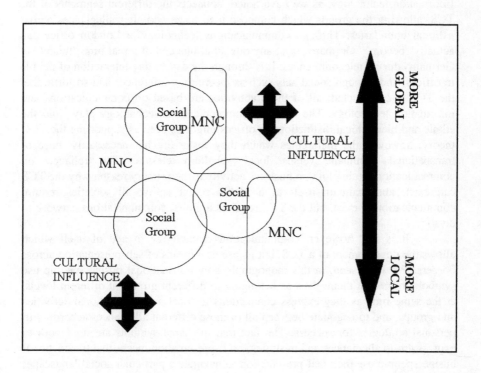

**Figure 7.1  The transnational capitalist society**

another. It enables us to take into account the similarities as well as the differences between, for instance, Sklair's TCC and Portes' (1998) Mexican and Dominican entrepreneurs: the small-scale actors are transnational businesspeople, most of them are elites in their home contexts, and, while they do not inhabit exactly the same social space as the German transnational businesspeople, they do take the same aeroplanes, live in the same "global cities," work for the same MNCs and so forth. Quack and Morgan (2000a) also speak of "national capitalisms," in the plural, indicating that capitalism, like transnationalism, takes different forms from group to group. It is also well-documented that MNCs take different forms, and have different ways of engaging with the local, in different cases (Bartlett and Ghoshal 1992; Doz et al. 2001). The TCS also fits Quack and Morgan's description of markets as a social system "consisting of social structures which emerge from recurrent exchange between different economic actors," and which are shaped by power struggles, external events and so forth (2000b: 44). To consider all of these actors as part of a transnational capitalist society is to include and take into account all of these distinctions, as well as the underlying similarities, between groups involved in transnational capitalism (Fig. 7.1).

The TCS, furthermore, is based upon the use of global communications. Information technology, as we have noted, connects the different segments of the TCS, allowing the groups which compose it to forge and alter allegiances across national boundaries. Through communications technology, a London office can actually "become" Germany, or at any rate sit at one end of a real-time "tunnel" to Germany, during teleconferences. It is through the day-to-day interaction of people in offices, and through social acts such as meetings, conferences and so forth, that the TCS is constructed; all of these activities are based on communications and information technology. The fact that communications technology plays into the ethnic and hierarchical distinctions in offices might be seen as supporting the TCC theory; however, the hierarchies which they foster are not necessarily those of transnational dominant versus local subaltern classes. The reliance on communications technology in business activity is the primary reason why the TCS can exist, and maintain itself as a global social entity; all societies require communication to exist, but the TCS requires a global communications network to do so.

It is not, however, communications technology in and of itself which allows the development of a TCS, but its use as a means of self-presentation across borders. We have seen, in this monograph, how transnational businesspeople use symbols to present themselves as belonging to different groups at different levels, at the same time as they express connections to local and transnational activities and groups, and to negotiate between all of these different allegiances according to personal strategies for success. The fact that the same symbols are used both to express group allegiances and in strategic self-presentation means that transnational businesspeople use their self-presentation to navigate a particular social landscape; in this case, the social landscape as it relates to transnational business activity. The self-presentation activities of transnational businesspeople thus do not define particular groups, so much as membership in different groups on different levels, and complex interconnections between them, suggesting that all of this negotiation activity defines a broader level of activity above and encompassing the national group level—in short, a transnational capitalist society.

In sum, then, the fact that groups within transnational business remain distinct, and yet have undeniable similarities, connections and shared histories, suggests that we are better off thinking of them, not so much as members of distinct and bounded social groups, but as collective participants in a globe-wide society above and beyond their immediate group of identification.

*Support for the TCS Hypothesis*

The merits of a TCS versus a TCC model can be seen in the case of the German businesspeople presented earlier in this book. The case of the City of London, for instance, reveals a pattern less like that of the solidary TCC, and more like the sort of complex patterns of different social interaction seen in wider societies. As noted in Chapter 4, the City appears—and is often said—to be a transnational business enclave which is separate from the rest of the UK, and which is engaged with other transnational business enclaves around the world, in keeping with Sklair's formulation (2001: 17-31). However, despite the City's external links, it has undeniable connections to the UK in that its local employees are British; the impact of the "Big Bang," interestingly, is mainly described by commentators in terms of its effect on the local system of social classes (Augar 2000: Introduction; Courtney and Thompson 1996: 167). Furthermore, the City's connections to the USA and Europe are not uncontested, and form the source of a continually changing discourse among City think-tanks (see Lascelles 2000). Finally, there are many different sorts of transnational businesspeople in the City, including not only expatriate businesspeople and information-technology specialists, but also such diverse groups as immigrant restaurant-owners, ex-military security guards, and tourists. The City, rather than an enclave for elite transnationalists, is a slice of a transnational capitalist society, which contains numerous different groups and maintains links with other local and transnational social formations.

Furthermore, the City achieves this engagement through strategic self-presentation. The objects and images which its members use to define it are deployed in ways which express connections to diverse groups; the emphasis on the City's "multiculturalism," for instance, in many of its popular histories (e.g. Merriman and Visram 1993), fits with transnational businesspeople's valuation of cosmopolitanism, and allows connections with non-UK cities (Corporation of London 2000b). However, at the same time this "multiculturalism" is defined in local terms. The displays at the Museum of London, for instance, focus on visible minorities in Elizabethan, medieval and Victorian times, whereas the prominent German community of all three periods is not mentioned, in keeping with present-day English popular definitions of "multiculturalism" as primarily involving skin colour. Furthermore, there seems to be a continual reinterpretation of the symbols used to present the City, with the Old City people focusing on their connections with the past, and the New City people focusing on their multicultural and international aspects. The City is based on a continually shifting ethos and an imperative requirement to keep up with trends; this makes the ability to shift allegiances essential, and favours actors who are able to present themselves in terms of multiple attachments. As put forward in the TCS theory, then, the City is not only multiply engaged and constantly changing, but achieves this form through the strategic self-presentations of the people who work in its institutions.

In the case of the historical German community in the City, the TCS model is also more relevant than that of the TCC. If we consider them as a TCC, for instance, both the Germans of the 19th century and those of the present-day appear to be members of the same group, and it further seems as if both are part of an unbroken line of German transnational communities in the UK which has lasted since the eleventh century. However, there have been a number of historical changes which break up the alleged "community" (Borer 1977: 89-90; Wraight 1991: 42; Mann 1993: 110-111). Panayi's descriptions of Victorian Germans suggest a quite different lifestyle and social position to those in London today (1993, 1995). At the same time, however, it must be acknowledged that all of these historical groups have a claim to both Germanness and transnationalism. There is also the fact that a number of City companies which were originally either German or begun by Germans (such as Reuters, Barings and Schroeders) and are today thought of as "domestic" by UK people, suggesting again a continual adjustment of self-presentation according to internal and external social influences (Read 1999; Panayi 1995: 17-18, 72, 140). The historical German community thus supports the idea of a connected, continually changing and dynamic TCS rather than an isolated, static and detached TCC.

This can also be seen in the case of the modern German business community. The people whom I interviewed have connections with each other, but at the same time are socially engaged with Germany, the UK host culture and other German (and non-German) transnationals. In their turn, the Germans also affect these groups in and of themselves; the presence of German businesspeople abroad is important to the domestic German self-image, for instance (Hughes 1994: 36-37), and the maintenance of the discourse of cosmopolitanism-as-Germanness among elites. Also, the presence of Germans contributes to the City's self-image as globally engaged, and reinforces its connections with Europe, itself an entity with complex global and local connections (Castells 1997: 267). In Richmond, it is difficult to differentiate absolutely between Germans and non-Germans, as many of the symbols used to present the speaker as German also could be taken as expressing elite social status. It is equally possible to be linked to more than one group at the same time: one of my interviewees was a former City person now working for a German social institution who was married to an Anglo-Asian. Furthermore, the symbols used in the presentation of Germanness are not uncontested, as witness the case of *Heimat*. We therefore see a group whose focus is neither exclusively, or even mostly, global or local, but whose members show a variety of different degrees and types of connection to both positions, sometimes even simultaneously, and which change over time (Skelton and Allen 1999; see also Tomlinson 1999a; Castells 1997; Doz et al. 2001). The example of Germans in the City of London thus suggests a transnational capitalist society which includes engagements to local and non-capitalist global activities as well as a degree of internal solidarity, rather than an isolated class.

The relationship of the Germans in the study with outside institutions also suggests a diffuse but linked "society" rather than a solidary "class." The cultural institutions, the DSL, and the various business organisations are all connected to the German transnational businesspeople working in the banks; furthermore, they appear to unite diverse elements under a transnational business remit. While there may be divisions between Embassy staff, short-term expatriates and long-term emigrants, for instance, all of them have children at the DSL; the DSL itself is talked of in terms of belonging to the "German" school system, with the differences between regional educational systems in Germany itself being glossed over. However, there are differences in the ways in which members of each group experience transnational capitalism. The adaptation of children, while they may all be attending the same school, varies from case to case, and differs from that of their parents. Similarly, different people going to conferences, using institutions and so forth gain different things from them and deploy them in different ways, as witness the behaviour and motivations of the diverse attendees of the GBF conference. Furthermore, all of the institutions discussed here may be transnational and capitalist, but they are transnational and capitalist in different ways to each other. The businesspeople and institutions therefore are better described as elements of a TCS, showing variation within a wider social grouping, than as fellow-members of a transnational business elite.

Moreover, it is also possible to see complex patterns of relationships in the interactions between businesspeople and cultural and business institutions. Even people who do not participate in or make use of an institution are affected by its presence, and indeed the very act of not participating may constitute a symbolic use of it. By defining themselves in opposition to the Embassy staff, for instance, businesspeople are acknowledging this group's claim to transnational elite status and, furthermore, are using this group's definition of themselves as part of their own self-definition. Furthermore, there are always exceptions; philanthropic contact between businesspeople and charity organisations, for instance. The diverse origins and agendas of the people at both conferences described here suggest members of a global society with different ways of relating to Germanness and cosmopolitanism; owing to the multivalency of symbols, even non-German people can in some circumstances lay claim to Germanness. Indeed, as in the case of the Goethe Institut pamphlet placed on the bulletin board at the bank, symbols of Germanness can also be used in the self-presentation of non-Germans. The relationship of the different groups to each other is thus not one of people unified within (or excluded from) a TCC, but of different members of a TCS, relating to each other in different ways.

The same can be said of ZwoBank. Again, this MNC appears to form a reasonably self-contained transnational community of the sort to which Sklair's description is most applicable (2001: Chapter 3). Even here, however, it is not so much a transnational social entity in and of itself as much as it is an acknowledged part of a wider transnational social formation partly defined through its own self-presentation. Companies change, as the matrix integration described in Chapter 5 demonstrates; during this process, the ways in which employees and organisations present themselves change as employees assume new roles and the relationships between branches and Head Office are re-examined, but this does not involve the construction of a new group so much as a rethinking of relationships between the old ones. Furthermore, companies also make use of strategic self-presentation to navigate between different social groups, transnational and local: Siemens, for instance, can be a global company, and/or a German company, and/or a symbol of German national affiliation—and for its UK employees and the surrounding town, their presentation of group allegiance—and also, particularly in the case of *Mittelstand* firms, discourses of affiliation pertaining to the German hometown. MNCs, ZwoBank included, are not self-contained transnational entities, but are engaged with others and change their self-presentation according to circumstances.

Furthermore, the flexible and constantly changing nature of self-presentation in ZwoBank again suggests a dynamic TCS rather than a static, unified and singular culture. The fact, as we have noted, that the ZwoBank employees described relationships within the company very much in terms of German versus English is largely down to the environment in which they found themselves (to say nothing of what they had been told about my purpose for being there). A competitor bank, whose director was also interviewed in connection with this project, presented itself at the time as a global organisation with German components rather than as a German firm with a UK branch. This flexibility also stems from the mobile nature of life in a City office, with its short-termist ethos and its employees continually shifting location while using their desks as symbolic bases. The fact that most corporations apparently go through restructurings, mergers or other changes regularly every few years also reflects the dynamic nature of the environment. In addition, the focus on self-presentation owes much to the information-focused nature of the City, in which companies and individuals communicate their self-images in strategic attempts to establish or re-establish themselves, and in doing so define themselves as parts of a wider transnational social entity (Jackall 1988: 163-170). Not only are both the City and the corporations within it focused around the constant changing of strategies and the possession of multiple allegiances expressed through strategic self-presentation, but in doing so, their members define themselves as a wide, diverse and transnationally-engaged group with an interest in business.

The description of ZwoBank in Chapters 5 and 6 also includes diverse ways in which to be transnational, rather than of simply being an elite enclave. ZwoBank contains a variety of different groups: there are long-term expatriates, short-term expatriates, non-German Germanophiles, Head Office employees whose remit includes all international branches even though they themselves seldom leave Frankfurt, trainees, spouses and children. The same organisation has more and less global sections, all of which relate to the global in a number of different ways. In fact, it was often difficult to pick out who were the "true" transnational businesspeople: the German expatriate who had never been to any country other than Germany and England, his wife, taking a leave of absence from her job to join him in the UK, the German manager with an English spouse, or the English contract employee with family connections all over the world and a job record which takes in stints in Hong Kong, South Africa and the Middle East. A number of other works on transnational businesspeople suggest that this is not atypical; both Sakai (2000: Chapter 2) and Kelly (2001) note distinctions between Japanese managers who are locally hired and those who are simply taking a job overseas for a couple of years. Comparing the work of both these researchers to Hamada's 1992 study of Japanese international managers, we can also see a change in the nature of the group as a whole over the intervening years, due to the increased emphasis on internationalisation in Japan and the shock of the 1996 financial crisis. In some ways, the bank studied here can be considered a unified entity; in others, a divided one; in still others, a subunit of a wider entity, be it German business, the global financescape, or whatever it may be. All of these groups have very different relations to the local, the global, and capitalism, rather than simply being part of a TCC, or part of a hierarchical system opposing elite transnational businesspeople to subaltern local hires. Consequently, the diversity of ways in which ZwoBank presents itself, and its members present themselves, suggest the kind of loosely-unified diversity typical of societies rather than subcultures.

The internal diversity exhibited by ZwoBank and other companies, furthermore, is often overlooked by researchers studying MNCs. While many articles and books exist on the relationship between branches and head offices, and on the nature of culture in MNCs (Mueller 1994; Ghoshal and Nohria 1989), little consideration (beyond some side remarks by Hofstede [1980: 105]) has been given to the fact that corporations also contain within themselves a variety of non-national groups with different relations to Head Office, the home country and each other, and quite diverse cultures. Using the TCS hypothesis, one can take into account these divisions, and the ways in which they shift as the company changes; according to this theory, any organisation is the intersection of different groups, and itself intersects with other organisations. The internal diversity of MNCs is thus better accounted for by a formulation which takes diversity as well as solidarity into account.

By looking at Germans in London as part of a TCS, divided and multiply engaged, we get a quite different picture than when we consider them as members of a self-contained transnational entity, and are therefore able to take their internal as well as external engagements into account. We shall now consider the implications for wider theories of culture in business studies.

*The TCS, Home and Host Country Cultures*

The TCS model also provides a more useful means of analysing of the respective influence of the home and host cultures on a corporation's culture than the more traditional, static models. Most research, even that which acknowledges that the relationships between the subsidiary and the headquarters are different in different circumstances (as in Ghoshal and Nohria 1989), frequently does not recognise that these relationships are actually dynamic, as are the degrees of influence of home and host cultures on any part of the organisation. More recently, critiques of this approach have developed, which, significantly, are focused on strategy and change; Kristensen and Zeitlin, for instance, discuss how a company's strategy is dependent on its context and history, and affects the outcomes of its dealings (2004). Birkinshaw (2001) also discusses how the corporation's strategy depends on its internal and external environment. In the case discussed here, prior to the restructuring of ZwoBank, the influence of the home country was evidently seen as something largely confined to particular areas of the bank. Subsequently, however, as the changes began to take hold, employees felt a greater sense of engagement with the home country. Similarly, prior to the restructuring the existence of London Branch was of little concern to most people at Head Office, who were afterwards forced into greater contact with it. Head Office and branch, also, had both developed different ways of presenting the organisation while at the same time remaining parts of the same group. The relationship between branch and head office is thus difficult to define in terms of a single culture, transnational or otherwise, but less so in terms of a transnational capitalist society which incorporates multiple, changing cultures.

The relationships within the corporation, furthermore, do not define a transnational elite and local underclass so much as they do a continuously negotiated dynamic between global and local cultures in a wider social context. While the relationship between groups in the office could be viewed in terms of dominant/subaltern, transnational/local conflict, in fact what took place seemed to be more of a complex negotiation between different groups in the office and the company of varying degrees of global engagement. Furthermore, not all of these were defined by nationality or control of resources. The use of language, for instance, or differences in meeting styles, involves other discourses than nationality, including section rivalry, age, the difference between private and public space, and many others. There are significant differences between the global engagement symbolised by speaking English, and the global engagement symbolised by speaking German, and yet people can express both discourses, even simultaneously in the case of, say, English-speakers who also know German. Again, what we have is not a case of bounded groups in a dominant/subaltern relationship, but of actors linked in different ways, interacting in a changing, symbolically defined environment.

This can also be seen in the case of communications both within the office and with outside groups. In the case of "wartime" humour, a joke can be at once or sequentially offensive and inoffensive, depending on the context, the intention, the interpretations of the listeners and so forth. The use of information technology, also, did not so much define a bounded transnational social formation as it did a variety of groups using technology in different ways to engage with global and local actors. The nature of communication in MNCs such as ZwoBank is thus an interaction of many groups, individuals and organisations in a system which is global, local and many things in between, simultaneously and at different times.

Communications technology thus does not define an isolated elite, transnational or otherwise, but a multiply engaged TCS comprising many different elite and subaltern groups, reproducing itself by means of strategically deployed information.

As well as providing a more flexible way of defining groups in transnational business, furthermore, the TCS theory also illustrates how members of such groups negotiate between local and global cultures. The German businesspeople may form an elite transnational enclave in some ways, but they also mediate between two or more geographical localities, and in ways which change over time. For instance, one of my friends from ZwoBank was living in London and maintaining a flat in Frankfurt when I met him, but by the end of the study had moved back to Frankfurt and was in a job which involved daily communication with many locations around the globe, but no travelling. There were also, as noted, quite different groups around the bank, who related to the local and the global in different ways. All of this, furthermore, was achieved through strategic self-presentation; by defining themselves symbolically, these individuals could maintain global and local contacts, but change the nature of these connections subtly as their circumstances change. The different groups in and around the bank mediate the global and the local in particular ways, through the fact that they draw on each other for their strategic self-presentation and in turn contribute to that of others. The TCS theory thus allows us to describe how the German businesspeople negotiate between the local and the global in their daily lives, by seeing it not as the detached interaction of one group with another, but of individuals moving from one position within a society to another through their self-presentation activity.

The sheer diversity of the ways in which this was achieved, finally, suggests that the relationship between global and local cannot be properly defined using the TCC theory alone. Rather than maintaining their own self-definition and imposing it upon local subordinates, the German transnational businesspeople would incorporate local UK modes of self-presentation into their repertoires. What it is to be "German" is determined in this case as much by the English definition of Germanness as the German one. The sheer complexity of ways in which the global and the local relate in the case of Germans in the UK thus necessitates the use of a symbolically engaged, broadly focused model such as the TCS theory rather than one predicated on dominant/subaltern relations between isolated groups.

While they can be seen in some circumstances as a solidary elite group, then, the examples given suggest that it is more useful to consider German businesspeople in the UK as part of a wider transnational capitalist society, internally divided and externally engaged, than as a transnational capitalist class. What seems, considered one way, as a closed-off, isolated elite can also be demonstrated, through an examination of its use of symbols in self-presentation, to contain a variety of subgroups and include external connections, transnational and local. The use of flexible self-presentation does not only provide a continuously changing way of navigating the business environment through the use of telecommunications, but also allows actors to negotiate between local and more global social formations which form part of the same TCS.

In sum, then, the examples discussed in the preceding chapters indicate that the German transnational businesspeople do not so much form a transnational capitalist class in and of themselves, detached from other groups, but instead form a part of a wider transnational capitalist society. This is a theoretical construct which defines a sprawling, worldwide, multiply connected social network, which is globally engaged in many ways, but which also includes various links to different sorts of local cultures; groups can thus remain distinct on one level while acknowledging their links to one another on other levels. The TCS model thus provides a way of understanding, and modelling, the complexity of culture in transnational business which is more in line with what we have seen than more monoculturally-focused theories.

## Multiple Engagements: The TCS, the Global and the Local

The TCS model, however, is not simply a means of explaining how people in the global financial world interact amongst themselves and with other transnational groups. It can also go some way towards helping to understand the elusive and multifaceted relationship between the concepts of "global" and "local" in business and elsewhere. In this section we will consider the wider implications of the concept, and how the transnational capitalist society model can provide a way of explaining of how the local and the global are related.

### Theories of Globalisation and the Global-Local Question

The question of how to consider the relationship between the local and the global has resulted in a number of diverse, even contradictory, answers among sceptics, hyperglobalisers and transformationalists. In the sceptical camp, Smith argues that there is no connection between the two, saying that global social formations, lacking signifiers of geography, history and so forth, cannot "support" identification in the same way that a region or a nation can (1995). Mintz, likewise, argues that globalisation is just colonialism by any other name (1998: 120, 117, 125). Proponents of the sceptical viewpoint, assuming that they acknowledge that the global exists, thus hold that there is little or no connection between the global and the local, and that, if there are, the local always dominates.

Hyperglobalisers, similarly, argue for a sharp distinction between global and local. In this case, however, the global frequently dominates. Robertson speaks in terms of localisation as the reverse side of globalisation, but which goes on at the same time as a kind of reaction to its processes (1992: 146). Waters, similarly, describes how the act of consumption is universalised and localised at once (1996: 58). Hyperglobalisers thus tend to argue that the local is an adjunct to the global, or else is a part of it rather than a distinct entity in its own right.

Within the transformationalist camp, however, there are several different ways of constructing the relationship between global and local. One response has been to define the two as distinct but connected: Hannerz, for instance, describes a scenario in which some, mainly elite, individuals are globalised and everyone else is localised, a formulation which agrees broadly with Sklair (1996; Sklair 2001). A second has been to suggest that the act of transnationalism is one of linking localities, as argued by Guarnizo and Smith, who propose the term "translocal" to define the act of building symbolic bridges between diverse areas (1998: 13). This would include the practice by nations which stop short of statehood, as Castells diplomatically puts it, of making use of the international media and global communications technology to support and further their cause (1997: 52, 80, 84). This definition can also include many different sorts of relationships, however; Yeung cites three such "region states," Wales, Northern Italy and Silicon Valley, all of which relate to the global in different ways and are quite different in and of themselves (1998: 294). The transformationalists thus have developed a theory which involves the acknowledgement of a variety of diverse relationships between the local and the global.

Castells, furthermore, puts forward an explanation of these relationships which is not simply a matter of global and local, but of an opposition between the Net (i.e. globalising social networks) and the Self (i.e. the individual), which includes global and local components (1996: 3). He points out commonalities between national groups, regional groups, and groups such as the green and gay rights movements, in that they have local aspects but also define themselves over space and time through symbolic self-presentation, using a variety of media (1997: 123, 215). In this formulation—again, considering the same phenomena as the other researchers mentioned here—Castells comes up with a model suggesting that we think in terms of multiply engaged social networks with local and global connections.

In business studies, the question of the relationship between global and local is also much debated through studies of home versus host country effect, and with similar results. Some writers tend to argue that the one dominates the other (Hickson and Pugh 1995; Bergsten et al. 1978). Others suggest that there are different kinds of firms incorporating different relationships to home and host countries, as in Ghoshal and Nohria's typology of scenarios (1989: 325). Still others debate the merits of ways of structuring a firm in particular conditions (Garth Morgan 1997). Business studies thus parallels the hyperglobaliser/sceptic/transformationalist debate seen in other social sciences.

It thus seems that there are a number of ways of describing the relationship between global and local social formations, all of which seem to hold true under their particular circumstances. Held et al., summing up their discussion of the impact of globalisation on local entities, conclude that "contemporary globalisation is not reducible to a single causal process but involves a complex configuration of causal logics" (1999: 436). They note that globalisation is uneven and inconsistent (442), and say that the impact of globalisation on state power is the "confluence of globalising tendencies" (437). They also note the difficulty of drawing the boundaries of a political community in a global/regional world order (446). Tomlinson, similarly, argues that globalisation should be considered in terms of "complex connectivity" (1999a: 2), that is, that the global and the local are connected in a variety of ways, not just through a simple all-defining process. While it seems to be generally agreed that there are many ways of explaining the relationship between the global and the local, it is less easy to explain how this is done, and how this multiplicity of relationships is in fact possible.

When considering business activity, then, social scientists have come up with a variety of different, even opposed, ways of relating the global to the local. It may thus be that we need to develop the transformationalist viewpoint further to encompass the diversity of links and oppositions between local and global, again, perhaps, by thinking in terms of a wider society rather than of isolated groups.

## Complex Connectivity, the TCS and the Global-Local Question

If we consider the connections between local and global in terms of strategic self-presentation, however, things become clearer. As we have noted, the flexible aspects of self-presentation allow one to express local connections—such as working for a German firm—and also global connections—such as the firm's UK subsidiaries, or its global reach—at the same time. We have also discussed how this same property means that what seems like the same sort of relationship—say, between German and UK employees in a bank branch—can differ quite strongly from each other at the ground level in terms of meaning and interpretation. It thus seems that, in transnational business, the "complex connectivity" which Tomlinson describes is achieved through the use of strategic self-presentation.

This model of complex connectivity through symbolic self-presentation is supported by the examples seen in Chapters 3-6. We have seen how the use of strategic self-presentation allows German businesspeople to be part of definite groups in some cases but not in others, to acknowledge more than one allegiance at the same time, and to develop complex webs of connection and division within a single organisation. Each of the four cohorts in ZwoBank had quite different connections with Germany, the UK and the firm, even though these were expressed through the same discourses. A comparison of Head Office and London Branch also reveals very different ways of defining the relationship between the local and the global, but in fact the symbols used to define these are common to both of them, and there is also much communication and social exchange between the two groups through interbranch meetings, exchanges and so forth. In the case of *Heimat*, furthermore, the flexible symbolic discourses associated with term can be used not simply to link the local with the global (by providing, say, an Argentinean German with an "imagined" homeland as a means of identification [see Goltz 1998: 6, 69]), but to link various sorts of global with various sorts of local entities (linking any combination of town, state, and country with any combination of firm, financescape, mediascape, cosmopolitan group and so forth). In the case of business, the way in which the relationship between home and host country, or branch and head office, is defined is symbolic, and therefore subject to change as the strategy in question changes. Through the use of strategic self-presentation, the Germans connect, mediate between and negotiate not only "the global" and "the local," but different ways of being global and local at different times and in different places.

The global and the local are thus connected not simply in terms of elite-subaltern relationships or direct contact between particular "cultures," but through the strategic self-presentation of particular actors in a complex, multiply engaged transnational capitalist society. The essential nature of communications technology to the existence the TCS, and the fact that this can be used in a variety of ways, provides the medium of self-presentation. However, the actors in this sphere can be more or less global in different contexts, and have diverse connections to the local and the global through their own activities and through their links to outside institutions. Through these activities and the symbols through which they present themselves, actors are continually constructing themselves and their environment, and are in turn being constructed by others. Consequently, the relationship between global and local is continually redefined to fit the situation through the self-presentation of individual and collective actors; furthermore, the concepts of the local and the global are symbolic constructs themselves, residing more in the collective definition and redefinition of people using the ideas. The multiply engaged, globalising nature of the TCS means that it is predicated on, and influenced by, the use of symbolic self-presentation, and consequently that actors within this society are able to link global and local activities through symbolic discourses.

At one point during my fieldwork, I asked the director of an Anglo-German business organisation to define globalisation. His response was to say that "Globalisation simultaneously forges bonds and allows for the actions of culture." Globalisation, at least in the context of transnational business, is something which allows for local connections, but also for the action of diverse sorts of culture, corporate, national and otherwise, of varying degrees of transnationalism. Transnational business cultures are thus not so much solidary and detached as they are fragmented, changing and engaged with the transnational, the local and the financescape in diverse ways, and which are constructed and developed through flexible self-presentation. The nature of the transnational capitalist society thus not only means that we have to consider transnational groups as networks of relationships rather than isolated, bounded entities, but also that, in order to understand the relationship between local and global, we must look to the ways in which these relationships are expressed in a wider social context including both local and global components.

It therefore seems that the transnational capitalist society theory does not simply provide a means of defining the webs of relationships which underpin global financial activities. Rather, the fact that the concept is predicated on the use of symbolic discourses of self-presentation means that it can explain the complexity and diversity of ways in which global and local social entities and activities are related, and provides a means of understanding these relationships. We shall now consider some of the theoretical and practical implications of the concept.

**What to Do about Culture: The Implications for Global Business**

Although based on a single, detailed case study, the TCS theory as outlined here can be generalised to other sorts of organisations to address practical concerns. In particular, it has general implications for the ways in which branch/Head Office relationships are conducted; for the carrying-out of transnational restructuring programmes such as the one considered in Chapter 5; and, finally, for cross-border mergers and acquisitions. We shall now briefly examine some of these issues.

In the case of branch/Head Office relationships, the ZwoBank example suggests that a different approach is needed to the monocultural approaches of the past, and perhaps even to the more complex "third-culture" position. Rather than considering the organisation as having a single culture, however much a product of individual circumstances, the TCS theory allows us to take full account of dynamic, complex cultures which emerge from particular historical circumstances and relationships. Also, rather than seeing branch and Head Office as isolated from each other, influenced only by different national cultures—or as united, linked by a solidary organisational culture—the TCS portrays both as participating in each other and in other cultures, subject to diverse linkages being closer to and more distant from each other at particular points in time. It also takes into account the possibility that there are subgroups within the organisation which may transcend individual branches (such as the putative transnational business elite), or which may be peculiar to a single branch (such as the cohorts of ZwoBank London), but which have an influence on the way in which the organisation is run and structured. The TCS theory thus provides a model by which one can consider organisations as the product of particular circumstances and containing particular dynamics within them, through acknowledging them as part of wider social networks rather than the process of simple interactions between two or more cultures.

The TCS theory also has implications for the way in which transnational restructuring programmes are carried out. The case of the ZwoBank matrix integration scheme, discussed in Chapter 5, indicated that the failure to take subcultures within the branch into account caused unnecessary tension within the branch, and between the branch and the head office. A good deal of the problems within the restructuring, moreover, stemmed from the fact that the employees in charge of cultural issues in the restructuring considered the organisation in terms of individual business cultures, one more "German" and one more "British," than taking the diversity of the organisation into account (Moore 2003). Had they instead looked at the organisation from the point of view of diversity, not assuming them to be single, solidary institutions but taking into account the different potential influences within and outside of the branch, they might have been able to draw up a complex map of the situation which would take the true nature of the organisation's culture into account (see Fig. 7.2). This approach would also have allowed them to consider the strengths and weaknesses of the new structure for the organisation; many employees argued, for instance, that it would be impossible for a branch of that size and degree of social integration to begin operating instead as a set of sections linked to a globalising Head Office, and indeed, follow-up work indicated

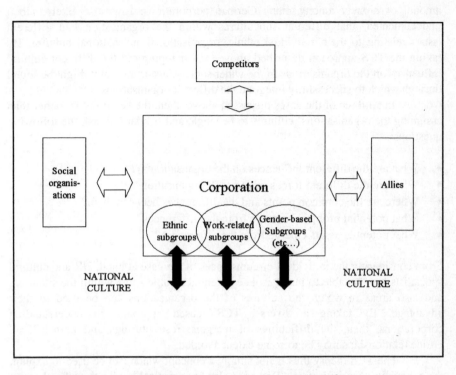

**Figure 7.2 Prototype TCS map of influences on a corporation**

that the branch had to be even more radically restructured than initially predicted in order to achieve this end. The TCS theory could thus be practically applied to the problem of cultural barriers to organisational restructuring, by allowing people to consider the diversity of influences on the corporation.

Similar issues apply, to a certain extent, to the conduct of mergers and acquisitions. Cody's account of the merger of two American medical-supplies companies indicates that most plans for mergers do not take into account the different histories and social forces which have an impact on the cultures of the organisation: although Cody does not indicate this, it seems that much friction within such ventures comes, not only from the tensions produced by the takeover situation, but from failure to take the cultural complexity of the organisation into account (1990). This can also be seen in the case of the Vodafone-Mannesmann takeover discussed briefly in Chapter 6: in that case, national culture, and the historical relationships between the countries of origin of the two companies, had a strong and unexpected impact on the takeover, causing it to be much more fraught and emotional than had been anticipated (Höpner and Jackson 2001). To this one might also add the nature of the IT sector, and the fact that takeover laws in Germany had then only recently been relaxed, a move which caused a certain amount of anxiety among many German corporations. It is also likely, albeit undocumented, that different subcultures within the organisation had different issues relating to their individual ethnic, organisational and national cultures. By taking the TCS approach described above, and mapping out the different cultural influences on the organisations in the wider society, a starting point might be found through which to successfully integrate the different organisations.

In all three of the cases discussed above, then, the key point is, rather than assuming the organisations' cultures to be single and solidary, to ask the following questions:

- What are the different influences on the organsation(s)?
- What are the different forces *within* each organisation?
- Where are the common points and the differences between them?
- What potential problems emerge from the differences?
- What potential assets emerge from the differences?

From considering the individual circumstances of the case at hand, HR and cultural specialists may be able to better isolate potential trouble spots within the situation, and also areas in which the cultures of the organisations can be used to their advantage. By taking a diverse, TCS-focused approach to understanding corporations, then, the difficulties of mergers, restructurings and branch-Head Office relationships may be to some extent avoided.

The TCS theory thus is not simply a concept which can be used to explain the behaviour of organisations. Rather, it also has practical implications for the way in which MNCs run branch/head office relationships, conduct M&A and restructure themselves. The application of the TCS to such situations highlights the need to take into account multiple influences and individual cases when making changes within organisations, rather than thinking in terms of paradigms and models which try and generalise for all organisations.

## Conclusion

In the case of the self-presentation of German transnational businesspeople, then, the situation appears, at first, to be a case of an emerging transnational business elite defining itself through possession of a particular "culture." However, the act of self-definition on their part requires an acknowledgement of, and engagement with, diverse ways of being German, transnational and a businessperson, as well as interactions with other groups, local and global. Furthermore, to look only at the one definition of this group is to fail to consider the place of German transnational businesspeople in the wider global financescape, and to avoid the question of how to define the complex and diverse ways in which these actors navigate between "the global" and "the local."

The fact that the presentation of self through symbols of national and transnational allegiance takes place in different ways in different contexts and on multiple levels suggests, therefore, that MNCs and businesspeople are best considered, not in isolation as individuals and corporations with a particular "culture," but as part of a wider transnational capitalist society incorporating many cultures with diverse links. More importantly, however, it seems that the TCS's symbolic nature is the key to understanding the relationships between different sorts of global and local social formations. Finally, this theory has practical implications: by viewing organisations as dynamic, complex mixtures of cultures, instead of in terms of single cultures acting in a vacuum (however complex the definition of these cultures may be), organisations may lay themselves open for problems and conflicts during restructuring programmes, mergers and the management of global and multinational corporations.

Chapter 8

# Conclusion:
# Defining Transnational Business
# Cultures

## Introduction

Over the past seven chapters, we have examined a variety of ways in which culture
is used strategically by German transnational businesspeople working in the City
of London. The results of this admittedly limited overview suggest that
transnational businesses are neither dominated by national cultures nor wholly
detached from them, but exist in a system of complex relations between different
global and local cultures, both national and organisational. More significantly,
however, the findings of this study have implications for both theoretical and
practical implications both for researchers in anthropology and international
business, as well as for practitioners conducting business in the globalising
environment. In this final chapter, I will restate my conclusions and consider the
theoretical contributions and limitations of this volume, along with the possibilities
that it opens up for future research.

   Throughout this work, I have argued that the empirical evidence does not
so much support the extant model of individual "cultures" belonging to particular
groups, as it does the concept of a "transnational capitalist society." This TCS is a
globe-spanning social construct comprising many different groups and subgroups,
all with varying degrees of global connectedness, and with links to each other of
different kinds and strengths. This model provides a more useful way of
understanding the influence of culture on organisations, and the way in which
globalisation affects business, than more monocultural theories; it is also more
accurate to the lived experiences of transnational managers, allowing us to take
into account their non-business connections (as outlined in Chapter 3) and the
internal fault-lines along which they align themselves (as discussed in Chapters 5
and 6). It also, through the discussion of the restructuring in Chapter 5, provides a
way of looking at transition periods in organisations which does not simply focus
on conflict between two cultures,  but on the different benign and negative
influences on the organisation. The TCS theory, by considering managers as part
of a society rather than as isolated groups, gives us a new way of looking at the
organisation which allows us to take individual contexts and situations into
account.

## Somewhere, Out There: Culture and the Transnational Capitalist Society

The unique contribution of this thesis is thus not only to cast light on the lived experiences of transnational businesspeople and to provide a comprehensive model of culture in the global financescape, but also to suggest a theoretical construct which may allow us to better understand the ways in which businesses operate transnationally. In this section, I will discuss how the TCC theory improves upon earlier ways of looking at transnational business activity, supported by the empirical evidence seen in the previous four chapters.

The TCS theory, as stated in the previous chapter, draws upon Sklair's "transnational capitalist class" theory, but adds to it Tomlinson's "cultural complexity" argument, Appadurai's "global landscapes" model, and Castells' discussions on the importance of social networks to globalisation. The resultant formulation considers transnational businesspeople of whatever nationality not as part of a global, detached "class," but as groups included within a globe-wide theoretical construct which comprises all actors who are engaging in business activity across borders at any given time. The TCS is constructed through the self-presentation of individuals, and also includes the links between different transnational business social formations, and particular local entities inasmuch as they engage in transnational capitalism. The TCS theory is thus one which presents a complex, flexible, multiply engaged picture of business activity under conditions of globalisation.

As noted in Chapter 7, none of the extant theories regarding culture in transnational organisations completely fits the case of the German transnational businesspeople considered here in the way that the TCS theory does. The home- and host-country-effect theories, while they do highlight the impact of outside cultures on those of organisations, tend to take a monocultural perspective, ignoring the level of diversity both within organisations and in terms of their outside influences. Certainly, it would have been inaccurate to have seen ZwoBank London as solely, or even predominantly, "British" or "German" in terms of its corporate culture, as my interviewees in Chapters 5 and 6 occupied a series of positions relative to the two cultures rather than having one or the other. The "third-culture" theories, while increasing the level of complexity and highlighting the fact that researchers should focus on the specific influences of individual organisations rather than in general terms of "national" or "organisational" cultures, nonetheless still tends to focus on outside influences, rather than on the political dynamics within the organisation (e.g. Doz et al. 2001); again, they also did not seem terribly applicable in a case where the employees did not possess a single "mixed" culture, but several different mixes of British and German influences. The influence of the four cohorts, consequently, would have largely gone unnoticed in an approach which focuses primarily on the corporation's history and national cultures. Theories which focus on the existence and makeup of particular national and/or organisational cultures thus do not take the level of complexity which I found into account in the same way as a theory focusing on the interactions of multiple cultures in a wider transnational social context.

Sklair's "transnational capitalist class" theory, while better able to address the transnational links of the businesspeople seen here, is ultimately little better. Sklair's proposition that a global elite is emerging which consists of transnationally-operating businesspeople, bureaucrats and media professionals (2001: 18-22), while it initially seemed to fit the case of the German transnational businesspeople better than theories based purely on national culture, proved on closer investigation to do so only at a superficial level, and failed to take into account the degree of complexity and of local engagement seen in the ethnographic evidence presented in Chapters 3-5. While the Germans of ZwoBank and elsewhere may be globally engaged, connected with each other through social networks and maintaining a cosmopolitan attitude which is arguably out of step with that of their fellow-citizens, the examination of their self-presentation and social interactions in London, the City and an individual business suggests that they are not as detached from the local as the above theory suggests. Furthermore, as individuals they can be seen to be "transnational" and "globally-focused" in quite different ways, without a single categorical way of relating to global and local entities. The conclusion of this study is therefore that, while the above theories can be used to describe the German transnational businesspeople in the case study in broad terms, it fails to take into account the complex, ongoing and flexible ways in which they use symbols to present themselves according to particular strategies. The TCS theory outlined above, however, is able to take into account this level of complexity and flexibility, as it situates the German transnational businesspeople in the context of their interactions with, and links to, other groups of varying degrees of Germanness, transnational engagement and local involvement.

Throughout this book, we have considered the application of various theories of culture at a variety of levels. After the theoretical background was established in the first two chapters and the TCS theory initially proposed, the ethnographic chapters considered the case of the German transnational businesspeople in progressively greater detail, beginning with Germans in the UK as a whole, then focusing in on those in the City of London, those at a particular company and then, finally, focusing on a single aspect of their self-presentation, that of language. This approach means that we are able to consider their case both in its specific aspects (as would be done in business studies) and in the wider social, historical and cultural context (as would be done in anthropology). Over the course of this investigation, theories which were applicable at certain levels, or under certain conditions, proved not to be quite as useful at others. In the final analysis, then, the main advantage to the TCS theory over the earlier theories is that it allows us to consider groups at multiple levels, and to take both the wider context and the specific cases of particular groups into account.

The TCS theory therefore fits the empirical evidence seen here much better than the earlier models of the role culture in business, as it is able to take into account the different forms and degrees of transnational engagement of people in this group, and to allow for their links to various other social formations, while at the same time acknowledging their distinct natures. By complementing and augmenting theories of culture in business with other theories drawn from anthropology and sociology, we can then build up a more detailed, comprehensive picture of life among transnational economic elites, one which allows researchers to apply the necessary degree of complexity to the study of transnational businesspeople. We shall now consider what the TCS theory contributes to the study of transnational business as a whole.

## Thinking Globally: Theoretical Contribution of the TCS Model

The TCS model not only builds upon and develops earlier work in international business studies, but adds to the general body of literature on culture and social organisation in business in particular ways. In this section, I will outline how this model modifies earlier work on culture in organisations, develops a more accurate model for analysing business organisation in globalisation, produces a new way of looking at culture in transnational business and international expatriation, and allows a different perspective on mergers, acquisitions and restructuring activities while contributing rare qualitative data on the daily social interactions of MNC employees.

### Modifying Earlier Work on Culture in Organisations

To begin with, the TCS theory builds upon, and develops, the work of earlier writers looking at culture in organisations. Most works on culture in business studies, following Deal and Kennedy (1988), tend not to acknowledge the degree of negotiation which takes place within organisations, and, in emphasising the role of managers in promoting cultural change, ignore the fact that people with less status in the organisation can also play a major role in defining and shaping its culture; by taking a TCS approach to the firm, the complexity and multi-level nature of cultural change can be taken into account. The firm differentiation between "national" and "organisational" culture, problematic in many of the classic works on culture in business (e.g. Trompenaars 1993), is also avoided through the TCS approach, which considers different influences on different parts of the corporation. In contrast to the more abstract and vague approach taken by anthropologists, however, the TCS theory also has practical applications in that, as we have seen, it can be used as a model for considering the different influences on organisations during restructuring, mergers or branch-Head Office negotiations. The TCS theory thus maintains the focused and practical nature of national/organisational theories of culture, while at the same time adding a level of complexity which the earlier works lack.

The TCS theory also adds to the third-culture theories by adding a dynamic quality to the equation. While such works as Ghoshal and Nohria (1989) acknowledge that organisational cultures are a synthesis of cultures, and those of Kristensen and Zeitlin (2004) consider that organisational cultures are built up out of different relationships and over time, it is worth adding to this that these cultures are constantly changing, in response to inside and outside pressures, and that simply thinking in terms of national and organisational cultures does not begin to capture the complexity of influences on the organisation. As businesses are affected, not only by specific cultures, but also by geopolitical events, other transnational organisations (economic and otherwise) and regional activities, we may need to consider not so much "third cultures" as "transnational communities" (Glenn Morgan 2001). The TCS theory thus develops the third-culture studies to suggest a way of regarding organisations in the wider social and historical context, rather than focusing on the culture of a single organisation.

This monograph, therefore, does not only modify earlier theories of culture and strategy in organisations along more practical lines suggested by the TCS theory, but it also provides an unusual perspective on well-studied events through the nature of the methodology used to conduct the study. We shall now turn to the issue of relating the global to the local through the TCS theory.

*Developing a Global Perspective*

The TCS theory, as well as contributing to earlier debates, can also provide researchers with a better understanding of globalisation and the role of organisations and individuals in its development. We shall here take a brief look at what this theory contributes to studies of globalisation, in business and in general.

The TCS theory, to begin with, addresses the question of the relationship of the local to the global. The fact that there are so many different ways of describing this relationship (as seen in Chapter 2) might appear to suggest different perspectives on a single phenomenon. However, according to the TCS theory, there exist a variety of different social connections and interactions which can all be said, broadly speaking, to relate to "globalisation." If we therefore consider globalising activities as forming a variety of diverse subsets of the same social phenomenon (as under the TCS theory), the different ways of describing it can be easily integrated as different facets of the same phenomenon. The relationship between the two spheres is therefore shown to be not so much one-to-one as it is complex and symbolically mediated, accommodating many ways of acting; indeed, when we consider the different ways of relating the global to the local seen in Chapters 4, 5 and 6, it is difficult for us to speak of a single "global" or "local," as there appear to be a number of ways of approaching and presenting these orientations. Ultimately, the TCS problematises the concept of "the local" and "the global" in business; under the TCS theory, we see a single, complex phenomenon incorporating many "globals" and "locals," with different relationships emerging between them, as it were, which are defined and redefined through the self-presentation of people and organisations. The TCS theory thus provides a way of reconciling diverse ways of relating global and local social entities under a single broad remit.

The case of the German transnational businesspeople also suggests that the reason for the diversity of relationships between global and local, and of the different sorts of transnational communities, lies in the importance of self-presentation to cross-border business activity. We have seen in Chapters 3 and 5 how symbols of a single national affiliation, Germanness, can be used to express different degrees of transnational engagement, different sorts of group allegiance, and different associations with localities, in ways which subtly change as the interpretations of the symbols used are changed and negotiated by the actors involved. Self-presentation appear to draw at least some of their power, in this context, from the importance of communications technology to globalisation; as was discussed in Chapter 6, the global financial world's dependence on such technology means that it is effectively a symbolically constructed entity. Consequently, as Castells notes in his volume *The Power of Identity*, strategic self-presentation and the ability to express belonging becomes even more powerful and significant (1997: 2). The complex, flexible nature of self-presentation, furthermore, makes it an ideal means for negotiating and navigating between group affiliations and positions: actors define social groups while presenting themselves, and the act of defining social groups affects self-presentation. This monograph thus highlights the fact that symbols, and self-presentation, are not simply amusing or interesting windows onto the cultures of organisations, but essential to social interaction in transnational business.

Combining the two points, furthermore, this monograph demonstrates that the symbolic nature of the relationship between global and local means that actors can use flexible self-presentation to negotiate between different sorts of local and global spaces. The individuals whom we have seen in this study possess links to local groups and to transnational ones—in this case, most notably, Germany and transnational businesses. However, the act of negotiating between groups—between London and Frankfurt, for instance, or a branch and its Head Office, or between expatriates and locally hired Germans—links the groups themselves, making for complex webs of communication between Germany, the UK and the transnational financial sphere, and taking in a number of variations along the way. It also means that the way in which culture is defined becomes more significant to business than ever before, as organisations struggle to define themselves relative not only to the global financescape, but to their supporters and competitors at different national, regional and global levels. Transnational capitalism is neither detached from the local, nor simply a case of "trans-local" activity, as there are components of it which do not take place in any one national setting, but which form the basis for a wide, diverse transnational society; had we simply focused on London Branch or Head Office in Chapters 5 and 6, we would have missed seeing the social and physical interconnections between them. The TCS theory thus takes into account the complexity of relationships between global and local social entities, and, in combination with the importance of self-presentation, indicates how symbols are used to construct and reconstruct social relationships in transnational business.

Finally, this study might even be taken to suggest that we should reconsider the concepts of "transnationalism" and "transnational," at least in the field of international business. The German case suggests that there is no blanket set of criteria through which people either "are" or "are not" transnational, but of different types, degrees and kinds of transnational activity. We could, for instance, ask whether a German who is more or less permanently settled in England and conducts most interactions in the UK, but still reads German newspapers online and asks colleagues to bring back consignments of *Weisswurst* for him when on business trips to Frankfurt, is more or less transnational than someone who commutes between London and Frankfurt on a weekly basis. Similarly, one might ask whether a small business located physically in the UK, but selling its products in Australia, Japan, China and North America, is more or less transnational than an organisation with representative offices in New York, Tokyo and Frankfurt. The difference, my findings suggest, is one of degree and type rather than one of categorically being or not being transnational. It might thus be worth doing further work which problematises, not only the concept of a transnational business elite, but that of transnationalism in general, asking whether the concept is really as accurate, or useful, as it could be.

By not simply looking at MNCs in as being either "global" or "local," therefore, we can develop a different way of looking at global business, which takes into account the sheer variety of ways of relating the global to the local.

## Formulating New Views of International Management

The nature of the TCS theory, plus the methodology used to develop it throughout this monograph, also develops new ways of looking at transnational business and transnational businesspeople. This consequently has implications for how we view expatriation, culture and restructuring in transnational organisations.

To begin with, this study addresses some of the limitations of earlier studies of transnational businesspeople, by making plain the level of diversity in the organisation. Most research on organisational cultures tends to focus instead on differences between national cultures, managers and workers and different branches in the organization. Furthermore, the case of the different cohorts of ZwoBank highlights the fact that the *internal* cultural divisions in organisations may be as important as the external ones: that sometimes the divide between, say, "British" and "German" can be less significant than that between recently-arrived expatriates and Germans who have settled in the UK. In any multinational organisation, the TCS theory implies, there will be a variety of national cultures influencing it, due not only to the nationality of the company, but the origins of its employees, the nationality of its clients and competitors, and many other things. This study also suggests, peripherally, that more attention needs to be given to the relationship between so-called "elites" and "subalterns." The tendency for researchers to fall into the trap of assuming that all subalterns are heroically resisting oppression has already been noted by Guarnizo and Smith (1998: 24), but it should also be apparent that the divide between elite and subaltern can be complex. Jews in the 19th-century City of London, for instance, were very much a financial elite, but were also an excluded group, subject to attack and rejection (see Panayi 1995: 140, 84, 256-257); today, non-white people face a similar (if less oppressive) combination of financial acceptance but social exclusion (Courtney and Thompson 1996: 169). By taking a more complex, nuanced view of organisations, some of these issues may be addressed. Much as recent research focusing on the possibility of the emergence of a single European business system has discovered that internal cultural differences apparently continue to exist, even when operating under region-wide legal edicts (Ferner and Hyman 1998), my research suggests looking at the organisation not as a single "multinational," but consider it, like Europe, to be a larger organisation with a variety of other influences within it.

This study also addresses one of the main problems with earlier research on international managers as individuals. Critiques of studies of expatriation have often pinpointed the fact that they assume a kind of "generic international manager," relatively young, white, American, single, male and globally engaged (Forster 2000; Linehan and Walsh 1999). By considering, in Chapter 5, a number of different individuals within the organisation who might broadly be described as "international managers," and, in Chapter 6, taking a closer look at ethnic and national divisions within the organisation and the impact of IT on such cultural boundaries, this monograph provides an alternative perspective. As well as demonstrating that such studies need not "genericise" their subjects to produce a viable result, this study provides an indication of the diverse nature and forms which international management can take, and the impact of these differences on the operation of transnational organisations.

This study also highlights the roles which self-presentation and individual strategy play in shaping and controlling businesses. Although Turner (1992) and Garth Morgan (1997) discuss the development of group identity through the use of symbols to some extent, and countless books exist encouraging businesspeople to improve their powers of self-presentation (Lurie 1981: 26), this seems to be the extent of the discussion. Furthermore, the latter works are less concerned with the actual use of self-presentation than how it should ideally be used, and the former focus on group formation at the expense of other uses of self-presentation—and, also, seldom discuss cases in which the use of self-presentation does not have the desired effect. This is surprising when one considers the increasing importance of self-presentation in business, with the processes of globalisation encouraging the rise of advertising, public relations and personal presentation (see Jackall 1988: 163-170). As the business world becomes increasingly communication-focused, so the strategic use of self-presentation becomes ever more important, and consequently more attention must be paid to its use in business. This monograph thus goes some way towards exploring and discussing the role of this process in international business.

The present monograph thus has contributed to the study of international business by suggesting new ways of looking at international managers and how they relate to the organisation. In the long run, these may prove more useful to people studying expatriation and international organisation than theories based on more quantitative research.

*Producing New Views of the Organisation*

Finally, in addition to allowing the development of the TCS theory, the methodology behind this work provides a near-unique view of organisations. At a time when researchers are looking for new ways of understanding companies in globalisation, a change in perspective may be valuable to researchers.

As noted in Chapter 1, there have been relatively few ethnographies of business per se, and virtually none at all on transnational business activity at the elite level. Even studies which have a high qualitative component tend to be focused on interviews and limited interaction with subjects rather than outright participation; studies of expatriates (e.g. Forster 2000; Harzing 2001a, b) tend to be survey-based and not to consider them in the wider social and political context. The nature of the methodologies used in this study thus provides a perspective on the organisation as a community, a cultural group and part of a wider society, which constantly sets it apart from many other studies of transnational organisations.

The fact that ZwoBank was undergoing a restructuring and merger at the same time also provides unique advantages. Leaving aside the fact that sociological, case-study-based monographs on mergers, acquisitions and restructurings are relatively rare in general, the position of the ethnographer as a partial outsider to the organisation means that this monograph produces a view of such events which is neither too quantitative, nor (as with such books as Cody 1990) strongly coloured by the emotional tensions produced in the wake of the restructuring. The circumstances of the case study thus provide up a limited, but still valuable, view on an organisation undergoing a period of transition.

In sum, then, this work contributes to international business as a field in a number of different ways. As well as advancing the TCS theory, which has consequences for the way in which social scientists view organisations and their activities, the methodology and premises of the study provides a useful counterbalance to the strong quantitative focus of earlier research. We shall now consider some of the limitations and problems of this monograph.

**The Trouble with Transnationalism: Limitations of the TCS Theory**

Like all such models, the TCS theory is not without its limitations. In this section, we will consider some of the difficulties thrown up by the theory itself, as well as by the material and methodology used to support it, and suggest ways in which these can be remedied.

One might, for instance, argue that the TCS theory, in addressing monocultural theories of social organisation, goes too far in the opposite direction, being too general where earlier theories were too specific. While such writers as Sklair and Hofstede do not take into account the diversity of connections of transnational businesspeople, for instance, it might equally seem that the TCS theory incorporates too much diversity, including so many forms of organisation that it might simply best be called "the global financescape" or simply "the global." While this is a good point, the words "transnational" and "capitalist" do provide definition to the social formation in question; the concept refers to social activity in the financial/capitalist and transnational spheres. Furthermore, referring to them as part of the TCS does not make social groups within it any more or less discrete; the Germans of ZwoBank were still Germans belonging to a particular organisation, even as they adopted and modified other social identities in the process of self-presentation. Rather, the TCS theory provides a model for exploring the ways in which these groups interact, and for understanding the role of their different connections and self-presentation in their daily activities. It must also be said that one of the aims of this exploration is to further expose the artificiality of the exercise of drawing boundaries between groups, a finding which may apply to non-transnational groups as well (see R. Jenkins 1996: 98). The case study in this monograph thus suggests that the TCS theory may at least provide a useful starting point for other researchers.

It might equally be suggested that the TCS theory is, in some ways, too limited. While I was able to highlight the different ways in which people related to British and German business cultures, this study does not even begin to cover the diversity of the organisation. The "British" employees, for instance, included a minority of Welsh, Irish and Scots within the organisation, to say nothing of Britons of Indian, Pakistani and West Indian descent, and the "Germans" also varied in terms of their regional origin, class background and religion. Despite the seeming monoculturality of Head Office, there were still non-Germans within the organisation (albeit largely unrecognised), and in Frankfurt itself there are many different ethnic groups, including, among many others, Turks, Vietnamese, Africans and Italians (see Vertovec 1996b). It might thus be that future research will find a way of expressing and incorporating this level of diversity

The ZwoBank case study also indirectly highlights the fact that we have to consider other influences on companies than simply, as here, the impact of national and organisational cultures. The ethnographic chapters, plus the conclusions expressed in Chapter 7, highlight the fact that ZwoBank did not exist in a vacuum; employees continually expressed the influence of outside political, economic and cultural events by referring to, for instance, BMW's problems managing its Rover subsidiary, and the Vodafone-Mannesmann takeover. However, even this level of detail cannot take account of the other factors influencing the bank, such as gender, departmental specialisation, outside those discussed in this book. Not only could ethnic relations within the bank be affected by something as simple as the European football championships, but the same event could impact differently on different departments (the championships being, for instance, a non-issue in the largely-female HR department but a source of fierce discussion in the largely-male and fairly "macho" dealing room). There is thus scope for expansion and development of this theory in terms of other forms of diversity than simply the ethno-national.

Finally, as noted in Chapter 1, while ethnographic methodology has provided a number of new insights into culture in transnational business, it also has certain drawbacks. The fact that the researcher was a relatively young woman undoubtedly influenced the responses people gave and how I was treated; it could therefore be worthwhile considering similar ethnographies by people in different demographic brackets, or of different ethnic backgrounds. The practical limitations of access to the organisation which I faced also means that it is difficult for me to say whether the behaviour which I observed is limited to the London Branch and Head Office contexts; again, a study of other branches of the same organisation might prove useful in addressing this. I was also aware that the responses which people gave to me were coloured by my position with the organisation; while I have been able to address this to some extent by doing follow-up interviews in a different social position (that of former associate of the organisation, now working elsewhere) the fact remains that the responses which I received are inevitably influenced by how I was perceived. In the end, also, all ethnographies are of necessity subjective, anecdotal and impressionistic; while this does not diminish their value as research tools, the nature of the research inevitably affects the conclusions drawn. While the quantitative research of Carroll and Fennema (2001) does back up my findings, more comparisons with quantitative research still need to be done. This work could thus be further developed in ways which address the study's limitations.

The limitations discussed here, while not invalidating the conclusions drawn, demonstrate that the TCS model is simply a starting point, a theory formulated on the basis of a single case; more research will be required in order to refine it into something more workable. Future development of this hypothesis may, however, allow researchers to develop more viable models of transnational business cultures, and practitioners to apply this to their own issues in business.

## Taking it from Here: Areas for Future Development

By suggesting different ways of looking at transnational business cultures to those previously employed in business studies, then, the TCS theory thus opens up possibilities for future research in theoretical, methodological and practical directions. I will here briefly consider a few of the directions in which this study could be taken.

### Areas for Theoretical Development

To begin with, it might be worth expanding this study into other areas, to test how far the TCS model applies under different conditions to those cited here. One possible direction would be to change a single variable within the study, and, say, consider Germans in other global financial centres, such as New York and Hong Kong, or consider transnational bank employees of other nationalities in the City of London., or Germans in a different business sector. I have been developing the study myself in this area, by doing comparative research with an Anglo-German manufacturing firm of a similar age and with a similar history of internationalisation to ZwoBank, with a view to developing such a cross-sector comparison of how well the TCS model works. My findings have thus far suggested that the TCS theory can be applied to the manufacturing firm as well: for instance, the managers and the workers in the plant are both engaged with transnational activities, but in quite strikingly different ways. Once again, also, the traditional distinction between English and German management was broken down into different groups: unlike in the bank, however, this group divided strongly along occupational lines and lines of seniority, confirming the hypothesis that these divisions, although present in most if not all organisations, vary strongly from company to company in terms of their form. Although the study is at an early stage, follow-up research in other sectors has suggested that the traditional factory studies of the early 20th century, focusing on management/worker conflict, can also be updated according to the TCS theory (Baba 1998). However, this does not mean that the research presented here could not be challenged or modified by a similar study in another sector, or another city, or with another set of ethno-national groups.

It might also, in light of this study, be worth reconsidering earlier studies of transnational *subaltern* businesspeople and organisations. Portes' Dominicans, for instance, are said by him to be engaging in a form of resistance to domination by a transnational capitalist elite (1998). However, the case of the German transnational businesspeople suggests that there are inextricable connections between elites and subalterns, which further implies that the Dominicans' resistance activities might be more problematic than it seems at first. Bridget Anderson's study of migrant domestic workers, also, describing as it does a group whose members originate in many diverse localities, form more or less focused and/or ethnically based social groups in other areas, and have links to the political and ambassadorial global elite, suggests another group which might be worth considering less in terms of community and network, than in terms of actors possessing multiple links and engagements united under a single collective designation (2001b). Many of the traditional anticapitalist works (e.g. N. Klein 2000) might also be worth revising, particularly in light of the changing power balance between First and Third-World countries in transnational economic organisations such as the WTO. It might thus be valuable to consider small multinational businesses, or local businesses, with a view to considering whether they experience similar effects to that felt by the large global bank. One might also look at other transnational groups which are not business-related, from a TCS theory-based perspective, to see if the model is restricted solely to business or whether it can be expanded into other areas. Comparative studies considering smaller, less powerful or non-business-related groups according to the same theory thus might prove useful for testing the TCS model, or for developing it into other areas of social interaction.

Finally, we have the issue of communication and communications technology. While the work of Reis (2004) and Piekkari (2004) has made some steps in this direction, this is an area which has received very little attention until recently in business studies. This is all the more problematic when one considers that the present monograph highlights the complexity which communications provide for organisations, resisting attempts to classify them into terms such as good/bad, tool of oppression/tool of resistance, despite attempts on the part of politicians and some researchers to do so. The same process can be both at once, as witness the use of German in ZwoBank, which simultaneously incorporates resistance by a local language to English hegemony, and the imposition of a different language on local subalterns by a globalising (German) elite. More studies which focus on the use and social value of communications technology and language use within the organisation, particularly in business contexts, are therefore urgently needed.

The present study thus throws up a number of potential areas for future development, either through doing comparative research, or through following up on some of the areas of interest highlighted by the research. We shall now consider the implications of this research in non-theoretical areas.

## Areas for Methodological Development

These conclusions also have methodological implications for the use of ethnography and other qualitative methodologies in the study of businesses. While this subject has been mentioned above, it is worth briefly highlighting some of the methodological issues which the study has produced.

Although it is a common business-studies critique of qualitative research that non-numerical, descriptive data are a sort of "noise" distracting from the main aim of the exercise (e.g. Hofstede 1980: 314, 339), this case suggests that it is much more significant than that. As we have seen, the German transnational businesspeople's connections to other groups of varying degrees of transnationalism and status are what allows them to carry out their strategies in the global financescape. By having local links and connections to other sorts of transnational groups, they are able to mobilise resources on many levels; by ignoring these connections, then, and focusing only on those aspects of their lives which can be quantitatively assessed, we miss out on one of the key aspects of organisation in multinational corporations (see Andersson et al. 2000). As Chapman argues, the use of extensive, broad-ranging data makes for a superficial treatment of the material even as it makes for greater possibilities of generalisation (1997: 11). It is worth noting that, whatever his expressed views on the subject, Hofstede backs up his empirical findings extensively with personal and anecdotal evidence. There is, therefore, support for d'Iribane, Chapman and others' claim that an ethnographic study yields insights which a nonethnographic one does not, which are nonetheless valuable to business (1997; 1997). In this case, it is only by looking at the qualitative data that one sees the connections and interactions which actually cause the phenomena measured by the more broad-level studies.

This project also suggests that the study of transnational and global social formations may require different sorts of methodologies to those currently in use. Increasingly, the divided and multiply engaged nature of transnational social formations is coming to be recognised, in business as in other areas, and several researchers are suggesting that changes in research methodology and descriptive writing may be necessary (Appadurai 1997: 115). This bears a striking parallel to developments in the study of identity in anthropology. Early ethnographies on the subject considered it to be a solid, possessible thing, but subsequently it was found to be more diffuse and subject to negotiation than had at first seemed (Banks 1996). Here too, the groups which were portrayed as solid units in earlier studies now appear as diffuse entities, multiply linked and internally divided. It might thus be worth taking another look at the way in which transnational businesses, social groups and other sorts of communities are described and considered by researchers, perhaps focusing on interdisciplinary studies rather than those involving a single perspective and/or set of methodologies.

It thus might be worthwhile conducting more qualitative studies in business, and following up earlier quantitative studies with qualitative research projects, in order to gain a fuller perspective on the organisation. This study thus highlights some of the advantages which qualitative studies can bring to the organisation, supporting the views of Chapman and d'Iribane on the subject.

*Areas for Practical Development*

Finally, this study has implications for the practical day-to-day operation of multinational corporations. It might therefore be worth considering some of these implications, and how they might affect managers in such organisations.

For instance, this study suggests that managers need to take a more qualitative and diversity-focused perspective on organisations. By treating ZwoBank as a unit with regard to the matrix integration described in Chapter 5, following the quantitative work of Hofstede and others, its managers ignored the different perspectives on, and issues relating to, the integration which the different cohorts possessed. This resulted, as we have seen, in an unnecessary amount of friction between Head Office and employees who feel that their needs are not being met, as well as a failure to exploit, for instance, the mediating role which could be played by the German local hires and Germanophiles. Hofstede defended his use of quantitative methodologies to study culture in organisations by saying that he was attempting to develop a broad overview of cultural difference; however, he has been criticised for missing out on important details due to his statistical approach (1980: 314; d'Iribane 1997: 36). While Harris' argument that ethnographic and nonethnographic methods should be combined to give a holistic picture of the organisation is well taken (2001), and while this may certainly be true in the case of some studies of culture in business, it is difficult to say what a statistical approach would have contributed to determining the issues and concerns of the employees of this particular group of German and British businesspeople. By not examining the cultural richness of the material relating to businesspeople, managers as well as researchers miss out on crucial issues which affect the success of their corporations.

There is also a tendency for managers, when considering the operation of their organisation and how to implement changes within it, to consider only the managerial sector. While some theoretical work has been done on secretaries (Pringle 1994) and on service-industry workers (Royle 2000), there is still very little which looks at power dynamics within organisations. Harzing's excellent studies of the use of expatriates as a means of social control in MNCs, (2001a, b), due to their quantitative focus, tend to ignore the possibility of resistance to this control on the part of the employees of the branches, nor to the possibility, indicated by Beaverstock's studies (2002), that the expatriates themselves have their own career agendas (Moore, forthcoming). Except within the field of gender studies, also, the differences between different groups and categories of managers is also seldom considered (Adler and Izraeli 1994). Although this monograph can only go a little way towards problematising this issue, it suggests that managers as well as social scientists need to pay less attention to particular groups in and of themselves, and more to the connections and transactions between them, if they are to reduce conflict, exclusion and discrimination in their multinational corporations.

The present study of German transnational businesspeople suggests that group formation among transnational groups, may be less a matter of solid, definite entities than of diffuse collections of links. Furthermore, it raises a number of issues relating to theory, epistemology and practice in business studies, which point the way to future research. It will be very interesting to see how future research is able to address the limitations of the present study and develop its conclusions in new areas.

## Conclusion

In sum, then, the key result of this investigation has been to suggest that that transnational businesspeople, like the Germans considered in the case study, use symbols to present themselves in ways too complex, shifting and subtle to define them simply as a single transnational elite. Rather, they should be considered as a part, or several parts, of a wider social organisation along the lines of a transnational capitalist society. This conclusion, however, raises interesting theoretical and practical issues which could impact on the way in which self-presentation is viewed and treated in business, the way in which managers operate in the branches and head offices of multinational corporations, and the way in which we think about transnational business cultures.

This monograph has thus not only provided a new perspective on the management of European multinational corporations and suggested a new theoretical model for viewing transnational business interaction for further consideration, but it has also produced new areas for research and practical development. The full implications of the TCS theory for international business will, therefore, become more apparent with the passage of time.

# Bibliography

Anonymous (1905) *The Address of the Anglo-German Conciliation Committee*, London, 4 December 1905, available from the Deutsche Bank Archive, Frankfurt

Anonymous (1916) *Trading with the Enemy Act*, 1914, amended 1915, 1916, available from the Deutsche Bank Archive, Frankfurt

Anonymous (1919) *Londoner Filiale [Documents Relating to Closure of London Branch of Deutsche Bank]*, unpublished manuscript, available from the Deutsche Bank Archive, Frankfurt

Anonymous (1994) *A Tribute to the Bank of England 1694-1994: Three Hundred Years of Banking and Investment*, London: Lookturn Ltd.

Anonymous (1995) *Banken und Bankkonzerne in Deutschland Jahresabschlüsse 1993*, Düsseldorf: IDW-Verlag GmbH

Adams, Scott (1996) *The Dilbert Principle: A Cubicle's-Eye View of Bosses, Meetings, Management Fads & Other Workplace Afflictions*, New York: HarperCollins

— (1998) *The Joy of Work: Dilbert's Guide to Finding Happiness at the Expense of Your Co-Workers*, New York: HarperCollins

Adler, Nancy and Izraeli, Dafna (1994) *Competitive Frontiers: Women Managers in a Global Economy*, Oxford: Blackwell

Ahrens, Thomas (1996a) *Talking Accounting: A Comparative Ethnography of British and German Practice*, Southampton: University of Southampton

— (1996b) *Management Accounting and Strategy: Practitioners' Temporal Integration into Emergent Organisational Action*, Southampton: University of Southampton

Aitken, Thomas (1973) *The Multinational Man: The Role of the Manager Abroad*, London: George Allen and Unwin Ltd.

Altmann, Rüdiger (1984) "Staats- und Geschichtsbewusstsein in der politischen Kultur der Bundesrepublik Deutschland," in Klaus Weigelt (Ed.), *Heimat und Nation: zur Geschichte und Identität der Deutschen*, Mainz: von Hase und Köhler Verlag, 220-226

Amin, Ash and Thrift, Nigel (1992) "Neo-Marshallian Nodes in Global Networks." *International Journal of Urban and Regional Research*, 16 (4), 571-587

Amiraux, Valérie (1997) "Turkish Islamic Associations in Germany and the Issue of European Citizenship," in Steven Vertovec and Ceri Peach (Eds.), *Islam in Europe: The Politics of Religion and Community*, London: Macmillan, 245-259

www.ananova.com (2002) "US Says It Captures Two Al-Qaida in Cave Complex," 8 January 2002

Anderson, Bridget (2001a) "State, Space and Human Relations: The Lives of Migrant Domestic Workers," paper presented at ESRC Transnational Communities Seminar, Oxford, 1 November 2001

— (2001b) "Different Roots in Common Ground: Transnationalism and Migrant Domestic Workers in London," *Journal of Ethnic and Migration Studies*, 27 (4), 673-683

Andersson, Ulf, Fosgren, Mats and Holm, Ulf (2001) "Subsidiary Embeddedness and Competence Development in MNCs: A Multi-Level Analysis," *Organization Studies*, 22 (6), 1013-1034

Anthony, Peter D. (1994) *Managing Culture*, Buckingham: Open University Press

Appadurai, Arjun (1990) "Disjuncture and Difference in the Global Cultural Economy," in Mike Featherstone (Ed.), *Global Culture: Nationalism, Globalization and Modernity*, London: Sage, 295- 310

— (1997) "Fieldwork in the Era of Globalization," *Anthropology and Humanism*, 22 (1), 115-118

Appelius, Stefan (1995) "Wir brauchen noch immer unseren Club," *Jüdische Allgemeine Zeitung*, 8, page 5

Appiah, Kwame Anthony (1998) "Cosmopolitan Patriots," in Pheng Cheah and Bruce Robbins (Eds.), *Cosmopolitics: Thinking and Feeling Beyond the Nation*, London: University of Minneapolis Press, 91-114

Applegate, Christina (1990) *A Nation of Provincials: The German Idea of Heimat*, Berkeley: University of California Press

Ardagh, John (1995) *Germany and the Germans*, London: Penguin

Arthur D. Little Ltd. (1979) *The EEC as an Expanded Home Market for the United Kingdom and the Federal Republic of Germany*, London: Anglo-German Foundation

Association of Social Anthropologists of the UK and the Commonwealth (1999) "Ethical Guidelines for Good Research Practice," available from http://les1.man.ac.uk/asa/ethics.htm

Augar, Philip (2000) *The Death of Gentlemanly Capitalism: The Rise and Fall of London's Investment Banks*, London: Penguin Books

Bade, Klaus J. (Ed.) (1992) *Deutsche im Ausland–Fremde in Deutschland: Migration in Geschichte und Gegenwart*, München: Verlag C. H. Beck

— (1992) "Einführung: Das Eigene Und Das Fremde–Grenzerfahrungen in Geschichte Und Gegenwart," in Klaus J. Bade (Ed.), *Deutsche im Ausland–Fremde in Deutschland: Migration in Geschichte und Gegenwart*, München: Verlag C. H. Beck, 15-25

Balibar, Etienne (1998) "The Borders of Europe," in Pheng Cheah and Bruce Robbins (Eds.), *Cosmopolitics: Thinking and Feeling Beyond the Nation*, London: University of Minneapolis Press, 216-229

Bank of England (2000) *Annual Report*, London: Bank of England

The Bank Relationship Consultancy (1997) *Relationship Banking*, London: Financial Times Finance Management Report

Banks, Marcus (1996) *Ethnicity: Anthropological Constructions*, London: Routledge

— (1998) "Visual Anthropology: Image, Object and Interpretation," in John Prosser (Ed.), *Image-Based Research: A Sourcebook for Qualitative Researchers*, London: Falmer Press, 9-23

Barley, Nigel (1998) "The Rehabilitation of Raffles," *High Life*, December 1998, pp. 52-56

Bartlett, Christopher A. and Ghoshal, Sumantra (1992) *Managing across Borders: The Transnational Solution*, London: Century Business

— (1993) "The Multinational Corporation as an Interorganizational Network," in Sumantra Ghoshal and D. Eleanor Westney (Eds.), *Organization Theory and the Multinational Corporation*, London: The Macmillan Press, 76-107

Beaverstock, Jonathan V. (1991) "Skilled International Migration: An Analysis of the Geography of International Secondments within Large Accountancy Firms," *Environment and Planning*, 23, 1133-1146

— (1994) "Re-Thinking Skilled International Labour Migration: World Cities and Banking Organisations," *Geoforum*, 25 (3), 323-338

— (1996a) "Migration, Knowledge and Social Interaction: Expatriate Labour within Investment Banks," *Area*, 28 (4), 459-470

— (1996b) "Revisiting High-Waged Labour Market Demand in the Global Cities: British Professional and Managerial Workers in New York City," *International Journal of Urban and Regional Research*, 20 (3), 422-445

— (1996c) "Subcontracting the Accountant! Professional Labour Markets, Migration and Organisational Networks in the Global Accountancy Industry," *Environment and Planning*, 28, 303-326

— (2002) "Transnational Elites in Global Cities: British Expatriates in Singapore's Financial District," *Geoforum* 33, 525-538

— and Smith, Joanne (1996) "Lending Jobs to Global Cities: Skilled International Labour Migration, Investment Banking and the City of London," *Urban Studies*, 33 (8), 1377-1394

Baba, Marietta L. (1998) "Anthropology of work in the Fortune 1000: A critical retrospective," Anthropology of Work Review, XVIII: 4, 17-28

*The Banker* (2000) "Foreign-owned Banks in London," October 2000, pp. 41-49

Baumann, Gerd (1996) *Contesting Culture: Discourses of Ethnicity in Multi-Ethnic London*, Cambridge: Cambridge University Press

Beevor, Antony (1999) "Tommy and Jerry," *The Guardian*, 16 February 1999, page 2

Behrman, Jack (1970) *National Interests and the Multinational Enterprise: Tensions among the North Atlantic Countries*, Englewood Cliffs: Prentice Hall Ltd.

Berghahn, Marion (1988) *Continental Britons: German-Jewish Refugees from Nazi Germany*, Oxford: Berg

Bernstein, Basil (1971) *Class, Codes and Control*, Theoretical Studies Towards a Sociology of Language vol. 1, London: Routledge and Kegan Paul

Bergsten, C. Fred, et al. (1978) *American Multinationals and American Interests*, Washington: The Brookings Institution

*Berliner Lokal Ausaiger* (1912) "Zur deutsch-englischen Verständigung," 26 June 1912

Best, Otto F. (1993) *Volk ohne Witz: über ein deutsches Defizit*, Frankfurt am Main: Fischer Taschenbuch Verlag

Biermann, Wolf (1991) *Über das Geld und andere Herzensdinge: prozaische Versuche über Deutschland*, Köln: Kiepenheuer und Witsch

Binney, George (1993) "The British Company and the German Company Compared," in George Binney (Ed.), *Debunking the Myths About the German Company*, London: Chameleon Press, 15-18

Birkinshaw, Julian (2001) "Reframing the Subsidiary's Competitive Environment: The Impact of Internal and External Actors on Subsidiary Competitiveness," paper presented at ESRC Conference on "Multinationals: Embedded Organisations, Transnational Federations Or Global Learning Communities?" Warwick Business School, Coventry, 6-8th September 2001

Blaschke, Monika (1992) "'Deutsch-Amerika' in Bedrängnis: Krise und Verfall einer 'Bindestrichkultur'," in Klaus J. Bade (Ed.), *Deutsche im Ausland--Fremde in Deutschland: Migration in Geschichte und Gegenwart*, München: Verlag C. H. Beck, 170-179

Bloch, Maurice (1974) "Symbols, Song, Dance and Features of Articulation: Is Religion an Extreme Form of Traditional Authority?" *Archives Europaiennes de la Sociologie*, 15, 55-81

Bloom, Matt, Milkovitch, George T. and Mitra, Atul (2003) "International compensation: learning from how managers respond to variations in local host contexts." *International Journal of Human Resource Management* 14: 8, 1350-1367

Boden, Deirdre (1994) *The Business of Talk: Organizations in Action*, Cambridge: Polity Press

Boll, Heinrich (1992 [1949]) "German Efficiency," trans. Shaun Whiteside, *Granta*, 42, 11-13

Borneman, John (1991) *After the Wall: East Meets West in the New Berlin*, New York: HarperCollins

— (1992) *Belonging in the Two Berlins: Kin, State, Nation,* Cambridge: Cambridge University Press

— and Peck, Jeffrey M. (1995) *Sojourners: The Return of German Jews and the Question of Identity,* Lincoln: University of Nebraska Press

Borer, Mary Cathcart (1977) *The City of London: A History,* London: Constable and Co.

Bott, Elizabeth (1957) *Family and Social Network: Roles, Norms, and External Relationships in Ordinary Urban Families,* London: Tavistock

Braun, Babette (1993) *German Subsidiary Companies in the UK/Deutsche Niederlassungen im Vereinigten Königreich,* London: German Chamber of Commerce in the United Kingdom

Breitenstein, Rolf and Hommerich, Angelika (Ed.) (1976) *German Sites in London: A Pictorial Guide,* London: Oswald Wolff

Brown, R. and Gilman, A. (1972) "The Pronouns and Solidarity," in Pier Paolo Giglioli (Ed.), *Language and Social Context: Selected Readings,* Harmondsworth: Penguin, 252-281

Bruhn, Joachim (1994) *Was deutsch ist: zur kritischen Theorie der Nation,* Freiburg: Ça-Ira Verlag

Burns, Tom (1992) *Erving Goffman,* London: Routledge

Burrus, Katrina (1997) "National Culture and Gender Diversity within One of the Universal Swiss Banks," in A. Sackman (Ed.), *Cultural Complexity in Organizations: Inherent Contrasts and Contradictions,* London: Sage, 209-227

Buruma, Ian (1989) "From Hirohito to *Heimat*," *New York Review of Books,* 26 October, 1989, pp. 31-2, 40-5

Carr, Christopher, et al. (1994) *Strategic Investment Decisions: A Comparison of UK and German Practices in the Motor Components Industry,* Aldershot: Avebury

Carroll, W.K. and Fennema, M. (2002) "Is there a Transnational Business Community?" *International Sociology* 17 (3), 393-420

Carroll, W.K. and Carson, Colin (2003) "The Network of Global Corporations and Elite Policy Groups: A Structure for Transnational Capitalist Class Formation?" *Global Networks* 3 (1), 29-57

Castells, Manuel (1996) *The Rise of the Network Society,* The Information Age vol. 1, Oxford: Blackwell

— (1997) *The Power of Identity,* The Information Age vol. 2, Oxford: Blackwell

— (1998) *End of Millennium,* The Information Age vol. 3, Oxford: Blackwell

— (2000) "Global Networks and Local Societies: Cities in the Information Age," paper presented at ESRC Transnational Communities Seminar, Oxford, 15 June 2000

Cesari, Jocelyne (1999) "Islam in the West: The Issue of Pluralism in the Context of Globalisation," paper presented at ESRC Transnational Communities Seminar, Oxford, 3 June 1999

Chapman, Malcolm (1997) "Preface: Social Anthropology, Business Studies and Cultural Issues," *Inernational Studies of Management and Organization,* 26 (4), 3-29

Chandler, Alfred D. (1977) *The Visible Hand: The Managerial Revolution in American Business,* Harvard: Belknap Press

Chetham, Jacqui (1994) *Issues in Banking: Problems, Strategies and Practices,* London: Financial Times Management Reports, Financial Times Business Information

Clifford, James (1994) "Diasporas," *Cultural Anthropology,* 9 (3), 302-338

Cody, Thomas (1990) *Strategy of a Megamerger,* New York: Quorum Books

Cohen, Anthony P. (1985) *The Symbolic Construction of Community,* London: Tavistock

— (1986) "Of Symbols and Boundaries, or, Does Ertie's Greatcoat Hold the Key?" in Anthony P. Cohen, *Symbolising Boundaries: Identity and Diversity in British Cultures,* Manchester: Manchester University Press, 1-22

— (1987) *Whalsay: Symbol, Segment and Boundary in a Shetland Island Community*, Anthropological Studies of Britain no. 3, Manchester: Manchester University Press

— (1994) *Self Consciousness: An Alternative Ethnography of Identity*, London: Routledge

Cohen, Robin (1997) *Global Diasporas: An Introduction*, London: UCL

Corporation of London (2000a) *The Review: The Work of the Corporation of London*, London: The Town Clerk's Office, Corporation of London

(2000b) *London-New York Study: The Economies of Two Great Cities at the Milennium*, London: Corporation of London

Courtney, Cathy and Thompson, Paul (1996) *City Lives: The Changing Voices of British Finance*, London: Methuen

Crystal, David (1997) *English as a Global Language*, Cambridge: Cambridge University Press

Cyert, Richard M. and March, James G. (1992) *A Behavioural Theory of the Firm*, Oxford: Blackwell

Czarniawska, B. (1997) *Narrating the Organization: Dramas of Institutional Identity*, London: University of Chicago Press

Dahlen, Tommy (1997) *Among the Interculturalists: An Emergent Profession and Its Packaging of Knowledge*, Stockholm Studies in Social Anthropology, 38, Stockholm: Stockholm University

Darnstädt, Thomas, et al. (1999) "Die Kampf Um Die Pässe," *Der Spiegel*, 11 January, pp. 22-32

Davies, Caroline (2000) "Bus Driver Dubbed 'Herman the German' Loses Racism Claim," *Daily Telegraph*, 6 July 2000, page 3

Deal, Terrence E. and Kennedy, Allen A. (1988) *Corporate Cultures: The Rites and Rituals of Corporate Life*, London: Penguin

Delacroix, Jacques (1993) "The European Subsidiaries of American Multinationals: An Exercise in Ecological Analysis," in Sumantra Ghoshal and D. Eleanor Westney (Eds.), *Organization Theory and the Multinational Corporation*, London: The Macmillan Press, 105-135

Deutsche Bank (1905a) Letter, to Herr Luecke, 31 May 1905, available from the Deutsche Bank Archive, Frankfurt

— (1905b) Letter, to Herr Luecke, 9 June 1905, available from the Deutsche Bank Archive, Frankfurt

Deutsche Schule London (1998) *Jahrbuch 1998-1999*, DSL: London

Dohmen, Frank and Kerbusk, Klaus-Peter (1999) "Vom Jäger zum Gejagten," 15 November 1999

Douch, Nick (n.d. [1990?]) "Foreign Exchange," in The Winchester Group (Ed.), *The Square Mile in 1990*, London: The Winchester Group

Douglas, Mary (1970) *Natural Symbols: Explorations in Cosmology*, London: Barrie and Rockliff

— (1983) "How Identity Problems Disappear," in Anita Jacobson-Widding (Ed.), *Identity: Personal and Socio-Cultural, a Symposium*, Uppsala: Almqvist and Wiksell International, 35-46

— (1987) *How Institutions Think*, London: Routledge and Kegan Paul

Doz, Yves L. Santos, Jose, and Williamson, Peter (2001) *From Global to Metanational: How Companies Win in the Knowledge Economy*, Cambridge (Mass.): Harvard Business School

Drainville, André C. (1998) "The Fetishism of Global Civil Society: Global Governance, Transnational Urbanism and Sustainable Capitalism in the World Economy," in Michael Peter Smith and Luis Eduardo Guarnizo (Eds.), *Transnationalism from Below,* Comparative Urban and Community Research vol. 6, London: Transaction Publishers, 35-63

Dumont, Louis (1994) *German Ideology: From France to Germany and Back,* Chicago: University of Chicago Press

Dyer, Colin (n.d.) *The Guild of Freemen of the City of London: A Record of Its Formation and History,* London: Guild of Freemen of the City of London

Ebster-Grosz, Dagmar, and Pugh, Derek (1996) *Anglo-German Business Collaboration: Pitfalls and Potentials,* London: Macmillan Press

*The Economist* (1962) "[Untitled Article]," July 14 1962, page 144

— (1995) "The Mittelstand Meets the Grim Reaper," 30 September 1995, pp. 77-78

— (1998a) "The Ties That Bind," 9 May 1998, pp. 5-8

— (1998b) "Reds at the Ready," 11 July 1998, page 53

— (1998c) "Salesman Schröder," 29 August 1998, page 16

— (1998d) "A New Mix," 26 September 1998, page 31

Edstrom, Anders and Galbraith, Jay R. (1977) "Transfer of Managers as a Coordination and Control Strategy in Multinational Organizations," *Administrative Science Quarterly,* 22: 2, 248-264

Egelhoff, William G. (1993) "Information-Processing Theory and the Multinational Corporation," in Sumantra Ghoshal and D. Eleanor Westney (Eds.), *Organization Theory and the Multinational Corporation,* London: The Macmillan Press, 182-210

Eisenberg, Christine (1985) *Frühe Arbeiterbewegung Und Genossenschaften,* Bonn: Verlag Neue Gesellschaft GmbH

Elias, Norbert (1996) *The Germans: Power Struggles and the Development of Habitus in the Nineteenth and Twentieth Centuries,* Oxford: Polity Press

Engelmann, Bernt (1991) *Deutschland-Report,* Göttingen: Steidl Verlag

Falham, David (1999) *Managing in a Business Context,* People and Organisations Series, London: Institute of Personnel and Development

Farrell, Jerome (1990) "The German Community in 19th Century East London," *East London Record,* 13, 2-8

Fay, Stephen (1988) *Portrait of an Old Lady: Turmoil at the Bank of England,* London: Penguin Books

Ferner, A. and Hyman, R. (eds.) (1998) *Changing Industrial Relations in Europe,* Oxford: Blackwell

Fetterman, David M. (1998) *Ethnography: Step by Step,* Newbury Park: Sage

*Financial Times* (1998a) "Merged Bank May Beat Its Costs Target: Bayerische Hypo-und Vereinsbank," 30 August, available from http://globalarchive.ft.com/globalarchive /articles.html

— (1998b) "Rover's Poor Return," 22 October 1998, page 20

— (1999) "Compensation for Nazi Era Labour to Rise," 7 October 1999

Firchow, Peter Edgerly (1986) *The Death of the German Cousin: Variations on a Literary Stereotype 1890-1920,* London: Associated University Presses

Foner, Nancy (1997) "What's New About Transnationalism? New York Immigrants Today and at the Turn of the Century," paper presented at Conference on Transnational Communities and the Political Economy of New York in the 1990s, The New School for Economic Research, February 21-22, 1997

Forster, Nick (2000) "The Myth of the 'International Manager'," *International Journal of Human Resource Management* 11 (1), 126-142

Forsythe, Diana (1989) "German Identity and the Problem of History," in Elizabeth Tonkin et al. (Eds.), *History and Ethnicity*, Vol. 27 London: Routledge, 137-156

*Frankfurter Allgemeine Zeitung* (2000) "HVB bleibt trotz schwachem Start optimistisch für laufende Jahr," 23 March 2000, available from http://globalarchive.ft.com/globalarchive/articles.html

Friends of Douglas House (1993) *Welcome: Tips für den Start in England,* London: Friends of Douglas House

Fröbel, Folker et al. (1980) *The New International Division of Labour: Structural Unemployment in Industrialized Countries,* Cambridge: Cambridge University Press

Gall, Lothar (1995) "The Deutsche Bank from Its Founding to the Great War 1870-1914," in in Lothar Gall, Gerald D. Feldman, Harold James, Carl-Ludwig Holtfrerich, and Hans-E. Büschgen (Eds.), *The Deutsche Bank 1870-1995,* London: Weidenfeld and Nicolson, 1-127

—, Feldman, Gerald D., James, Harold, Holtfrerich, Carl-Ludwig and Büschgen, Hans-E. (Eds.) (1995) *The Deutsche Bank 1870-1995,* London: Weidenfeld and Nicolson, xii-xx

Ghoshal, Sumantra and Nohria, Nitin (1989) "Internal Differentiation within Multinational Corporations," *Strategic Management Journal,* 10, 323-332

Gillespie, Marie (1995) *Television, Ethnicity and Cultural Change,* London: Routledge

Goffman, Erving (1956) *The Presentation of Self in Everyday Life,* Edinburgh: University of Edinburgh

— (1961) *Encounters: Two Studies in the Sociology of Interaction,* Indianapolis: Bobbs-Merrill Ltd.

— (1963) *Behaviour in Public Places: Notes on the Social Organization of Gatherings,* London: The Free Press of Glencoe

— (1970) *Strategic Interaction,* Oxford: Basil Blackwell

— (1979) *Gender Advertisements,* Macmillan, London

Goltz, Joshua (1998) "Memories of *Heimat*: National Socialist Propaganda and the Homelands of German Emigres in Argentina," M.Phil Thesis, ISCA, University of Oxford, Oxford

Goodman, Roger (1993) *Japan's "International Youth": The Emergence of a New Class of Schoolchildren,* Oxford: Clarendon Press

Gordon, Robert (2000) "Not Much of a New Economy," *Financial Times,* 26 July 2000, available from http://www.globalarchive.ft.com/

Graham, Laurie (1995) *On the Line at Subaru-Isuzu: the Japanese Model and the American Worker,* Ithaca: ILR Press

Grass, Günther (1990) *Deutscher Lastenausgleich: Wieder das dumpfe Einheitsgebot: Reden und Gespräche,* Frankfurt am Main: Luchterhand Literaturverlag

Greverus, Ina Maria (1979) *Auf der Suche nach Heimat,* München: Beck

Guarnizo, Luis Eduardo and Smith, Michael Peter (1998) "The Locations of Transnationalism," in Michael Peter Smith and Luis Eduardo Guarnizo (Eds.), *Transnationalism from Below,* Comparative Urban and Community Research vol. 6, London: Transaction Publishers, 13-34

Habermas, Jürgen (1994) *The Past as Future,* Cambridge: Polity Press

Hagen, Stephen (1998) "Panel Discussion," at the Doing Business with Germany Conference, Goethe Institut, London, 21 October 1998

Hamada, Tomoko (1992) "Under the Silk Banner: The Japanese Company and Its Overseas Managers," in Takie Sugiyama Lebra (Ed.), *Japanese Social Organization,* Honolulu: University of Hawaii Press, 135-164

Hannerz, Ulf (1983) "Tools of Identity and Imagination," in Anita Jacobson-Widding (Ed.), *Identity: Personal and Socio-Cultural, a Symposium*, Uppsala: Almqvist and Wiksell International, 347-360
— (1992) *Cultural Complexity: Studies in the Social Organization of Meaning*, New York: Columbia University Press
— (1996) *Transnational Connections: Culture, People, Places*, London: Routledge
Harris, Simon (2000) "Reconciling Positive and Interpretative International Management Research: A Native Category Approach," *International Business Review*, 9, 755-770
Hartley, Paul and Robins, Gertrud (1996) *Manual of Business German: A Comprehensive Language Guide*, London: Routledge
Harvey, David (1989) *The Condition of Postmodernity: An Enquiry into the Origins of Cultural Change*, Oxford: Blackwell
Harzing, Anne-Wil (2001a) "An Analysis of the Functions of International Transfer of Managers in MNCs," *Employee Relations* 23: 6, 581-598
— (2001b) "Of Bears, Bumblebees and Spiders: the Role of Expatriates in Controlling Foreign Subsidiaries," *Journal of World Business* 36: 4, 336-379
Head, David (1992) *"Made in Germany": The Corporate Identity of a Nation*, London: Hodder and Stoughton
van Hear, Nicholas (1998) *New Diasporas: The Mass Exodus, Dispersal and Regrouping of Migrant Communities*, London: UCL
Held, David, McGrew, Anthony, Goldblatt, David and Perraton, Jonathan (1999) *Global Transformations: Politics, Economics and Culture*, Cambridge: Polity Press
Heller, Robert (1995) *The Naked Manager for the Nineties*, London: Warner Books
Henrich, Dieter (1993) *Nach dem Ende der Teilung: über Identität und Intellektualität in Deutschland*, Frankfurt am Main: Surkamp Verlag
von Herder, Johann Gottfried (1969) *Johann Gottfried Herder on Social and Political Culture*, Cambridge: Cambridge University Press
Hickson, David J. and Pugh, Derek S. (1997) *Management Worldwide: The Impact of Societal Culture on Organizations around the Globe*, London: Penguin
Hirst, Paul Q. and Thompson, Grahame (1996) *Globalization in Question: The International Economy and the Possibilities of Governance*, Cambridge: Polity Press
Hoecklin, Lisa Marie (1996) "(Re)Constructing Hausfrauen: Gender, Ideology, 'the Family' and Social Welfare in Southern Germany," M.Phil Thesis, ISCA, University of Oxford, Oxford
— (1998) "Motherhood in the Fatherland: Towards Understanding a Mother Centre in Southern Germany," D.Phil Thesis, ISCA, University of Oxford, Oxford
Hofstede, Geert (1980) *Culture's Consequences: International Differences in Work-Related Values*, London: Sage
Holmes, Colin (1988) *John Bull's Island: Immigration and British Society, 1871-1971*, London: Macmillan
Holtfrereich, Carl-Ludwig (1995) "The Deutsche Bank 1945-1957: War, Military Rule and Reconstruction," in Lothar Gall, Gerald D. Feldman, Harold James, Carl-Ludwig Holtfrerich, and Hans-E. Büschgen. (Eds.), *The Deutsche Bank 1870-1995*, London: Weidenfeld and Nicholson, 357-521
Höpner, Martin and Jackson, Gregory (2001) *An Emerging Market for Corporate Control? The Mannesmann Takeover and German Corporate Governance.* Köln: Max-Planck-Institut für Gesellschaftsforschung Discussion Papers Series
Horovitz, Jacques Henri (1980) *Top Management Control in Europe*, London: Macmillan
Hughes, Terence (1994) *The Image Makers: National Stereotypes and the Media*, London: Goethe Institut London

Hunt, John (1998) "Go Abroad, Young Manager," *Financial Times*, 7 October 1998, page 17

Hussey, D. E. (1995) *How to Manage Organisational Change*, London: Kogan Page

Hutton, Will (1996) *The State We're In*, London: Vintage

d'Iribane, Phillipe (1997) "The Usefulness of an Ethnographic Approach to the International Comparison of Organizations," *Inernational Studies of Management and Organization*, 26 (4), 30-47

Irwin, Jonathan (2000) "The Hateful Welcome," *Daily Mail*, 8 June 2000, page 41

Iyer, Pico (2000) *The Global Soul: Jet Lag, Shopping Malls and the Search for Home*, London: Bloomsbury

Jackall, Robert (1988) *Moral Mazes: The World of Corporate Managers*, Oxford: Oxford University Press

Janoski, Thomas and Glennie, Elizabeth (1995) "The Integration of Immigrants in Advanced Industrialized Nations," in Marco Martiniello (Ed.), *Migration, Citizenship and Ethnonational Identities in the European Union*, Aldershot: Avebury, 11-39

Janssens, Maddy (1994) "Evaluating International Managers' Performance: Parent Company Standards as Control Mechanism." *International Journal of Human Resource Management* 5: 4, 853-873.

Jenkins, Alan (1988) *The City: London's Square Mile*, London: Viking Kestrel

Jenkins, Richard (1996) *Social Identity*, London: Routledge

Jones, Sheila (1998) "A Cauliflower Will Cost You 56 Centimes–in Rothsham," *Financial Times*, 11 November, page 12

Kasimir, Sharryn (2001) "Corporation, self and enterprise at the Saturn automobile Plant," *Anthropology of Work Review* XXII: 4, 8-12

Kelly, William (2001) "Japanese Expatriate Managers: The Coordination of Overseas Subsidiaries in the United Kingdom," paper presented at Nissan Institute Seminar, Oxford, 9 March 2001

Kerfoot, Deborah and Knights, David (1994) "The Gendered Terrains of Paternalism," in Susan Wright (Ed.), *Anthropology of Organizations*, London: Routledge, 124-139

Klein, Michael (1997) *Leben, Werk und Nackwirkung des Genossenschaftsgründers Friedrich Wilhelm Raiffeisen (1818-1888)*. Schiffenreihe des Vereins für Rhenische Kirchengeschichte, 122, Köln: Rheinland-Verlag

Klein, Naomi (2000) *No Logo*, London: Flamingo

Klein, Wolf Peter (1998) "Pidgin als Weltsprache," *Frankfurter Allgemeine Zeitung*, 14 October, page 5

Kluthe, Klaus (1985) *Genossenschaften und Staat in Deutschland: symbolische und historische Analysen deutscher Genossenschaftspolitik bezogen auf dem Zeitraum 1914 bis zur Gegenwert*. Schriften zum Genossenschaftswesen und zur öffentlichen Wirtschaft, Band 12. Berlin: Duncker und Humbolt

Kogat, Bruce (1993) "Learning, or the Importance of Being Inert: Country Imprinting and International Competition," in Sumantra Ghoshal and D. Eleanor Westney (Eds.), *Organization Theory and the Multinational Corporation*, London: The Macmillan Press, 136-154

König, Johann Gunther (1994) *Wem nutzt Europa? Banken und Konzerne: Fit für den Weltmarkt-- wer behält Gelt und Arbeit in Deutschland*, Bremen: SachBuch Verlag

Kosnick, Kyra (2001) "'Good Guys and Bad Guys': Turkish Migrant Broadcasting in Berlin," paper presented at European Forum Summer School, Cecina, 8-17 July 2001

Krauthammer, Charles (1999) "Planet Amerika," *Der Spiegel*, 27 December 1999

Kristensen, P.H. and Zeitlin, D. (2004) *Local Players in Global Games: The Strategic Constitution of a Multinational Corporation*, Oxford: Oxford University Press.

Kynaston, David (1995) "The Bank of England and the Government," in David Kynaston and Richard Roberts (Eds.), *The Bank of England: Money, Power and Influence 1694-*

*1994*, Oxford: Clarendon Press, 19-55

Lane, Christel (1989) *Management and Labour in Europe: The Industrial Enterprise in Germany, Britain and France*, Aldershot: Edward Elgar

Larsen, Peter Thal, Waters, Richard and Lewis, William (2000) "Vodaphone-Mannesman: Making the Connection," *Financial Times*, 5 February 2000, available from http://globalarchive.ft.com

Law, John (1994) *Organizing Modernity*, Oxford: Blackwell

Lawrence, Peter (1980) *Managers and Management in West Germany*, London: Croom Helm

Lascelles, David (2000) "Should Great Britain Join the Euro?" paper presented at Foreign Banks and Securities Houses Association Annual Conference, London, 27 November

Lakoff, Robin (1979) "Language and Woman's Place," *Language and Society*, II, 45-80

Leach, Edmund (1976) *Culture and Communication: The Logic by Which Symbols Are Connected*, Cambridge: Cambridge University Press

Leeson, Nick (1996) *Rogue Trader*, London: Little, Brown and Company

Lewis, Michael (1989) *Liar's Poker: Two Cities, True Greed*, London: Hodder and Stoughton

Leyshon, Andrew and Thrift, Nigel (1997) *Money/Space: Geographies of Monetary Transformation*, London: Routledge

Lindisfarne, Nancy (2002) "Fieldwork, Gender and Imperialism Now," *Critique of Anthropology* 22 (4), 403-444

Linehan, Margaret and Walsh, James S. (1999) "Recruiting and Developing Female Managers for International Assignments," *Journal of Management Development* 18 (6), 521-530

Lippert, Werner (Ed.) (1997) *Future Office: Corporate Identity und Corporate Culture, Geist und Stil der Firma*, Düsseldorf: Metropolitan Verlag

Lurie, Alison (1981) *The Language of Clothes*, London: Heinemann

Lynn, Eric (1997) "German Business Culture," in Roderick Millar and Jonathan Reuvid (Eds.), *Doing Business with Germany*, London: Kegan Paul Ltd., 57-69

MacDonald, Sharon (2001) "Trafficking in History: Multitemporal Practices," *Anthropological Journal on European Cultures* 11, 93-116

Mai, Gunther (1993) "Vom Obrigkeitsstaat zur Demokratiefähigkeit? westdeutsche Einstellungen seit Kriegsende," in Axel Knoblich et al. (Eds.), *Auf dem Weg zu einer gesamtdeutschen Identität?* Köln: Verlag Wissenschaft und Politik, 66-84

Major, Tony (2000) "Dust Settles on Failed Merger," *Financial Times*, 22 May, available from http://globalarchive.ft.com/globalarchive/

Mann, Kay (1993) *London: The German Connection*, Bridgwater: KT Publishing

Mars, Gerald (1982) *Cheats at Work: An Anthropology of Workplace Crime*, London: George Allen and Unwin

Marsh, David (1994) *Germany and Europe: The Crisis of Unity*, London: Heinemann

McDowell, Linda M. (1997a) "A Tale of Two Cities? Embedded Organizations and Embodied Workers in the City of London," in Roger Lee and Jane Willis (Eds.), *Geographies of Economies*, London: Arnold, 118-129

— (1997b) *Capital Culture: Gender and Work in the City*, Oxford: Blackwell

McSweeney, Brendan (2002) "Fundamental Flaws in Hofstede's Research," *EBF* 9, pp. 39-43.

Mead, George (1994) *International Management*, London: Blackwell

Mehr, Max Thomas and Sylvester, Regine (1992) "The Stone-Thrower from Eisenhuttenstadt," trans. Michael Hoffman, *Granta*, 42 (Winter), 134-142

Merriman, Nick and Visram, Rozina (1993) "The World in a City," in Nick Merriman (Ed.), *The Peopling of London: Fifteen Thousand Years of Settlement from Overseas*, London:

Museum of London, 1-27

*The Metro* (2000) "Germans Poised for Blitz on C&W," 6 July 2000, pp. 43

Micklethwait, John and Wooldridge, Adrian (2000) *A Future Perfect: The Challenge and Hidden Promise of Globalisation,* London: William Heinemann

Millar, Jean (1979) *British Management Versus German Management: A Comparison of Organisational Effectiveness in West German and UK Factories,* London: Saxon House

Miller, Daniel and Slater, Don (2000) *The Internet: An Ethnographic Approach,* Oxford: Berg

Mintz, Sydney W. (1998) "The Localization of Anthropological Practice: From Area Studies to Transnationalism," *Critique of Anthropology,* 18 (22), 117-133

Mitchell, J. Clyde (1983) "Case and Situation Analysis," *Sociological Review (N.S.),* 31 (2), 187-211

Mikes, George (1953) *Uber Alles: Germany Explored,* London: A. Wingate

Moore, Fiona (1999) "Ethnicity, Transnationalism and the Workplace: Expressions of Identity among German Business Expatriates," M.Phil. Thesis, ISCA, University of Oxford, Oxford

— (2003) "Internal Diversity and Culture's Consequences: Branch/Head Office Relations in a German Financial MNC," *Management International Review* 43, 95-111

Morgan, Garth (1997) *Images of Organization,* London: Sage

Morgan, Glenn (2001) "Transnational Communities and Business Systems," *Global Networks* 1: 2, 113-130

*Morning Post* (1908) "The Anti-English Feeling," 1 July 1908, page 9

Mueller, Frank (1994) "Societal Effect, Organizational Effect and Globilization," *Organization Studies,* 15 (3), 407-428

Nader, Laura (1974) "Up the Anthropologist—Perspectives Gained from Studying Up," in Del Hymes (ed.), *Reinventing Anthropology,* New York: Random House

Naughton, John (1999) "Techie Speak," *High Life,* January 1999, page 24

Nash, June (1979) "Anthropology of the Multinational Corporation," in G. Huizer and B. Mannheim (Eds.), *The Politics of Anthropology: From Colonialism and Sexism toward a View from Below,* Paris: Mouton Publishers, 421-446

Nicholson, Sally and Hill, Joyce (1992) *German Telephone Skills for Business,* Gerrards Cross: LETA Telephone Training

Norderhaven, Niels G. and Harzing, Anne-Wil (2003) "The 'Country of Origin Effect' in Multinational Corporations: Sources, Mechanisms and Moderating Conditions,' *Management International Review* 43, 47-66

Oberg, Kalervo (1960) "Cultural Shock: Adjustment to New Cultural Environments," *Practical Anthropology,* 7, 177-182

Ohmae, Kenichi (1990) *The Borderless World: Power and Strategy in the Interlinked Economy,* London: HarperCollins

Ong, Aiwah (1998) "Flexible Citizenship among Chinese Cosmopolitans," in Pheng Cheah and Bruce Robbins (Eds.), *Cosmopolitics: Thinking and Feeling Beyond the Nation,* London: University of Minneapolis Press, 134-162

Owen, Jenny (1999) "The City and Identity: News Frames and the Representation of London and Londoners in the *Evening Standard*," in Tracey Skelton and Tim Allen (Eds.), *Culture and Global Change,* London: Routledge, 117-123

Panayi, Panikos (1993) "Germans in London," in Nick Merriman (Ed.), *The Peopling of London: Fifteen Thousand Years of Settlement,* London: Museum of London, 111-117

— (1995) *German Immigrants in Britain During the Nineteenth Century, 1815-1914,* Oxford: Berg

Pelissier, Catherine (1991) "The Anthropology of Teaching and Learning," *Annual Review of Anthropology,* 20, 75-95

Peppercorn, Gillian and Skoulding, Gill (1987) *Profile of British Industry: The Manager's View,* London: British Institute of Management

Peraino, Kevin (1998) "Websites Help Expats Feel Less Away from Home," *Wall Street Journal Europe,* 10 Nov. 1998, page 4

Piekkari, Rebecca (2004) "Language and International Management: A Review and Extension," in *International Studies of Management and Organization* 34 (4)

Plender, John and Wallace, Paul (1985) *The Square Mile: A Guide to the New City of London,* London: Century Publishing

Pohl, Manfred and Burk, Kathleen (1998) *Die Deutsche Bank in London 1873-1998,* Munich: Piper Verlag

Portes, Alejandro (1998) *Globalisation from Below: The Rise of Transnational Communities,* Oxford: ESRC Transnational Communities Programme Working Paper

Posen, Adams (1993) "Less Than a Universe of Difference: Evaluating the Reality of German Finance," in A. Bradley Shingleton, et al. (Eds.), *Dimensions of German Unification: Economic, Social and Legal Analyses,* Oxford: Westview Press, 43-56

Prahalad, C.K. and Doz, Yves L. (1987) *The Multinational Mission: Balancing Local Demands and Global Vision,* London: Macmillan

Pringle, Rosemary (1994) "Office Affairs," in Susan Wright (Ed.), *Anthropology of Organizations,* London: Routledge, 115-123

Pryke, Michael and Lee, Roger (1995) "Place Your Bets: Towards an Understanding of Globalization, Sociofinancial Engineering and Competition within a Financial Centre," *Urban Studies,* 32 (2), 329-344

Quack, Sigrid and Morgan, Glenn (2000a) "National Capitalisms, Global Competition and Economic Performance: An Introduction," in Glenn Morgan, Richard Whitley and Sigrid Quack (Eds.), *National Capitalisms, Global Competition and Economic Performance,* Philadelphia: John Benjamins Publishing Co., 3-24

— (2000b) "Institutions, Sector Specialization and Economic Performance Outcomes," in Glenn Morgan, Richard Whitley and Sigrid Quack (Eds.), *National Capitalisms, Global Competition and Economic Performance,* Philadelphia: John Benjamins Publishing Co., 27-52

Rampton, Ben (1995) *Crossing: Language and Ethnicity among Adolescents,* London: Longman

Randlesome, Colin (1993) "The Business Culture in Germany," in Colin Randlesome et al. (Eds.), *Business Cultures in Europe,* Oxford: Butterworth-Heinemann, 1-85

Räthzel, Nora (1990) "Germany: One Race, One Nation?" *Race and Class,* 32 (3), 31-48

Read, Donald (1999) *The Power of News: The History of Reuters,* Oxford: Oxford University Press

Reis, Cristina (2004) "Power Implications of Language Diversity in Multinational Corporations," paper presented at EURAM 2004 Conference, St Andrew's, Scotland, 5-8 May 2004

Renton, Jane (1998) "Corporate Citizenship: A High Life Special," *High Life,* pp. 1-16

Roberts, Celia et al. (1992) *Language and Discrimination: A Study of Communication in Multi-Ethnic Workplaces,* Harlow: Longman

Robertson, Roland (1992) *Globalization: Social Theory and Global Culture,* London: Sage

Rose, Harold (1994) *London as an International Financial Centre: A Narrative History,* London: City Research Project

Roth, Ranier A. (1979) *Was ist typisch deutsch? Image und Selbstverständnis der Deutschen,* Würtzberg: Verlag Plötz

Rovan, Joseph (1983) "Staat und Nation in der deutsche Geschichte," in Werner Weidenfeld (Ed.), *Die Identität der Deutschen,* Bonn: Bundeszentrale für politische Bildung, 229-247

Royle, Tony (2000) *Working for McDonald's in Europe*, London: Routledge

Sakai, Junko (2000) *Japanese Bankers in the City of London: Language, Culture and Identity in the Japanese Diaspora*, London: Routledge

Sassen, Saskia (1991) *The Global City: New York, London, Tokyo*, Princeton: Princeton University Press

Schegloff, Emanuel A. (1972) "Sequencing in Conversational Openings," in John J. Gumperz and Dell Hymes (Eds.), *Directions in Sociolinguistics: The Ethnography of Communication*, New York: Holt, Rinehart and Winston, Inc, 346-380

Schein, Louisa (1998) "Forged Transnationality and Oppositional Cosmopolitanism," in Michael Peter Smith and Luis Eduardo Guarnizo (Eds.), *Transnationalism from Below*, Comparative Urban and Community Research vol. 6, London: Transaction Publishers, 291-313

Scheuermann, Agnes (1997) "'Typical German, Typical British': Differences in Communication Style," *Initiative*, pp. 20-21

Schnyder, Alfons Beat (1989) *Unternehmenskulture: die Entwicklung eines UK-Models und der Berücksichtigung ethnologischer Erkentnisse und dessen Anwerkung auf die Innovations-Thematik*, Frankfurt am Main: Peter Lang Verlag

Scholtz, Christian (1987) "The Symbolic Value of Computerized Information Systems," paper presented at the Third International Conference on Oral Symbolism and Corporate Culture, Milan, June 24-26 1987

Schwartzman, Helen B. (1993) *Ethnography in Organizations*, Quantitative Research Methods Vol. 27, London: Sage

Schwarz, Gunther (1989) *Unternehmungskultur als Element des strategischen Managements*, Betriebswirtschaftliche Forschungsergebnisse vol. 92, Berlin: Duncker und Humbolt

von See, Klaus (1994) *Barbare, Germane, Arier: die Suche nach der Identität der Deutschen*, Heidelberg: Universitätsverlag C. Winter

Seger, Frank (1997) *Banken, Erfolg und Finanzierung: eine Analyse für deutsche Industrieunternehmen*, Wiesbaden: Deutscher Universitäts-Verlag

Skelton, Tracey and Allen, Tim (1999) "Culture and Global Change: An Introduction," in Tracey Skelton and Tim Allen (Eds.), *Culture and Global Change*, London: Routledge, 1-10

Sklair, Leslie (1995) *Sociology of the Global System*, Hemel Hempstead: Prentice Hall

— (1998a) *Transnational Practices and the Analysis of the Global System*, Oxford: ESRC Transnational Communities Programme Working Paper

— (1998b) "The Transnational Capitalist Class and Global Capitalism: The Case of the Tobacco Industry," *Political Power and Social Theory*, 12, 3-43

— (2001) *The Transnational Capitalist Class*, Oxford: Blackwell

Smith, Anthony D. (1995) *Nations and Nationalism in a Global Era*, Cambridge: Polity Press

Sorge, Arndt (1996) "Societal Effects in Transnational Organization Studies: Conceptualizing Diversity in Actors and Systems," in Richard Whitley and Peer Hull Kristensen (Eds.), *The Changing European Firm: Limits to Convergence*, London: Routledge, 67-86

— and Warner, Malcolm (1986) *Comparative Factory Organisation: An Anglo-German Comparison of Manufacturing, Management and Manpower*, Aldershot: Gower

Sparke, Matthew (2001) "Networking Globalization: A Tapestry of Introductions," *Global Networks*, 1 (2), 171-179

Sperber, Dan (1974) *Rethinking Symbolism*, Cambridge: Cambridge University Press

*Der Spiegel* (1998a) "It's a Trick," 20 April 1998, pp. 124-125

— (1998b) "Ferien für den Euro," 27 April 1998, pp. 100-107

— (1998c) "Ich bleibe Deutscher," 7 September 1998, pp. 88-89

— (1998d) "Der Hunne träumt," 21 September 1998, page 269

Stack, John F. (1981) "Ethnicity and Transnational Relations: An Introduction," in John F. Stack (Ed.), *Ethnic Identities in a Transnational World*, London: Greenwood Press, 3-15

von Stein, Joachim Heinrich (1998) "Bankensystem in Deutschland: Kreditbanken, Sparkassen, Genossenschaftsbanken, Kreditinstitute mit Sonderaufgabe und die Bundesbank," in Heinrich von Stein, Karl-Heinz Nassmacher, Hans-E. Büschgen et al. (Eds.), *Banken in Deutschland; wirtschaftspolitische Grundinformation*, Oplanden: Leske und Budrich, 35-49

Stewart, Rosemary, et. al. (1994) *Managing in Britain and Germany*, New York: St Martins' Press

Stockdale, E.V.M. (1957) "Some Notes on the Bank of England and Her Connection with the Chamber of London, and Certain Other Aspects of Civic Life," *Transactions of the G.H.A.*, II, 39-45

Stopford, John (1998/9) "Think Again: Multinational Corporations," *Foreign Policy*, 113, 12-24

Strecker, Ivo (1988) *The Social Practice of Symbolization: An Anthropological Analysis*, London: Athlone Press

Thrift, Nigel (1994) "On the Social and Cultural Determinants of International Financial Centres: The Case of the City of London," in *Money, Power and Space*, Stuart Corbridge, Ron Martin and Nigel Thrift (Eds.), Oxford: Blackwell, 327-355

— and Leyshon, Andrew (1994) "A Phantom State? The De-Traditionalization of Money, the International Financial System and International Financial Centres," *Political Geography*, 13 (4), 299-327

Tomlinson, John (1999a) *Globalization and Culture*, Cambridge: Polity Press

— (1999b) "Globalised Culture: The Triumph of the West?" in Tracey Skelton and Tim Allen (Eds.), *Culture and Global Change*, London: Routledge, 22-29

Torbiörn, Ingemar (1982) *Living Abroad: Personal Adjustment and Personnel Policy in an Overseas Setting*, Chichester: John Wiley and Sons

Trompenaars, F. (1993) *Riding the Waves of Culture*, London: Nicholas Brealey.

— and Hampden-Turner, Charles (1994) *The Seven Cultures of Capitalism: Value Systems for Creating Wealth in the United States, Japan, Germany, France, Britain, Sweden, and the Netherlands*, London: Piatkus

Tugendhat, Christopher (1971) *The Multinationals*, Harmondsworth: Penguin

Turner, Barry A. (1971) *Exploring the Industrial Subculture*, London: Macmillan

— (1992) "The Symbolic Understanding of Organizations," in Michael Reed and Michael Hughes (Eds.), *Rethinking Organization: New Dimensions in Organization Theory and Analysis*, London: Sage, 46-66

Vertovec, Steven (1996a) "Comparative Issues in, and Multiple Meanings of, the South Asian Religious Diaspora," paper presented at the Conference on the Comparative Study of the South Asian Diaspora: Religious Experience in Britain, Canada and USA, London, UK, 4-6 November 1996

— (1996b) "*Berlin Multikulti*: Germany, 'Foreigners' and 'World-Openness,'" *New Community*, 22 (3), 381-399

— (1999) "Conceiving and Researching Transnationalism," *Ethnic and Racial Studies*, 22 (2), 447-462

— (2001) "Transnational Social Formations: Towards Conceptual Cross-Fertilization," paper presented at Workshop on "Transnational Migration: Comparative Perspectives," Princeton University, Princeton, New Jersey, USA, June 30-July 1 2001

— and Rogers, Alisdair (1998) "Introduction," in Steven Vertovec and Alisdair Rogers (Eds.), *Muslim European Youth: Reproducing Religion, Ethnicity, Culture*, Aldershot:

Ashgate, 1-33

Viehoff, Felix (1978) *Zur mittelstandbezonenen Bankpolitik des Verbundes der Genossenschaftsbanken teil I: Zum Begriff und zur wirtschaftlichen Bedeutung des Mittelstandes,* Veröffentlichungen der Deutsche Genossenschaftsbank vol. 11, Frankfurt am Main: Fritz Knapp Verlag

Vogel, Ezra (1979) *Japan as Number One: Lessons for America,* Cambridge (Mass.): Harvard University Press

Wade, Robert (1996) "Globalization and its Limits: Reports of the Death of the National Economy Are Greatly Exaggerated," in Suzanne Berger and Ronald Dore (Eds.), *National Diversity and Global Capitalism,* London: Cornell, 60-88

Wallman, Sandra (1986) "Ethnicity and the Boundary Process in Context," in John Rex and David Mason (Eds.), *Theories of Race and Ethnic Relations,* Cambridge: Cambridge University Press, 226-245

Warner, Malcolm and Campbell, Adrian (1993) "German Management," in David J. Hickson (Ed.), *Management in Western Europe: Society, Culture and Organization in Twelve Nations,* Berlin: Walter de Gruyter, 89-108

Waters, Malcolm (1995) *Globalization,* London: Routledge

Watson, Alan (1995) *The Germans: Who Are They Now?* London: Methuen

Weidenfeld, Werner (1983) "Die Identität der Deutschen: Fragen, Positionen, Perspektiven," in Werner Weidenfeld (Ed.), *Die Identität der Deutschen,* Bonn: Bundeszentrale für politische Bildung, 13-49

— and Korte, Karl-Rudolf (1991) *Die Deutschen: Profil einer Nation,* Stuttgart: Klett-Cotta Verlag

Weigelt, Klaus (1984) "Einleitung," in Klaus Weigelt (Ed.), *Heimat und Nation: zur Geschichte und Identität der Deutschen,* Mainz: von Hase und Köhler Verlag, 15-25

Westney, D. Eleanor (1993) "Institutionalization Theory and the Multinational Corporation," in Sumantra Ghoshal and D. Eleanor Westney (Eds.), *Organization Theory and the Multinational Corporation,* London: The Macmillan Press, 53-76

White, Jenny (1997) "Turks in the New Germany," *American Anthropologist,* 99 (4), 754-769

Whitley, Richard (1992) "Societies, Firms and Markets: the Social Structuring of Business Systems," in Whitley, Richard (ed.), *European Business Systems: Firms and Markets in their National Contexts,* London: Sage, 5-45

Whitley, Richard (ed.) (1992) *European Business Systems: Firms and Markets in their National Contexts,* London: Sage

Willis, Paul E. (1977) *Learning to Labour: How Working Class Kids Get Working Class Jobs,* Farnborough: Saxon House

The Winchester Group (n.d. [1990?]) *The Square Mile in 1990,* London: The Winchester Group

Wolff Olins Identity Research (1995) *Made in Germany: A Business Survey of the Relevance of the National Badge and Its Image Associations,* Wolff Olins

Wraight, John (1991) *The Swiss in London: A History of the City Swiss Club 1856-1991,* London: City Swiss Club

Wright, Susan (1994) "'Culture' in Anthropology and Organizational Studies," in Susan Wright (Ed.), *Anthropology of Organizations,* London: Routledge, 1-31

Yeung, Henry Wai-Chung (1998) "Capital, State and Space: Contesting the Borderless World," *Transactions of the Institute of British Geographers,* 23, 291-309

Zachary, G. Pascal (2000) *The Global Me: New Cosmopolitans: The Competitive Edge: Picking Globalism's Winners and Losers,* London: Nicholas Brealy Publishing

# Index